An Evangelical Among the Anglican Liturgists

Founded in 1897, the Alcuin Club seeks to promote the study of Christian liturgy and worship in general with special reference to worship in the Anglican Communion. The Club has published a series of annual Collections, including *A Companion to Common Worship*, volumes 1 and 2, edited by Paul F. Bradshaw, and most recently a new edition of *Christian Prayer through the Centuries*, (SPCK 2007) by Joseph Jungmann. The Alcuin Liturgy Guide series aims to address the theology and practice of worship, and includes *The Use of Symbols in Worship* (SPCK 2007), edited by Christopher Irvine. The most recent in this series are the twin volumes covering the celebration of the Christian Year: *Celebrating Christ's Appearing: Advent to Christmas* (SPCK 2008), and *Celebrating Christ's Victory: Ash Wednesday to Trinity* (SPCK 2008), both by Benjamin Gordon-Taylor and Simon Jones. The Club works in partnership with GROW in the publication of the Joint Liturgical Study series, with two studies being published each year.

Members of the Club receive publications of the current year free and others at a reduced rate. The President of the Club is the Rt Revd Michael Perham, its Chairman is the Revd Canon Dr Donald Gray CBE, and the Editorial Secretary is The Revd Canon Christopher Irvine. For details of membership and the annual subscription, contact The Alcuin Club, 5 Saffron Street, Royston, SG8 9TR. Email: alcuinclub@gmail.com

Visit the Alcuin Club website at: **www.alcuinclub.org.uk**

An Evangelical Among the Anglican Liturgists

Colin Buchanan

Alcuin Club Collections 84

First published in Great Britain in 2009

Society for Promoting Christian Knowledge
36 Causton Street
London SW1P 4ST

British Library Cataloguing-in-Publication Data
A catalogue record for this book is available from the British Library

ISBN 978–0–281–06026–9

10 9 8 7 6 5 4 3 2 1

Designed and typeset by Kenneth Burnley, Wirral, Cheshire
Printed in Great Britain by Ashford Colour Press

Produced on paper from sustainable forests

Contents

Foreword

Colin Buchanan and I served alongside on the Church of England Liturgical Commission for the best part of 20 years. I believe during that time we learnt a good deal from each other.

It is a fact that by the time Colin joined the Commission he had already acquired an extensive knowledge of Christian worship and liturgy.

He was discovered, as a theological student, by Charles Whitaker. Canon Whitaker told Ronald Jasper, then Chairman of the Commission, that he had recently maked a GOE (General Ordination Examination) Worship paper which was the most outstanding he had ever come across![1] So, only three years after ordination, the young librarian of the London College of Divinity was sitting among the liturgical luminaries and participating to the full from day one.

Never shy in expressing his opinions he quickly became a significant member of the Commission. 'Never shy' of course fails to convey the style of his interventions. Archbishop Runcie characterized Colin as being the only bull he knew who brought along his own china shop!

The Alcuin Club is pleased to add this volume to its long series of Collections. It allows us to recognize, among other things, Bishop Buchanan's fruitful co-operation with the Club in the production of our series of Joint Liturgical Studies, now in their twenty-third year.

Colin Buchanan has always worthily represented an important strand of Anglican tradition and scholarship. While doing so he has, most importantly, opened up to recent generations of Evangelicals the challenges and opportunities of liturgical worship.

CANON DR DONALD GRAY
Chairman of the Alcuin Club

---

1 An account of this is found in the booklet by Bill Kelly, *Charles Whitaker, Pastor and Liturgical Scholar: A Memoir* (Carlisle diocese, Carlisle, 2002), pp. 12–13.

Acknowledgements

The New Communion Service – Reasons for Dissent was published in 1966 by the Church Book Room Press, the publishing arm of Church Society, and is reprinted by kind permission of Church Society.

'Infant Baptism – The Atomized Sacrament' was originally published in Clifford Owen (ed.), *Reforming Infant Baptism* (Hodder & Stoughton, 1990) and is reprinted by kind permission of the editor and publishers.

'Confirmation' is reprinted from David R. Holeton (ed.), *Growing in Newness of Life: Christian Initiation in Anglicanism Today* – copyright 1993 the Anglican Consultative Council for the International Anglican Liturgical Consultation. Published by ABC Publishing (Anglican Book Centre, Toronto). Used with permission.

What Did Cranmer Think He Was Doing? was published by Grove Books, Bramcote, as Grove Liturgical Study 7 in 1976, and all copyright belongs to the author, who was also proprietor of the press.

The End of the Offertory was similarly published by Grove Books, Bramcote, as Grove Liturgical Study 14 in 1978, and copyright of the condensed version here belongs to the author.

NOTE ON PRESENTATION

All use of standard or square brackets is original to the various texts reproduced in this volume. Editorial footnotes, with the numbers, are placed in square brackets. At the beginning and end of each chapter I have added a brief Foreword and Postscript.

Author's note

To put together for re-publication various past writings of my own on liturgy, as the Alcuin Club has generously invited me to do, is a privilege I was not expecting. Careful reflection with the Editorial Secretary of the Alcuin Club, with a necessary eye to constraints of space, has led to the actual contents of this Collection. The aim has been to provide a fairly wide range of materials, and the topping and tailing of each which I have been permitted to do will, with the bibliography, give an idea of the fuller range of issues I have addressed over the years. So this volume includes, from a 40-year period, both baptismal and eucharistic issues, and, while it relates closely to the Church of England in most cases, it also has an international Anglican essay. There is the strictly academic, the polemic and the pastoral, and also two lectures which were given to limited numbers and are now published for the first time. I hope that within it all, my concern to follow the biblical revelation will be clear. One item, *What Did Cranmer Think He Was Doing?*, has become near to an academic fixture in its 32 years of life, and so it has been reproduced verbatim, as a kind of centre-piece to the whole. Most items have to be read strictly in the context of their times. This proviso covers a whole series of historically conditioned factors – as, for example, the issue of inclusive language did not surface until the early 1980s, the authorities I cite in each piece come inevitably from a date prior to that piece's composition, and (less obviously) all the earlier writings were originally set in hot metal and I have transcribed them into modern technology. Much of the setting of them into their historical context is done in my recent work, *Taking the Long View: Three and a Half Decades of General Synod* (Church House Publishing, London, 2006), and I refer to that at intervals. My role as a street-level journalist of liturgy I would not venture to summarize myself, but am duly grateful to my good friend James Steven, himself a liturgy teacher, in Chapter 8 for making the 'blog' appear more attractive than it was in its original form.

During these 40 and more years, I have as a Christian minister been above all a liturgical practitioner, but I have also had additional opportunities which come to few people, and they have provided enormous scope for bringing my own priorities onto a larger scene, for which I am duly grateful. I have lived, by necessity and choice, having to straddle both the academic and the practical. It has been an unexpected and very welcome bonus that the Alcuin Club have wished upon me Christopher Cocksworth to open the door upon the collection. I am deeply grateful to him – and wish him well as he sets out this same week to become Bishop of Coventry.

COLIN BUCHANAN

Introduction

by Christopher Cocksworth, Bishop of Coventry

CONNECTING WITH COLIN BUCHANAN

It is a privilege to have been asked to write this introduction to Colin Buchanan's *An Evangelical Among the Anglican Liturgists* (Alcuin Club Collections 84). Indeed, it is also a particular pleasure because Colin (and I shall keep to the informality in what follows) has had a major influence on my life, as he has had on so many lives. My own association with him began when I joined St John's College, Nottingham to train for ordination and to research the place of the eucharist in evangelical thought and practice, under his supervision.[1] Up to that point, no one in my evangelical formation as a Christian had taught me about the Lord's Supper or told me to expect 'a personal interview with the Lord', as a great evangelical leader of an earlier generation exhorted his readers to do.[2] So I had supposed that my own experience of meeting the risen Christ in the breaking of the bread was somehow contrary to evangelical identity, even though I knew it to be thoroughly scriptural and full of the gospel. Colin, though, opened my eyes to a rich sacramental vein in evangelical history and theology from the Reformers onwards that tells of a deep compatibility between evangelical and eucharistic life.

Furthermore, he opened – quite literally – the doors of a large Narnia type wardrobe in his study to the world of Anglican liturgy. The

---

1 This work, begun under Colin's supervision and completed under the supervision of Kenneth Stevenson and Richard Bauckham, was later published in a shortened form as *Evangelical Eucharistic Thought in the Church of England* (Cambridge University Press, Cambridge, 1993). Much of Colin's involvement in the revision of the eucharistic rite of the Church of England is told here. For another third party account of his contribution not only to eucharistic liturgy but to other rites, see R. C. D. Jasper, *The Development of Anglican Liturgy 1662–1980* (SPCK, London, 1989), pp. 146ff.

2 H. C. G. Moule, *The Pledges of His Love* (Seeley & Co., London, 1907) and *At the Holy Communion* (Seeley & Co., London, 1914).

wardrobe held some of the secrets of the early days of his own involvement in liturgical revision. Inside I found such gems as draft anamneses typed (usually rather badly) by key protagonists of the mid- to late 1960s, and various personal letters to and from him, including a letter, heavily scented with disappointment, from Arthur Couratin, telling him that he had resigned from the Liturgical Commission, and that his departure was partly the result of the success of Colin's dissent, the story of which can be found in Chapter 1 of this collection.

The historical, theological and liturgical lessons I learnt in those years have shaped the course of my life since then.[3] I am only one of very many people, not only up and down the land but across the world, who have been encouraged and inspired to engage deeply with the practices of the Church through the example of Colin Buchanan. We have benefited immeasurably from Colin's critical contribution to the shaping and resourcing of people, evangelical and otherwise, with interests in the worship of the Church. As a founding member of the Latimer House Liturgy Group in 1961 (known since 1976 as the Group for the Renewal of Worship – GROW), the Society for Liturgical Study (SLS) in 1978 and the International Anglican Liturgical Consultations (IALC) in 1985, Colin has initiated and sustained networks for liturgists, and aspiring liturgists, enabling us to engage with and learn from each other. As founder of Grove Books, and through various other publishing ventures, especially his trilogy on the changing eucharistic rites of the Anglican Communion, Colin has not only made available an invaluable array of primary sources and scholarly comment, together with practical liturgical advice, he has also provided a platform for many writers to cut their publishing teeth. Colin's writings have given us an inside view of almost every stage of the evolution of the recent liturgical life of the Church of England, whether – as he likes to call it, and fairly – the 'accurate journalism' of *News of Liturgy*, his own Grove Booklets and

---

3 Indeed, in a strange sort of way my life and interests have followed a slightly similar course to Colin's, though only ever as a faint echo. My years in theological education and on the Liturgical Commission were far fewer. My writings, though in similar areas to his, make for a very short list compared with the several pages of Colin's writings that you can see listed on pp. 181–7 (and those are only his liturgical pieces). I am one of those bishops Colin describes in his personal record of General Synod as parachuted into Synod, never having had any involvement in – or appetite for – it in previous lives, compared with his remarkable commitment to the decision-making processes of the Church of England over four decades. And I only have ten volumes of Nathaniel Dimock's works compared with his 12! But our similar preoccupations make me especially delighted to be able to introduce this collection of writings and the person behind them.

other articles on the various stages of liturgical revision in the Church of England since 1964, or his own semi-autobiography in which he reflects on the history of General Synod and his own involvement in it – *Taking the Long View: Three and a half decades of General Synod.*[4]

So it is a fitting tribute to Colin's influence on individuals, Church and Communion that the Alcuin Club has gathered this collection of some of his seminal writings. As I open the door on them I would like to give some clues worth looking out for as one steps into them. I begin with some suggestions on what the articles tell us about the sort of person Colin is. (For example, what do they tell us about the particular concerns and capacities of the person behind them?). I then move on to give some signposts to help one navigate through his method. (For example, what do they tell us about how this particular writer plies his trade?). I end by posing some questions that remain in my mind after reading the articles afresh, to encourage others to bring their own to them – not that much encouragement is needed, because Colin's interrogative style naturally elicits an interrogative response.

THE SORT OF WRITER TO LOOK FOR BEHIND THE WRITINGS

Colin is a communicator. A life-long teacher, prolific writer and seasoned debater, he enjoys, and makes good use of, the power of words. The papers in this collection show him exercising his rhetorical craft skilfully in a variety of settings. What struck me as I read them again is the effective, sometimes devastating, use of analogy and metaphor, usually made more piercing in their effect by humour – a humour that ranges from observation of the ironic to scathing wit. In Chapter 3, baptism, in much Anglican practice, is likened to 'a dollop of grace or (preservative)' given to an infant much as she or he is inoculated soon after birth against all manner of things. He berates the sort of individualizing of the sacrament that lies behind this sort of approach. Gregory Dix, his long-time sparring partner to whom we shall return later, is blamed in Chapter 6 for an offertory theology that became 'a beacon which has led a whole fleet astray'. My favourite, though, is more on the lines of a parable which runs through most of Chapter 7, leaving – if I may play on his parody – a lot of egg on the face of a lot of priests.

At the same time, the articles in this collection, replete as they are with memorable turn of phrase and high-speed style, are also rich and

---

4 Colin Buchanan, *Taking the Long View: Three and a Half Decades of General Synod* (Church House Publishing, London, 2006).

deep in scholarship. Indeed, it would be difficult to guess that their author does not even, in fact, hold a first degree in theology, for they show the mind and training of a serious scholar at work, and that is worth observing.[5] One test of a scholar is the disciplined use of primary sources. This is very much in evidence in Chapter 5 and gives credibility to its ambitious title: '*What did Cranmer think he was doing?*' Of course, the Study remains, 'What Colin Buchanan thought Cranmer was doing' or, as some might say, unfairly I hasten to add, 'What Colin Buchanan would have liked Cranmer to have thought he was doing!' Nevertheless, what allows Colin to be remarkably successful (in my view) in this piece of trans-century mind-reading is the way he uses Cranmer's liturgical activity *alongside* his theological writings. Colin's attention to Cranmer's complete writings, as well as his sensitivity to both the historical setting and the way liturgy is constructed, gives him the feel of an archaeologist, painstakingly sifting the evidence, or of a detective piecing together the separate bits of information until they build up into a coherent and convincing picture.

In some chapters, the extensive search of sources, and the magnifying glass hovering over what is uncovered, are put to work on a very different historical period, and one in which evangelicals are usually less adept: the patristic age. This can be seen most clearly in Chapter 6 when Colin seeks to put an end to the offertory.[6] Here we can see with particular precision one of the basic scholarly purposes of historical excavation: to expose assumptions that have improperly influenced thought and practice because they have not been based on an accurate reading of the evidence. This exercise of 'clearing the undergrowth' (as he calls it) has always been an important aspect of Colin's work in print, lecture or debate. The sharpness of his theological scythe can be seen in action in Chapter 4 as he tackles some of the interpretative principles on which the (recently) inherited Anglican two-stage theories of initiation are based. To use another analogy, this time a boxing one taken from his synodical semi-autobiography, he has been committed to 'squaring the ropes for two opposite views to contest'.[7] In other words, he has wanted different views to have a fair fight and not to allow one corner to have an unfair advantage through unwarranted assumptions, or through any

---

5 It should not go unnoticed, though, that in 1993 Colin gained a Lambeth DD for his contribution to liturgical scholarship.

6 For a more recent, and impressive, example of Colin's patristic scholarship, see his *Justin Martyr on Baptism and Eucharist*, Joint Liturgical Studies no. 64 (SCM-Canterbury Press, Norwich, 2007).

7 Buchanan, *Taking the Long View*, p. 195.

other manipulation of the match, such as allowing one side to carry extra weight by dint of rank, reputation or custom. The fight is to be contested on the strength of the argument and by the power of persuasion arising from its own logic. At the same time, once the ropes are lined up, Colin seldom refrains from 'entering the ring as one of the opposed contestants'.[8] We will see more of this later when we look at how he takes Gregory Dix's powerful legacy head on.

A good deal of the passion that drives Colin's communicative energy and scholarly activity is his commitment to teaching, not only in the sense of correcting what he regards to be incorrect (see particularly his opening chapter explaining why he believed that the Liturgical Commission was in error in 1964, and his aforementioned *The end of the offertory*), but also in the more routine life of the classroom, where teachers and students need the support of reliable texts and studies. Personally, out of all his writings, I have found his essay on Cranmer's programme of liturgical revision the most helpful for teaching purposes, not least because of its very clever diagrams.

Important though teaching has been to Colin's scholarly endeavours, the revision of the Church's liturgy on a level unparalleled since Cranmer's day fuelled his passion both to uncover what is true and then seek to communicate it fiercely and fearlessly. Colin was brought onto the Liturgical Commission in 1964 when just out of his curacy in order to ensure that the views of more conservative evangelical voices were heard. Chapter 1 tells of the dilemmas that he was faced with immediately and how he chose to handle them. Chapter 2 gives a feel of the enjoyment he had on the Commission and the sense of opportunity that he and others had, especially in the years 1965 to 1971. The other chapters deal with most, but by no means all, of the theological themes which he pursued in the meetings of the Commission and in the various processes of General Synod: baptism, confirmation, eucharist (especially matters concerning offering or sacrifice) and ordination. Some of the papers were written alongside the revision process and their publication was expertly timed to maximize their influence upon it. It would be worth reading the articles alongside the various stages of the revision of the liturgy in the sort of way that Colin himself does with Cranmer's writing and the revisions of the sixteenth century. It is fascinating to see the battles that Colin won, and the ones that he lost, as well as where, in the words of John Bullimore, who chaired the synodical debate on a less-liturgical subject (establishment, in fact), he 'won the argument and lost the vote'.[9]

---

8 Buchanan, *Taking the Long View*, p. 195.
9 Buchanan, *Taking the Long View*, p. 225.

There are a number of other personae of Colin Buchanan that are worth noting as one reads the Collection, not only because they are interesting in their own right, but also because they help to place the writings in a larger context. Space does not allow for much more than mentioning them. One such persona is the publishing entrepreneur. I have already drawn attention to Colin's founding of Grove Books and to the careful timing of certain publications. It is the combination of these that made his influence so strategic. Colin's capacity to be the first word on a subject, if not the last, to use what became the strapline of Grove Books itself,[10] pre-dated the founding of his own publishing house (see, for example, his note about the fast writing and key timing of 'Reasons for Dissent' in the foreword of Chapter 2). But his creation of a publishing organ under his control gave him a guaranteed outlet for publications at monthly points in the revision processes. Similarly, his instigation of *News of Liturgy* through the same outlet gave him, as James Steven describes so well on pages 169–80, the sort of regular hearing in the latter decades of the twentieth century that anticipated the bloggers of the twenty-first.

Colin as an international Anglican and as an ecumenical Christian are both characteristics that are worth exploring in this collection. His commitment to the Anglican Communion is clear in Chapter 4, a text delivered to the Communion (following the 1991 International Anglican Liturgical Consultation), where his critique of two-stage patterns of initiation in which confirmation is necessary for full Christian status fell on more receptive ears than it did in much of the Church of England. A reading of some other of Colin's writings would highlight more clearly his significant ecumenical activity. Nevertheless, some of the principles with which he worked are evident in Chapter 7 in his comments on priesthood. Essentially, he remained committed to a robust reformed doctrine of presbyteral ministry which, on the one hand, disallowed any priestly accretions to ordained ministry that could not be applied equally to other members of the body of Christ and, on the other, insisted on the validity of the orders of those ordained by responsible churchly processes whether or not their orders had been conferred directly through the historic episcopate. Certainly behind the first, and probably behind the second, lies the classic Protestant position

---

10 My understanding is that the description of Grove Books as, 'Not the last word . . . but often the first', was coined by Michael Vasey. Colin's tribute to Michael's influence on him and on the liturgy of the Church can be found in *Michael Vasey: Liturgist and Friend* (Grove Books, Cambridge, 1999) which he edited on behalf of GROW.

which pervades his thought – that Rome had corrupted several of the catholic truths of the faith, and requires reform.[11] As he states elsewhere, if he believed otherwise he would become a Roman Catholic.

THE SORT OF METHOD TO LOOK FOR IN THE WRITINGS

Colin's method is one of close combat with a particular argument or position. Rather like an agile and determined fencer, he engages in sustained attack on those who support, actively or passively, a position that he suspects of being weaker than is generally assumed. His weapon is carefully targeted to test how well his opponent's view is defended, how far it will stand up to incisive critique and whether it represents more show than substance, erroneous for all its apparent elegance. His tactic is to subject the position to the analysis of Scripture, the evidence of actual patristic practice and the lessons of later history. Before we look more closely at these, it is worth noting that although each position and its proponents that he takes on are engaged with on their own terms, there are two schools of thought and practice with which Colin regularly finds himself in combat. The first is the most obvious one and is there in the foreground of Chapters 4 (Initiation), 6 (Offertory) and 7 (Priesthood) – mid-twentieth century Anglican liturgical orthodoxy in general, and the legacy of Gregory Dix in particular. The second is more hidden in this collection but, despite surface indications to the contrary, is in the background of Chapter 1 (Dissent), and also very much in the sight lines of Chapter 3 (Baptism) – the inherited practice of much contemporary Anglican evangelicalism.[12] Colin's overriding concern is to determine whether a particular liturgical principle, together with its theological rationale and its outworking in the life of the Church, is *scriptural*. Despite an apparent simplicity, Colin's hermeneutical methods are, in fact, sophisticated. His support of infant baptism and the ordination of women shows that he is well able to look through the surface level of Scripture to its deeper and determinative undercurrents. At the same time, his theological convictions about the place of the Bible in the life of the Church, and his capacities for historical

11 For a classic example of this position, see William Perkins, *A Reformed Catholike* (John Legat, London, 1598).

12 Like a skilled fencer, his assault is only designed to expose the flaws of the opposed view, not to harm the opponent. Although many may have been bruised by the encounters with Colin over the years, many (though perhaps not quite as many) have remained good friends with him, mutually committed to the common cause of the health of the Church of England and the promotion of the gospel.

reconstruction, ensure that he attends to the evidence of apostolic (that is, *scriptural*) practice and weighs the evidence accordingly. In other words, the theologian and the historian in him will only allow the worship of the Church the amount of rope that is justified by scriptural evidence. Other, looser, measurements influenced by perceived longevity of tradition, apparent pragmatic necessity or, worse still, sentimental association, run the serious risk of twisting the Church's worship into theological knots, and squeezing out its biblical breath.

Various examples of Colin's scriptural assault on a number of positions heavily defended by the received Anglican-Dixian school could be given, but his war on the front of evangelical practice is arguably more interesting at this point, given evangelicalism's commitment to biblical norms. His justification of infant baptism in Chapter 3 is relatively brief and relies on the fuller argument that can be found in a number of his other writings, but it does get to the driving contentions of his thought.[13] These are that, according to scriptural practice, baptism is 'fundamentally missionary'. It is practised by a 'missionary fellowship' and involves incorporation into ecclesial life and activity, including its fellowship meals and ongoing missionary practice. It is therefore necessary not only that children of believing parents are included within this missionary body and are expected to take their full part, but also that children of unbelieving parents who are not themselves active members of the missionary people should not be treated as candidates for baptism themselves until their parents have been evangelized. Evangelicals who were suspicious of infant baptism, as well as evangelicals (among others) who practised infant baptism indiscriminately on the grounds that, as it did not actually do anything, it could not harm anyone, were wrong-footed by a stance that placed more emphasis on what the Church is doing in baptism rather than on what the individual gains. Colin's ecclesial and missionary understanding of baptism anticipated several liturgical and theological developments around the turn of the century from the initiation rites of *Common Worship* (with their heightened profile for the Church), to the 'New Perspective on Paul' (with its contentions for the place of membership of the messianic community in the justification of the sinner).

Following on from Colin's testing of a position for its scriptural strength is his probing of its patristic stability. It is commonplace in theological and liturgical thought, and second nature in Anglicanism, to

---

13 For other of Colin's writings on infant baptism see e.g. *Is the Church of England Biblical?: An Anglican Ecclesiology* (Darton, Longman & Todd, London, 1998) and *A Case for Infant Baptism* (Grove Books, Cambridge, 1973, new edn 2009).

assume that patristic understanding and practice is a reliable guide to the intended meaning of Scripture and, often, to the actual practice of the apostles. In line with classic Protestant Anglicanism, Colin does not accept this principle entirely and, in the final analysis, is always prepared to turn the argument around and judge any later practice by the data of Scripture. However, for the most part he is happy to accept that patristic practice is significant theologically and historically, and is worthy of respect and serious engagement. On a purely pragmatic level, he knows that his arguments on straight scriptural grounds will be more difficult to win unless he can prove that patristic writers are also on his side. The way he goes about doing so is particularly clear in Chapter 6 where he takes on his main protagonist, Gregory Dix, and seeks to expose what he perceives as fatal flaws in one of Dix's favourite positions – the place of the offertory in the eucharist.

Colin is convinced that Dix misinterpreted the evidence and, in so doing, misled other scholars, framers of liturgy and the worship of large sections of the Church. In Chapter 6 Colin sets about the task of purging every 'bit of "patristic mythology" from our systems'. He does so because he believes that there are substantive biblical, liturgical and theological issues at stake. Biblically, he believes that Dix misconceived the dominical example, confusing the Lord's taking of bread and wine with some other action by which the elements are brought or given by the participants. Liturgically, he argues that Dix's attention to the bread and wine before the eucharistic prayer usurps the prayer itself. Theologically, he accuses Dix of overlaying an action about which the early history is uninterested with a theological meaning that allegedly belongs to the essence of the rite and, without which, in Dix's words, 'the primitive significance of the whole eucharist would not be incomplete but actually destroyed'.

Standing where we do now, relying on the work of Paul Bradshaw and a new generation of liturgical scholars who have shown us that patristic practice is much more complex than their predecessors thought, it is difficult to appreciate fully the assumptions which dominated much of twentieth-century scholarship.[14] Colin's revisiting of the evidence to assess whether it could bear the weight that had been built upon it (especially his concern 'to let the second century writers speak for themselves') anticipated the work of later scholars. In so doing he helped to uncover some unstable assumptions which had led to some

---

14 See, for example, Paul F. Bradshaw, *The Search for the Origins of Christian Worship: Sources and Methods for the Study of Early Liturgy* (SPCK, London, 1992, 2nd edn 2002) and *Eucharistic Origins* (SPCK, London, 2004).

clear misinterpretations of patristic history, including some of Dix's readings of the evidence about the offertory.

In addition to scriptural analysis and patristic assessment, Colin subjects liturgical arguments and positions to the light of the lessons of history. This is evident throughout his writing and debating, and no more so than right at the outset of his liturgical contribution. Chapter 1 describes the reasons for his dissent over the words proposed for the anamnesis in the draft order of the Second Series eucharistic rite, 'we offer unto thee this bread and this cup'. A major element in Colin's argument that such Hippolytan-type wording was improper was that, although it might have been perfectly acceptable in the third century, the history of eucharistic thought and practice made its contemporary use not only inadvisable in the Church of England but actually unworkable. We simply cannot return to the innocence of the third century and ignore the accretions of later centuries. History, Colin argues, teaches us that certain forms of wording at an earlier stage of the Church's life set in motion a line of theological and liturgical development that is to be avoided rather than encouraged.

SOME QUESTIONS TO POSE TO THE WRITINGS

It will be clear not only that I admire Colin Buchanan's contribution to liturgical study in general, and to the liturgical life of the Church of England in particular, but also that I sympathize with many of his views. So the questions that I would like to pose to this collection of papers and to their author will be different from, and more limited than, those asked by people who share less common theological ground with him. Wherever one stands, however, there is no doubt that close engagement with Colin's arguments, and particularly with the scriptural and historical evidence, is the best compliment that can be paid to his work. I will concentrate my main questions on 'confirmation and the signification of the Spirit', 'ritual expression during the preparation of the gifts in the eucharist', 'the veracity of Cranmer's eucharistic theology', and 'priestly associations to presbyteral ministry'. But first a word about context and style.

I have used a fencing analogy to describe Colin's method. He uses, among others, a boxing analogy. Both are adversarial. Historically, Christian debate has been pretty adversarial. Occasion has often demanded it: Paul and the Judaizers, Irenaeus and the Gnostics, Luther to the right and left of the Reformation, Barth and the German Christians and so on. Colin is part of this honourable tradition and it has borne good fruit, even if people did not always think so at the time. But what happens when times change and the atmosphere is different? What happens when the culture shifts, when, for example, modernity begins to fade and a new set of attitudes which more naturally permit a greater diversity than before sets in? What happens when the Church finds itself engaging with the issues that the world is throwing up and more instinctively unites itself around the deep themes of worship than it did previously? And what happens when the theological ground is revived by a common rediscovery of a major doctrine, such as the doctrine of the Trinity, in a way that mutually energizes different traditions and produces common liturgical interests?

All of this has happened over the course of Colin's liturgical career, and this partly explains why Colin's evangelical successors on the Liturgical Commission operated in a different, less adversarial manner than he did. This is not to criticize the positions or strategies that Colin has taken. Indeed, those of us who followed him were at times able to take a more relaxed position because of the stakes that he had already driven into the ground as, to be fair, was he for a large part after the 1964–1966 debacle.[15] Nevertheless, it is to raise a question worth posing to the texts regarding their contextuality. Likewise, it is to raise a question to pose to the process of liturgical truth-finding in the present stage of history in terms of how we discern where the limits of diversity of opinion and practice lie. How do we best dig more deeply into the deep core of the common Christian *Tradition* that lies beyond our competing *traditions*?

As for more detailed questions to ask of the writings, let me begin with confirmation. While I find myself almost entirely convinced by the case for the completion of sacramental initiation in baptism, I cannot quite dispel a remaining niggle. I can certainly see no justification for a separate *initiatory* rite of sacramental completion of baptism whether viewed in terms of personal appropriation of baptism or the giving of the Spirit. On the other hand, the ease with which initiation into the life

---

15 Once the battle over the proposed Second Series anamnesis was over, Colin worked creatively and irenically with other members of the Commission on the Series 3 anamnesis, gaining respect not only for his clear views but for his capacity to work with others across the Church of England, a process that culminated in his chairing of the *Alternative Service Book*'s eucharistic Rite A Steering Committee, and thereby piloting the rite successfully through General Synod (in what Colin describes as 'the drone's brief flight', that is the only opportunity he had to speak regularly from the platform, rather than the floor, of General Synod; see *Taking the Long View*, p. 75). Nevertheless, it would still be fair to say, certainly on the basis of the papers in this Collection, that Colin's style of writing and debate is combative, seeking to hunt out the weaknesses in other points of view, rather than conciliatory, searching for common ground behind the apparently opposing views.

of Christ can forget the dynamic of the Spirit's life in the believer makes me cautious about losing a critical spiritual reality.

Similarly, the repeated nagging of historical evidence of a distinctively pneumatological dimension to the living out of baptism pulls at my instinctive tendency to want to keep Christian initiation neat and tidy. Whether it is the cumulative effect of those biblical texts beloved of the two-stagers, problematic though they may be in isolation, or the dramatic stories of fourth-century bishops grabbing hold of new Christians as they emerged from baptism to pray in the Spirit that had been given in the waters, or contemporary charismatic experience of the newly-baptized receiving the gift of tongues as the elders lay hands immediately upon them, I am left wondering whether some sort of post-baptismal signification of the presence and power of the Spirit to Christian living is a worthy component of Christian initiation. Of course, it must not undermine the work of the Spirit in baptism. But might it not reinforce it? Might it not be a sign that the life of the Spirit into which we have been plunged in baptism is a life that needs to be continually sustained, and continually filled? Might it not signify the sort of spiritual valve that is essential to Christian living to show that the ongoing strengthening of the Spirit is part of the daily life of Christians? Might it not be the marker that this strengthening is administered ecclesially whether by the prayer of a friend, the laying on of hands at a time of particular challenge, or a major pastoral rite at the coming of age or renewal of faith? Hence, I remain satisfied with the inclusion in the *Common Worship* baptismal rite of a signification of the Spirit (with or without anointing with chrism) in close proximity to the preceding baptism but distinguishable from it, and to which later (in my mind, pastoral) rites for the strengthening of the Spirit can be, as it were, attached.

My next question is about Cranmer's eucharistic theology; and it is not a question about whether Colin got Cranmer right (I think he did), but whether Cranmer himself got it right. A supplementary question, more directly to Colin, is whether he thinks that Cranmer was right in a specific point of his eucharistic liturgy. That point is over the consecration. Colin's argument that by 1552 Cranmer had dispensed with the need for a liturgical consecration is entirely convincing. But was Cranmer right, or was later Anglican tradition right to correct him? To continue with the personalization of the issue, did Gregory Dix have more of a point than Colin allows in saying, 'This was what it all came to in the end – the bread had nothing to do with the Body – That was what [Cranmer] was dying for'?[16] In other words, even though theologically – as Dix fails to recognize and Colin seeks to prove – Cranmer certainly believed in a real encounter with the

---

16 G. N. Dix, *The Shape of the Liturgy,* 3rd edn (Continuum, London, 2005) p. 674. Also quoted by Colin in Chapter 6.

presence of the risen Christ in the eucharist, did he do enough to link *liturgically* the gift of the presence of Christ to the actual bread and wine of the Supper by demonstrating the intrinsic relationship between them within the sacramental event? In other words, did Cranmer close the loophole in reformed eucharistic theology which, because of its proper emphasis on the place of faith in meeting the risen Christ, finds it very difficult to relate the reception of the presence to the act of eating and drinking in remembrance of him? I have argued elsewhere that the liturgical consecration is the means by which the Church stays faithful to Christ's command to tie this particular remembering of Christ in faith to the actual bread and wine of his Supper, and that without it there is little to counteract, theologically and practically, the tendency in evangelical Christianity to push the eucharist to the optional edges of its life.[17]

My next question revolves around ritualization, particularly in relation to what happens before the eucharistic prayer. Colin's campaign to cut the connection between a convoluted process, with attendant theological overlays, by which the eucharistic elements are brought into the sphere of the sacramental activity and the first dominical command of taking bread and wine seem to me to be correct. However, his preferred liturgical expression is problematic in itself. Its purest form is found in Rite A of the ASB where 'The taking of the bread and cup' is distinguished by way of clear headings from 'The Preparation of the Gifts' and by a rubric instructing the President to 'Take the bread and wine into his/her hands and replace them on the holy table'. As Simon Jones notes in his introduction to the recent edition of Dix's *Shape of the Liturgy*, in practice this looks awkward and confusing. Unless the elements are already on the holy table and, as it were, ready for the action (as they are, of course, in the BCP rite), the separate taking of bread and wine simply seems to repeat what has already been done. And even where they are in place and ready to go, my observation is that by far the majority of presidents simply ignore the rubric in its present *Common Worship* form and move straight into the eucharistic prayer.

So, my question to Colin's analysis of the phenomenon of the so-called offertory is how his reform – which I generally support – can be expressed ritually? One way (and this is a practice I use myself) is to use a simple text which expresses what we are doing at this point of the action, such as, 'Following Jesus' example, we take bread and wine, and we give thanks to God'. But my supplementary question to Colin is: providing the simplicity and functionality of the preparation of the table is maintained, is it as necessary as he maintains to distinguish the preparation of the table from the taking of bread and wine? Indeed, is it really possible?

---

17 See my *Evangelical Eucharistic Thought* (Cambridge University Press, 2002), especially chapters 12–14.

The final question I want to pose to the writings is whether there is a proper sense in which priestly language may be applied to presbyteral ministry. Of course, we should begin in the right place, and that is by rooting the second order of ministry in presbyteral language as the New Testament and the early Fathers do, and as do the Reformers and the Second Vatican Council. Nevertheless, the activities of presbyteral ministry – watching over the people of God (Acts 20.28), building up their life through sound teaching (2 Timothy 4.1-4), modelling authentic discipleship and the striving after blameless conduct (1 Peter 5.3), equipping the saints for the work of ministry (Ephesians 4.12), leading the missionary people of God in the 'priestly service of the gospel' (Romans 15.16) – are all directed towards the realization of the calling and true identity of God's people to be a priestly nation that will bless all the nations of the earth. It is this Christ-like identity that presbyters long to see formed in the people of God (Galatians 4.19). An integral element of this ministry of ecclesial activation to which the presbyter is called is the being and doing of it in the actual person of the presbyter. Presbyters are to be 'examples to the flock' (1 Peter 5.3) who 'watch over themselves' (Acts 20.28), guarding their sanctity, and who do the work of evangelists ministering the gospel to the Gentiles so that all the peoples of the world will be sanctified and their offering to God made acceptable (Romans 15.16). In this sense, is it not permissible to see in presbyters signs of the priestly people of God who both embody and enable the priestly identity of the body of Christ? Is not their ministry of signification and realization of the Church's identity, through the Spirit who leads us into the life of Christ, a priestly ministry? Priestly identity and activity is a distinctive mark of presbyteral ministry but not in any sort of exclusive way. Quite the reverse: the priestly ministry of presbyters is, through the Spirit, expressed and fulfilled in the fulfilment of the Church as it reaches out to 'the measure of the full stature of Christ' (Ephesians 4.13).

While committed to the logic of his theological position in argument, Colin has proved to be a realist in practice, at least within certain clearly defined limits. The nomenclature of the second order of ministry is one example among many. For, albeit with some theological reluctance, Colin is, in fact, ready to allow presbyters to be 'also called priests'. It is this combination of penetrating and passionate theological argument with generosity in practice that has made Colin Buchanan such an influence upon the Church of England and on those who, with him, love it deeply and care for its worship. We will remain indebted to him.

Christopher Cocksworth, Bishop of Coventry

Revising Liturgy

Chapter 1

The new Communion service – reasons for dissent

FOREWORD

Having joined the Liturgical Commission in 1964, I was almost immediately confronted with a draft eucharistic text containing proposals I could not in conscience use, and therefore could not recommend. The Commission, however, proved unshakeable in their chosen dependence upon Hippolytus, and I was driven on 31 March 1966 to dissent from their final text. As that text was going to the Convocations in early May, I drafted against the clock a booklet explaining my dissent. This was published sufficiently fast for copies to go to every member of the two Convocations before the debate. It soon went to a second printing, and was also reprinted in The Churchman, *vol. 80, no. 2 (Summer 1966).*

In joining with the Commission in generally commending this Report, I reluctantly dissent from the last paragraph but one of section 24. Enquiry has shown that the phrase 'we offer unto thee this bread and this cup' in this paragraph is unacceptable to many Anglicans. I could not use it myself.

I also dissent from the proposed optional petition for the dead in section 14 for doctrinal reasons.

The above words are the text of the dissenting note I added to the report on the Communion service submitted to the Archbishops after the March meeting of the Liturgical Commission. I write now to express more fully my reasons for that dissent. It was not a step to be taken lightly and one which I would have far preferred to have avoided. I have sufficient grounds of principle to have taken it on my own. Nevertheless I am confirmed in my decision by enquiries I was able to make after the publication of the interim draft text in December 1965. I now know that I express the convictions of a wide section of the Church of

England. My detailed reasoning is of course my own. My conclusions are held by many. The results of my enquiries are summarized in an appendix.

'WE OFFER UNTO THEE THIS BREAD AND THIS CUP'

The Communion text is laid out so that the sacramental section of the service clearly expresses the acts instituted by our Lord. These are, in order, the taking of the bread and wine, the thanksgiving over them, the breaking of the bread, and the administration or sharing of them both. These are the only 'acts' which can be called 'instituted'. The 'Thanksgiving' here, as traditionally, includes a narrative of the Lord's institution of the sacrament, containing (with respect to both bread and cup) his command to 'do this in remembrance of me' (1 Corinthians 11.24–25). The next paragraph is traditionally an 'anamnesis' – that is, an echoing of his command, with a statement of how we intend to fulfil it. Hippolytus, in the most ancient liturgical text we possess (about AD 215), at this point said, 'Therefore in remembrance of his death and resurrection we offer to thee the bread and the cup, giving thanks to thee because thou hast found us worthy to stand before thee and minister to thee.' Here is the direct ancestor or archetype of the Commission's text. Cranmer in 1549 wrote: 'Wherefore . . . we . . . do celebrate and make here before thy Divine Majesty with these thy holy gifts, the memorial which thy Son hath willed us to make . . .' This, of course, though conceivably involving a Godward 'movement', does not resolve the then debated question of *how* we make memorial of Christ. To this extent the Commission's proposals lie well to the further side of the 1549 ambiguity. Cranmer however was moving in the opposite direction. In 1552 he resolved the question – the vital thing that we *do* in remembrance of Christ is to eat and drink. Not content with merely describing our eating and drinking at this point, he went further yet. The very acts of eating and drinking were moved to this place in the service and made into an anamnesis. The words of administration were altered to bring out this anamnesis aspect – 'Take and eat this *in remembrance* . . .' (This has been obscured by later changes.) For myself, whilst I gladly use Cranmer's rite, I am equally happy to follow a more traditional outline. That difference is not the point at issue. The question here is – what are we in fact to do or say we do 'in remembrance of him'? The traditional answer in liturgy from Hippolytus onwards was 'we offer . . .'. But this, as Cranmer saw, is *not* what our Lord commanded. 'Offering' is not one of the instituted acts of Christ, and is therefore an intrusion.

It is not only an intrusion, it is in fact a regrettable one. The initiative in a sacrament lies with God. He provides the elements ('these thy creatures'), he interprets them with his word, and he gives the inward grace they convey. We give thanks over them, but in so doing we should acknowledge them as provided primarily *by* God *for* us, if any question of their origin is to be raised at all. In a secondary sense we do of course literally provide them ourselves, but if any liturgical expression needs to be given to this (which I very much doubt) it could only properly come at the 'Preparation of the Bread and Wine'. After that the sacramental elements are at God's disposal not ours, and further giving them to God by us is redundant and badly misleading. The context provided by the narrative of our Lord's institution neither encourages nor permits a 'movement' of the bread and wine from us to God. To 'offer' is *not* the logical fulfilment of our Lord's command which the linking 'wherefore' claims it to be.

This in itself might be reasonably innocent even if illogical. But a set of words cannot now be wrenched free from its historical associations. The associations which this set of words has gathered are various expressions of one or more doctrines loosely covered by the term 'eucharistic sacrifice'. These doctrines, whether ancient, medieval or modern, sophisticated or crude, must, if they are to obtain liturgical expression, at some point link an offering of *ours* with *this* bread and *this* cup. The anamnesis is traditionally the place where this is done. It is hardly possible therefore to take 'we offer unto thee this bread and this cup' as just an archaizing return to Hippolytus, as distinct from an expression of a modern doctrine of eucharistic sacrifice. Hippolytus merely provides a convenient peg on which to hang the modern doctrine, and would surely never have been copied otherwise. Most such modern doctrines seem to me to be defective in just the very point of wanting to ensure that we have something to offer God which is peculiar to a Communion service. Certainly there are responsive sacrifices which we are to offer. Thanksgiving is one such sacrifice, the offering of our whole selves to God is another. But such sacrifices are in no way peculiar to the eucharist. They should no doubt find liturgical expression at the eucharist, for they are very appropriate to it. They do in fact have liturgical expression at other points in the text under consideration. But they cannot properly be offered by, with, or under the bread and the wine. This particular offering is in fact additional to those, and I have found myself unable to think of any doctrine of eucharistic sacrifice which I could both believe and want to express this way.

The Commission has of course been well aware of the different schools of thought in the Church of England. Its claim (as in *Alternative Services Second Series*, p. 147, or in the speech of Canon Couratin at the

Liturgical Conference in February 1966) is that a liberty of interpretation will allow all Anglicans to use this text equally happily. That claim
was made without all schools of thought being equally heard. Many
Anglicans regard an oblation such as this as unambiguously wrong for
today, and others again can only accept it at the cost of real unhappiness
at what is one of the most solemn points of the service. In other words,
what this text needs is not interpretation but alteration. Men who fear
that doctrinal novelty is being imported will be confirmed in their fears
by the Commission's insistence that this form of words, and nothing
less than this form of words, must be recommended to the Church. For
myself I was and am ready to recommend at this point different texts
giving varying emphases, and some of these I add as an appendix [see
end of chapter]. I would not myself insist on any one particular set of
words, but the Commission in effect does. As I could not accept the
Commission's set, I think an onus now lies on those who so immovably
insist on this form of words to show *why* it is so vital to a proper fulfilling of our Lord's command.

   Here Hippolytus (and, for that matter, Clement, Justin, Irenaeus,
etc.) must come up for reconsideration. A full treatment of their
eucharistic doctrine is beyond my present task. But the application of a
guiding principle will enable us to get their writings into perspective.
The principle is that before controversy has arisen men often express
themselves in ways that would later be regarded as unguarded and misleading. This is obviously true with regard to the doctrine of the Trinity.
We would be unwise to take our creed from pre-Nicene writings – we
cannot 'get behind' Nicea. Eucharistic controversies of course have
never had so thorough and decisive resolution given to them. The
Reformation however saw many issues brought to a head, and the Hip-
polytean form of words, so far from 'getting behind' the Reformation,
in fact takes sides in the Reformation disputes. Hippolytus obviously
used the words innocent of all offence (as the ante-Nicenes did in their
sub-trinitarian statements about God), but that does not mean in either
case that we can. The innocence is lost when they are imported into our
present context.

   The principle further means that men of Hippolytus' times are often
simply wrong in their use of Scripture. Liturgy was not in fixed form
but great respect was paid to 'the tradition'. This means that liturgy
grew and changed slowly with the passing of the years. The oblation terminology arose and developed alongside two other dubious ideas. One
was the notion that the eucharist was the fulfilment of the 'pure
sacrifice' prophesied in Malachi 1.11, the other that in some sense the
Christian ministry held a sacrificing priesthood. How much these ideas

sponsored each other and affected liturgical expression of the eucharist is difficult to say. But they seem to be interrelated, and they are all equally a departure from the New Testament. Hippolytus himself calls the bishop a 'high priest', and links with this title the bishop's offering to God the gifts of the church. By parity of reasoning with that which has given us this eucharistic text, is the bishop to be called a 'high priest' in any future ordinal? If so, then further controversy must be expected. If not, then why is Hippolytus' terminology so sacrosanct in the eucharist?

None of what I have written above means that I despair of finding in the future a rite in which all Anglicans can agree. Quite the reverse. It is that very hope which makes me wish all the more that this text should not be passed in its controversial form. These are days of great change in the Church of England, and times when different schools of thought are genuinely on far better terms with each other than has often been true up to now. We are also beginning to learn from each other biblical truths which separately we have tended to overlook. In this situation I, as an evangelical, find a new flexibility among anglo-catholics. Today, to the question 'What do we need, and what do we *not* need, to say in a eucharistic liturgy?', the answer that many will give is 'We *do* need to give thanks over the bread and the cup, but we do *not* need to make specific verbal reference to offering the elements to God in that thanks-giving.' This eirenic approach (the spirit of which I would warmly wish to reciprocate) seems to me to hold great hope for the future, and to make the present text all the more regrettable. For it is not only the *spirit* of this sort of approach which an evangelical must applaud, it is also the actual content of it. It suggests that if we are to express the thanksgiving *totally* in terms of thanksgiving we might well be able to agree a text. And this I know to be true from personal experience. I can agree with at least some fairly representative anglo-catholics in a text which says *all* that both sides feel must be said and includes *nothing* that would give offence to either side. I remain hopeful that even the Com-mission itself, which has for the moment abandoned the quest for an agreed liturgy, will return to it and succeed in the future.

Some of the factors that have produced the situation in which I have found it necessary to dissent may not recur, and this may make the task slightly easier in the future. On this occasion the unexpected need for immediate and final action after the Liturgical Conference has been one reason, and perhaps the lack of a clear spelling out of the unacceptable nature of these words at that Conference has been another, why the Commission has settled for a text less than unanimously.

THE PRAYER FOR THE DEAD

My dissent in this case differs from that in the preceding one, in that here the matter I oppose is only optional. Thus its mere existence in the eucharistic text will not of itself stop those who will not pray for the dead from using the text. Nevertheless its existence raises a serious doctrinal problem. The same question is of course raised by *First Series* and by the Occasional Prayers and The Burial of the Dead in *Second Series*. I came onto the Commission at the point when the latter service was reaching its final stage of approval. I had had no part in the discussion leading up to its production, so, rather than dissent, I asked that I should be treated for these purposes as having not yet joined the Commission. I anticipated that a list of members would be attached to the report without my name appearing. In the event *Second Series* was not printed in this way, so now it appears as though I may well have assented to The Burial of the Dead Report. This was not so. I dissented from its historical introduction, its agnosticism about the state of even the Christian departed, and its prayers for the dead.

What then is the status of prayers for the dead in the Church of England? Three points of view are to be found. One is that, as not being explicitly condemned in the Articles, they are perfectly permissible liturgical material, though not in point of fact appearing in any Anglican liturgy from the Reformation onwards until this century. Another view is that, as being excluded from the 1552 and 1662 Prayer Books and denounced by the Book of Homilies, they are forbidden in the Church of England. A third and mediating point of view, to which I would subscribe, sees them as neither forbidden nor encouraged as private opinions or individual practices, but not eligible for inclusion in official liturgies. Liturgy expresses doctrine, and official liturgy official doctrine. It is true that no declaration of assent will be required to experimental services, yet such services can only be authorized as being 'in their doctrine neither contrary to, nor indicative of any departure from, the doctrine of the Church of England' (Alternative Services Measure 1965, section 1, para. 1). To authorize prayers for the dead even experimentally is to make them part of Anglican doctrine, and to rule out two of the three points of view I have listed above. It is for this reason that I cannot commend them.

It is freely acknowledged on all sides that the New Testament contains no prayers for the dead. To urge that Onesiphorus (2 Timothy 1.18) was dead when Paul prayed for him is to write one's conclusions into one's premises. We do not know, and must therefore decide on other evidence what the apostolic practice was. And here there is silence throughout. Prayers are offered for hosts of other objects, but none on behalf of the departed. Rather the reverse – for the New Testament *does* have a doctrine that we would call 'the communion of the saints'. It was just a lack of such a doctrine that unsettled the church at Thessalonica. Paul therefore writes to reassure the Thessalonians (1 Thessalonians 4.13–18). They need have no sorrows or fears on behalf of the departed. Yet he never tells them to express their unity with the departed by praying for them. His comfort to the bereaved is a declaration of eschatological confidence. For the moment the departed 'sleep', one day we shall be reunited with them joyfully at Christ's return. The situation was one that cried out for a commendation of prayer for the faithful departed, if that was an apostolic practice. Modern advocates of the practice would hardly have missed the opportunity if they had been addressing the same situation.

The point is frequently made and easily taken that prayer for the dead does not automatically entail belief in a purgatory (which is certainly contrary to the New Testament and the doctrine of the Church of England). This approach allows us to have absolute confidence in the blessed state of the faithful departed whilst still praying for them. It is certainly thoroughly in accord with the New Testament to pray that God will do what he has definitely promised to do. 'Lead us not into temptation' is a good example of this. On these grounds prayer for the faithful departed is not contrary to the New Testament, but a natural inference from it. These grounds may well be acceptable, provided that two further safeguards are observed.

The first safeguard is that, even when we are praying to God to do what he has promised to do, we only pray thus with respect to things that are still future. We do not pray that God should do something yesterday. Neither do Christians pray that they should be incorporated into Christ. Past events are accepted as having happened, and we either give thanks for them or repent of them. The logic of this safeguard is that we only ask for the departed those things which are really future. 'Grant them a share in thy eternal kingdom' does not fall into this category. 'Grant them a joyful resurrection on the last day' would (as might Paul's prayer in 2 Timothy 1.18 even if Onesiphorus were dead). To become sharers in God's eternal kingdom may be seen as occurring in this life ('in knowledge of whom *standeth* our eternal life'), or on departure from this life ('and *in the world to come* life everlasting'), or, and this is admitted, on the last day. The future reference of the prayer is therefore possible, but not so sufficiently clear as to make the prayer fall into the category of permissive prayers for the departed. The prayer might be amended, even as it stands, to read 'Grant them at the last day to inherit thy eternal kingdom'. This would draw out the future perspective it needs in order to be legitimate.

However, there is another safeguard to be considered. The argument above still only admits prayers for the dead of this particular sort as possible forms of private prayer for the theologically sophisticated. Public prayer is a different question. Here we must keep Paul's distinction between what is lawful and what is expedient. We have a moral duty to consider those who are not theologically sophisticated. They are easily caused to stumble by *any* forms of prayer for the dead. They become unsure of heaven, or distrustful of the authority that sanctions such prayer. We live in days when there is little certainty about heaven, little confidence in the ecclesiastical powers-that-be, and little theological sophistication in ordinary congregations. So even lawful forms of prayer for the dead should still be reckoned inexpedient.

They are also inexpedient because they seem to admit a larger principle. The present debate about prayers for the dead tends to deal in block judgements for or against them. It is thus inevitable that any allowance of the legitimate forms of such prayer will open the door to the illegitimate forms. No proper grounds can be alleged for praying that the dead may currently enjoy rest or light. Prayers like this prima facie teach that they lack these blessings and that is why we are praying for them. The Church of England perhaps needs a doctrinal commission (perhaps with an ecumenical composition) to define which prayers for the dead are possible and which not. Until such a distinction is officially made, they must be viewed under one heading as changing the official doctrine of the Church of England if they are authorized. That is why I am opposed to their inclusion in the text.

What should happen then when congregations want such prayers? Are they to be refused their desire for the sake of some perhaps mythical 'weaker brethren'? Clearly the only sensible answer to this question is 'no'. No one wants to be purely negative about this. But it is not necessary to write such prayers into the text. The Commission's form of intercessions allows great liberty of interpolation. Those who wish, for reasons of their own, to pray for the faithful departed may easily do so under the heading of the Church. Prayers may be inserted here at will. And such prayer here would give better expression to the communion of saints. An insertion would not become expressive of Anglican doctrine, but remain a private opinion within the Church. Only in this way can full justice be done simultaneously to all three points of view listed earlier.

It is interesting to notice that the new Roman Catholic form of corporate intercessions at the mass has no section for the departed at all.

They are commended to the intercession of the Virgin Mary in a final petition and that is all. They are also still the subject of intercession in the canon, but this is said silently by the celebrant and is not part of 'The Prayer of the Faithful'. The Roman intercessions have four main sections of prayer, the first three of which correspond with the Commission's first three. Where however the Commission has the section for the departed, the Roman form has a section 'For the local Christian Community'. Something like this would be sheer gain for us.

Canon Couratin stated publicly at the Liturgical Conference that the intercessions did not necessarily represent the Commission's final mind. They now do, but once again it is pressure of time which has made it so. I have been unable to accept the final form, not through any desire to obstruct the wishes of those from whom I differ. I dissent because it goes too far towards closing what the Church of England has up to now left as an officially open question.

THE UNITY AND POLICY OF THE
CHURCH OF ENGLAND

Thus far I have tried to express my personal reactions only, and my arguments would stand even if no one else shared them. However, the situation is far more serious than that. Through enquiry I have good reason to think that a large majority of evangelicals, and a small minority of other churchmen will agree with me in at least one of the two questions over which I have dissented. The Commission has therefore been facing a problem which is not simply a liturgical one. That problem now in turn faces the Convocations and the House of Laity. Members are being asked not simply 'Do you like this liturgy?' but rather 'Are you prepared to commend liturgy which will prove divisive?' The Commission, not without regrets, has been so prepared. This policy seems to me very questionable, so that even if I personally had been prepared to sanction the text, I would still have been given pause by the opposition to it. We live in a time that sees an unprecedented drawing together of evangelicals and anglo-catholics. It is a cause for regret that the Commission is prepared to forfeit or at least obstruct this progress by a liturgy that will tend to divide men into parties once more.

The case has been put to me that the matter is not as serious as this. Evangelicals, it is said, are not being asked to give up anything they wish to keep, nor to use anything they personally dislike. They have frequently professed themselves satisfied with the 1662 rite, and they will be able to continue using it. As 1662 lacks certain emphases which others desire, it is only right and fair that a new rite should be produced for these others. This argument has a specious plausibility, but a closer examination will show that it is disastrous. It is a proposal to isolate and fossilize evangelicals. They are by no means so committed to the structure, language and emphases of 1662 that they want no part in progressive experiment. They are as enthusiastic for liturgical revision as anyone. But if the policy of the Church of England is to produce 'party' liturgies, then two, three or more commissions ought to be asked to produce them. That policy would stand self-condemned, yet the case that 1662 is to become one 'party' liturgy and the new text another is only a variant on the same theme. The quest for an agreed text is far and away more sensible, and that is the Commission's task. Men concerned that the whole Church of England should move together and pray together will perhaps want the Commission to be told its task more plainly.

The Church of England today is not an isolated entity in Christendom. As the ecumenical movement involves us in ever closer relations with Methodists, Presbyterians and so on, it is vital that our liturgy be ecumenical and eirenic. Ecumenical relations in the past have frequently been disturbed by the ability of a party representing less than the whole Church of England to present its own case as the official Anglican one. That will be the case if this liturgy passes into use in its present form.

The actual strength of opposition to the text is extremely difficult to assess accurately in the very short time that has been available. Because of the very small initial printing in December clergy in many places did not receive copies till late in February. This has meant there has been little opportunity for thorough study, and no chance of taking thorough sampling of opinion. The Church may have been somewhat misled by the hesitant nature of the opposition at the Liturgical Conference (where perhaps it was not anticipated that the text would be reaching its final form so soon). On the Commission itself, whilst I have been heard with the greatest patience and understanding, for which I am grateful, yet my numerical representation as one among twenty is not such as to suggest that a large section of the Church of England has similar objections to these critical points in the text. Lest there should be further misunderstanding of the extent of the opposition I have attempted to systematize in an appendix [see end of chapter, at foot of p. 15, where the original appendix is briefly reported] the evidence I have to hand.

In many respects opposition to the interim draft ran far beyond the two matters on which I have dissented. Some of these objections have been met by the Commission. For instance, the ten commandments

(and the two), and the old words of administration have been option-
ally included. Other objections I have felt unable to press. I have tried
to meet the rest of the Commission by sinking many matters of
emphasis or preference for the sake of agreement.

My present dissent therefore only arises on matters of principle. My
hope is that even men who do not share those principles, or would not
apply them as I have done, will yet sufficiently respect them not to
authorize this service in its present divisive form.

APPENDIX 1: THE TEXT OF AN ANAMNESIS

How are the various possible texts of the anamnesis to be classified? In
the light of the foregoing arguments the most helpful division is
between those which describe a Godward action with reference to the
bread and cup and those which describe a movement from God to man.
The classification would then be as follows:

Godward action

1 'We . . . offer unto thy most excellent Majesty of thine own gifts a
   pure victim, a holy victim, a spotless victim, the holy bread of
   eternal life, and the cup of everlasting salvation.' (Roman mass)
2 'We offer thee thine own from what is thine.' (Eastern Orthodox
   Liturgy of St Chrysostom)
3 'We offer to thee this bread and this cup.' (Liturgical Commission
   following Hippolytus)
4 'We do this as thy Son commanded, offering to thee, with this holy
   Bread and Cup, our praise and thanksgiving for his one sacrifice . . .'
   (Liturgy for Africa)
5 'We . . . do celebrate and make here before thy Divine Majesty, with
   these holy gifts, which now we offer unto thee, the memorial which
   thy Son hath commanded us to make.' (Scottish Liturgy following
   1549 but adding an offering)
6 'We . . . set before thee this bread and this cup to be that memorial
   which he has commanded us to make.' (Southwark Liturgy for discussion following ancient Alexandrian Liturgy of St Mark)
7 'We here present unto thee, through thy Holy Spirit, this bread of
   eternal life and this cup of everlasting salvation.' (G. Cope, J. G.
   Davies and D. A. Tytler, *An Experimental Liturgy*, Lutterworth
   Press, London, 1963)

Despite the attempts to break away from the word 'offer', each of these texts contains in substance the same thought, and none could well carry assent throughout the Church of England.

Manward action

> We in obedience to thy Son's command do break this bread and drink this cup in remembrance of him. (L. E. H. Stephens-Hodge, *An Evangelical Eucharist*)[1]

This is one sample of the sort of words that more genuinely describe our Lord's instituted acts. Perhaps a little more consistency could be obtained by saying either '. . . eat . . . drink . . .' or '. . . break . . . bless . . .'. The rigorous purist might criticize such words by saying that they only describe one, or perhaps two, of the instituted acts, but they are surely the right ones to describe, and the previous forms describe none of them at all. It might also be said that this form does not describe what we are doing at the moment we are saying the words. The logic of this criticism would bring us back to Cranmer's method of making the administration the anamnesis. Otherwise Cranmer himself would no doubt have had a similar form. For the sake of unity however we are prepared to be a little less logical than Cranmer, and the criticisms do not seem overwhelming. I would like to see this tried.

Neutral forms of words

> 1   'We . . . do celebrate and make here before thy divine Majesty, with these thy holy gifts, the memorial which thy Son hath willed us to make.' (1549)

This would be possible, though with some discomfort as it seems to veer towards the 'Godward' side.

> 2   'We . . . entirely desire thy fatherly goodness mercifully to accept this our sacrifice of praise and thanksgiving.' (*Alternative Services First Series* following the 'Interim Rite')

[1   This was a draft text produced in 1963 by Leo Stephens-Hodge, my predecessor at the London College of Divinity, at the request of the staffs of the evangelical theological colleges, and its text only existed in duplicated form. It was written up by its author in *Studia Liturgica*, vol. III, no. 3 (Winter 1964), pp. 175–7. It came, of course, from days when evangelicals were thought to be opposed on principle to any service other than 1662.]

This involves a play on words (which have been moved from the context they had in either 1549 or 1552), and in the upshot either says the wrong things about the bread and cup or else says nothing about them at all. It is therefore unsatisfactory.

3　'We . . . do this.' (CSI, and draft Irish rite)

This is probably the neatest and simplest form possible, but it may well say too little. There is no explicit reference to the bread and the cup, and the question of what we do is left totally unresolved. It smacks of contrived vagueness.

My own strong preference would be for something in the second category, but it is probable that somewhere in the last category a way will emerge. None of the listed texts quite meets the case, but I have reason to think that a text expressed more definitely in terms of thanksgiving might command widespread assent. An example would be:

We give thanks to thee over this bread and this cup.

This describes one of the instituted acts, and the one we are doing at that very moment. It steers clear of both offering and receiving whilst saying something positive and relevant in unambiguous terms. The full text might then read something like this:

Wherefore, O Lord, having in remembrance his saving passion, his resurrection from the dead, and his glorious ascension into heaven, and looking for the coming of his kingdom, we give thanks to thee over this bread and this cup; and we pray thee to accept this our thanksgiving, and to grant that as we eat and drink we may be filled with thy heavenly benediction and grace, through the same Christ our Lord . . .

Appendix 2 – 'The Extent of Opposition' – was a collating of all the evangelical responses I had been able to get to the draft text between mid-February and the end of March. Time had been very short as the original Alternative Services Second Series *had only had a tiny printing, and texts had thus not got round the country till February. The responses were overwhelmingly hostile to the oblation of the bread and cup in the eucharistic prayer, and only marginally less so to the petition for the departed.*

POSTSCRIPT

The Convocations took the booklet seriously, and initiated attempts to find a unitive text (see my Taking the Long View, *chapters 5 and 7). Theology in October 1966 contained four essays on 'We offer this bread and this cup . . .'. With Roger Beckwith, who had helped me draft the booklet, I asked the editor why we had been omitted from these essays. He invited a reply. We wrote '"This Bread and this Cup": An Evangelical Rejoinder',* Theology, *June 1967.*

Series 2 Communion was finally authorized with a far more unitive anamnesis in July 1967, and 'we offer unto thee . . .' passed into history. Quite apart from a responsible concern in the Convocations and, particularly, the House of Laity, for unitive texts, it should be noted that the zeal to replicate Hippolytus, which had motivated Ratcliff and Couratin (and was found soon after in the new Roman Catholic Prayers, and consequently, though somewhat amended, in the Third Eucharistic Prayer in Rite A), slowly went off the boil. In more recent years the work of Paul Bradshaw, Maxwell Johnson and Edward Phillips in The Apostolic Tradition: A Commentary *(Fortress Press, 2002) has raised further serious questions over the transmission, integrity and provenance of the text which has for the last century been attributed to Hippolytus.*

During my early years on the Liturgical Commission I was simultaneously putting together my first volume of eucharistic liturgies collected from round the Anglican Communion, Modern Anglican Liturgies 1958–1968 *(Oxford, 1968). This worldwide coverage not only fulfilled its role as a work of reference, but it also demonstrated that revision of eucharistic liturgies was not, as I was frequently told in the 1960s, all moving in the direction of 1549. Changes also followed within the Liturgical Commission (see the next chapter), and, although the drafting of eucharistic prayers, and particularly of the anamnesis, remained a very sensitive and delicately balanced task, it was always possible after 1967 to pursue it in good hopes of finding texts which the whole Church of England could use with good conscience.*

The petition for the departed was also amended, and the Archbishops referred the issue to the Doctrine Commission, who produced the eirenic report, Prayer and the Departed, *SPCK, London, 1971 (see* Taking the Long View, *chapter 7).*

[NB: Readers nearly half a century later may be confused by my use here of *'Second Series'* and, in the next chapter of 'Series 2' and 'Series 3'. The nomenclature changed in a somewhat ragged way fairly early in the actual authorized life of *'Second Series'*, and, although rare instances of calling the next round *'Third Series'* can be found, I have chosen as the neatest solution to use the italicized label *'Second Series'* only for the text which was drafted, debated and amended, and then to denote it, once in authorized use, as 'Series 2'. The term 'Series 3' for the next round then follows naturally.]

Chapter 2

Liturgical revision and Geoffrey Cuming

FOREWORD

Geoffrey Cuming was not only an expert but also a friend, as this previously unpublished lecture shows. He left the Liturgical Commission (possibly at his own request) in 1981, but I pressed that we needed him as a consultant, and this was arranged. Then, as he approached 65 in 1982, David Wilcox, the principal of Ripon College, Cuddesdon, offered him a guest lecture as his farewell – and a choice between Ronald Jasper and me to deliver it. For reasons probably more to do with levity than learning, he chose me. Some counter-attraction in Oxford kept the numbers present down, but Geoffrey himself was of course there. I also wrote 'Liturgical Revision in Retrospect' for the Festschrift to Geoffrey, which Kenneth Stevenson was editing (The Liturgy Reshaped, SPCK, London, 1982), and have drawn on it to reconstruct the final paragraphs of this lecture, missing from my records.

I first met Geoffrey Cuming at St Katharine's Foundation, Stepney, in December 1965, when he, along with such notables as Charles Whitaker (who has so often worked in double harness with Geoffrey) and John Wilkinson, first joined the Liturgical Commission. I was already there – and had been cutting my teeth for fifteen months on the drafts of Second Series Communion, and fronting up to the old guard who remained from the 1950s, many of them still muttering about the infamy of Eric Milner-White.[1] I will not unfold that infamy now, lest I too mutter about the 1950s, when I come not to bury an era but to praise Geoffrey Cuming. I merely note that Geoffrey's entry has remained in my mind as a turning-point in liturgical revision, not wholly because of Geoffrey's appointment (though the significance of that will emerge), but certainly

---

[1 The infamy sprang from the manner of his opposition to the Commission's 1959 *Baptism and Confirmation* services.]

coincident with it; and thus the era of actual revision is well marked in my mind, and, I hope, in the history books. The latter it ought to be – for, when it comes to the history books of recent liturgical revision, it is Geoffrey and I who write them . . .[2]

I shall return to December 1965. But first I introduce Geoffrey himself – a man of many parts, of which I highlight five.

First, there is Geoffrey the scholar and author. An historian by his original trade, in the 1960s he busied his odd moments editing *Studies in Church History,* which I, as librarian, purchased for the old London College of Divinity.[3] It was as historian that he was originally drawn to *The Durham Book* when he was vice-principal of St John's College, Durham. There are few, if any, such satisfying works as this on anyone's shelves, if you look for impeccable scholarship deployed for no other end than to display the whole work to which he had given himself. Indeed, I doubt whether any publisher would accept such a recondite book today. And from Geoffrey's deep intimacy with the seventeenth century have come other smaller works, such as his delightful contribution to both the tercentenary symposium for the 1662 Prayer Book, and those *Studies in Church History* mentioned above.[4] When he joined the Commission it was rumoured that he was writing a successor to 'Procter and Frere'; and so he was. His *A History of Anglican Liturgy* proved to be gold that drove out all other currencies; and it can only be the recent shortage of such gold that has led the SPCK to republish that brontosaurus, *Liturgy and Worship*. Happily gold, high-quality gold, will soon be back in circulation – we are promised that bumper second edition of *A History of Anglican Liturgy* later this year. I would say little more about Geoffrey as author, save that in the last five years I have been privileged to join the select company of his publishers – and Grove Books has given you (and I hope you possess and cherish) superb but typical examples of Geoffrey's work in *Hippolytus: A Text for Students* (1976), *Essays on Hippolytus* (1978), and now, to crown it all, *He Gave Thanks* (1981).

[2 At the time this was broadly true. I had written booklets and edited the monthly *News of Liturgy,* and Geoffrey had produced his definitive volume, *A History of Anglican Liturgy.* Later that year Kenneth Stevenson's Festschrift for Geoffrey added several other names. Ronald Jasper's *The Development of Anglican Liturgy 1662–1980* (SPCK, London, 1989) was a magisterial addition, itself bodied out by Donald Gray's *Ronald Jasper: His Life, His Work and the ASB* (SPCK, London, 1997).]

[3 He edited the volumes of *Studies in Church History* from no. 2 in 1965 to no. 9 in 1972.]

[4 Geoffrey's Alcuin Collection, *The Godly Order: Studies in the Book of Common Prayer* (Alcuin/SPCK, London, 1983), was then in preparation.]

Second, I pay tribute to Geoffrey as lecturer. Cuddesdon students will know his lecturing merits as virtually no one else can. For myself, in 18 years teaching liturgy I have had Arthur Couratin to lecture for me twice, Henry de Candole once, a Roman Catholic or two, and a musician and an architect occasionally, but Geoffrey Cuming as often as I can get him. Again, his scholarship is always there (he is marvellous on the period from 1904 to 1928, for instance), but his lucidity is superb, and he has been appreciated as much by the essay-course older students as by high-flying graduates. He is of course generally dispassionate, and ready to smile at both the human race and the Christian Church, and it would take a lot to make him into a propagandist like Gregory Dix (or even like me). But these very qualities inspire enormous confidence – you never check Geoffrey out by some more judicious scholar. How could you? He is the plumb line against which judiciousness has to be measured in others.

Third, I pay tribute to Geoffrey as 'liturgiographer' (a neologism?). He has been deeply involved in the creative work of the Commission. Liturgical creativity is an area in which no Anglican has had any fun or job satisfaction since Thomas Cranmer (and he was the only one who did in his day, and he paid a higher price for the privilege than most members of a latter-day Commission would wish to). Happy those who saw the years 1965–80 through – they are in fact only Ronald Jasper, Geoffrey Cuming, Charles Whitaker and I. And happy too those who hear others praying with words they themselves have written – which Geoffrey does more often than I, as my composings have exceeded my fair share of bureaucratic rubrics and permissive opening 'Notes'.

Fourth, I pay tribute to Geoffrey as statesman. He once wrote about the 1661–2 conflicts that Cosin wanted this and Baxter that, but 'Sheldon had a more accurate sense of the nation's religious temper'.[5] (I once used that quotation from him for an exam question.) Right now, I suspect that historians of our times may say that Geoffrey had a more accurate sense of the Church of England's religious temper than most, if not all, other members of the Commission. This has led him into common-sense political stances. If this proposal is going to cause trouble (as, e.g., on one occasion, the proposal to include All Souls Day in an early calendar draft), then, he will say, let us omit it rather than endanger the whole package. He is great at cooling controversy, and finding agreed routes through apparent impasses. The ASB is deeply indebted to Geoffrey's statesmanship.

[5 *The English Prayer Book 1549–1662* (SPCK, London, 1962), p. 110.]

Fifth, Geoffrey has been a good friend, someone with whom it is delightful to relax, to swap the odd story, to imagine oneself back into the catacombs, or the Chertsey shotgun enterprise which produced the 1549 Prayer Book, or the Lambeth Palace episcopal goings-on from 1925 to 1927, when the new Prayer Book was virtually revised from beginning to end by episcopal hands, without a hint of a Liturgical Commission in sight. Geoffrey, I have greatly valued all your informal friendship – long may it continue.

But I revert to the question: why was December 1965 a turning-point?

First, the Commission had originally convened in December 1955, so that exactly ten years had elapsed of the 'phoney war' period – technically in action, but with nothing public to do. The Commission had in fact put one major item into the public arena (perhaps comparable to the battle of the River Plate in the phoney war period of 1939–40, although much less successful as an action), but no more.[6] Members had almost come to believe that there would be no real war. The truth was otherwise – 15 years of non-stop activity were about to fall upon it.

Second, the archbishops had known this before it reached the guts of that dons' dining club. They hoisted grave signs of impending action – Donald Coggan resigned as chairman in September 1964, to get a more active chairman, Ronald Jasper, into the saddle. Geoffrey Willis, that learned and perverse scholar whose birth certificate said '1914' but about whom everything else shrieked he was a contemporary of St Augustine of Hippo – well, Geoffrey was relieved of the secretaryship of the Commission and a full-time ecclesiastical civil servant was appointed in December 1964. *Crockford's* tells us that Geoffrey Willis lectured in liturgy at Cuddesdon from 1962 to 1968 (when Robert Runcie was principal), and I would love to find out what he taught. He was perverse to the last, and rumour said he refused to yield up his secretarial files to his successor.[7] Certainly he departed while Ronald Jasper was forbidding the notion that the Commission was the place for making last-ditch stands for 1662. Instead the Commission began girding itself for the creative task, the new appointments in Autumn 1965 concluding this preparation for action.

Third, the Prayer Book (Alternative and Other Services) Measure was about to become law. It had been long gestating – it derived from the 1928 debacle, the Cecil Commission's report on Church and State

---

[6 These were the services of *Baptism and Confirmation* (SPCK, London, 1959).]
[7 This departure is reported with just a hint of Geoffrey Willis's intransigence in Jasper, *The Development*, p. 242.]

(1935), the Canon Law Commission's report (1947) – and from the 17 years following 1947 while the Church Assembly deadlocked about the form of the Measure. Finally, the Measure passed the Assembly in July 1964, and Parliament in March 1965 (held up, I think, as its successor, the Worship and Doctrine Measure, was ten years later, by a parliamentary election). It was to begin on a date to be named by the two archbishops. They named 1 May 1966, and the era of experimental services came into sight.

Fourth, putting these things together, a change of gear was needed by a Commission, which until then had discussed as though the phoney war would last for ever. Suddenly, in June 1965, we were ordered to produce, to produce whatever we had, and to produce it instantly. Ronald Jasper must have told the archbishops that it was not as easy as that, as the Commission had only had ten years' life so far (*sic*!), and obviously could not be expected to produce texts quickly. The archbishops replied that for years they had been urging first the Assembly and then Parliament to complete and approve the Alternative Services Measure, because the Church of England was bursting for life with new services – and yet the Commission was apparently saying that, when 1 May 1966 came, there would be precious few proposals to show. They also asked the Commission to edit the 1928 services, and the Commission declined – we had no heart for 1928 stuff. The archbishops then edited these themselves, and commanded from the Commission not only the tiny tadpoles already completed (Morning and Evening Prayer, Occasional Prayers and Thanksgivings, Burial, and the Churching of Women), but also an interim, unsigned, draft text of the eucharist. The two books, *First Series* from the House of Bishops, and *Second Series* from the Liturgical Commission (including that draft eucharist), were published in the very month December 1965. In November 1965 I spoke to a clergy gathering about 'Holy Communion in the Church of England', and the agenda was simply 1662. Never again would that be so – since December 1965 there have always been alternative eucharistic texts, and they have started to dispossess the old book and its rite.

The years 1965 to 1971 were perhaps the Commission's vintage years. There were hard and strong debates, but the Commission knew it had an almost decisive say in the authorized texts – whereas in later years the Synod committees (admittedly aided and abetted by opportunist members of the Commission) have rewritten services from beginning to end, and the Commission has known that its own efforts were largely ephemeral, being simply a trigger to the true creative explosion in Synod. But until 1971 – and a little while after it – this was not so. *Second Series* Communion was admittedly controversial, and a conference between the Commission and the Assembly led to vital changes, but, even so, only three actual textual amendments occurred from its publication on All Fools' Day 1966 to its being authorized by the Laity in July 1967.

July 1967 not only ushered in Series 2 Communion, but also said farewells to the pre-1965 era. Edward Ratcliff died in late June and Arthur Couratin resigned from the Commission in near despair at both Ratcliff's death and the loss of the oblation of the bread and cup in the anamnesis, for which he and Ratcliff ('old men in a hurry' – far more dangerous than young men ditto) had worked for years. The curtain was rising on a scene of liturgical revision which at crucial points differed from that which Arthur had envisaged. These departures brought the drafting of Series 3 services into different hands from those which had determined Series 2. We worked this point into the Commission's *Commentary* on Series 3 Communion – it was the product of the junior team, after the senior team had retired or gone to glory.

After 1967 the Commission worked on modern language in the liturgy. This was occasioned in England by many factors (as, e.g., addressing God as 'you' came partly from changing fashions in extemporary prayer), but it chimed in remarkably with changes all round the English-speaking world; thus before 1968 virtually no texts existed addressing God as 'you', and since 1968 virtually no new texts have been written which address God as 'thou'. The Liturgical Commission, hitting exactly the hinge-point of history, in August 1968 published *Modern Liturgical Texts*. This included our own submissions to the International Consultation on English Texts (ICET), then just beginning. We took some bold stances – 'Father in heaven', 'Give us today the bread of life' (no one else dared a variant on 'daily bread', except the Australians who, briefly, tried 'the bread of the morrow'), 'save us from the devil', 'one in godhead with the Father', 'went down to the dead' and so on. Geoffrey made very significant contributions, including the first line of the Te Deum – 'You are God: we praise you' – an attempt at the nuance of the original 'Te' and 'Deum'. A course principal, at a joint staffs conference in January 1981, said to Geoffrey that 'You are God: we praise you' was awful, and asked Geoffrey's own view (assuming that, as an ICET text, it came from America). Geoffrey said he personally liked it, and it had an exactness. When the point was pressed, Geoffrey admitted, 'Actually I like it because I wrote it!' (though certainly he had other reasons). The other man should have blushed.

Geoffrey's great contribution then was his modernization of Series 2 Communion – a straight 'translation' attributed simply to 'one member'. Some of it reads datedly today, but other parts have made a continuing contribution. Most distinctive is Geoffrey's Agnus Dei:

Jesus, Lamb of God, have mercy on us;
Jesus, bearer of the world's sin, have mercy on us;
Jesus, redeemer of the world, give us your peace.

This, with one tiny change, became in turn the ICET text, and in Series
3 Communion was the *only* Agnus Dei. Since then tradition has
reasserted itself, and Rite A has a text more like the Latin original
provided by the ICET 1974 publication. However, the Cuming text
lives on also, and musical settings may well give it further currency.
Later stages will see scholars trying to re-establish the variant Latin
original from which Geoffrey drew his translation – a Cuddesdon
Codex, or even a Steeple Aston papyrus? Certainly it has become irre-
movable, as I discovered in *Sound of Living Waters – Fresh Sounds*. There
it is at *Fresh Sounds* no. 41:

Jesus, Lamb of God . . .
Jesus, bearer of our sins . . .
Jesus, redeemer of the world . . .

But the attribution there? Marvellously and memorably, it is 'Traditional'![8] Geoffrey himself will understand that material written
yesterday may become the 'tradition' today – when Synod debated
Series 3 in 1971, members complained: 'They have changed the
tradition.' On inspection, that tradition was Series 2, then just four
years old! Then when Synod came to Rite A in 1979, some bright spark
defended a change from Series 3 on the grounds that Series 3 was now
fossilized. This wrung the response from Geoffrey that six years must be
the all-time record for the creation of a fossil.

But I anticipate. Series 3 differed from Series 2 in many ways, reflecting the different hands at work. We gave special emphasis to the
all-sufficiency of Calvary, without losing more traditional contents of
the anamnesis. We got bolder about the second coming.[9] We got shot of

---

[8 I diverted here into the exact opposite at St John's, Nottingham, where a student
song sheet featured Bishop Ken's Doxology. But, no doubt inadequately taught, and
without pre-charismatic history, they attributed it to 'Come Together', a latter-day
Christian travelling roadshow.]
[9 Here I diverted into the interchange I had had with Mervyn Stockwood in the
drafting of the Second Series text 'looking for the coming of his kingdom'.
See Michael de la Noy, *Mervyn Stockwood: A Lonely Life* (Mowbray, London, 1996),
p. 145; it is mentioned in passing in my *Taking the Long View* (Church House
Publishing, London, 2006).]

'make the memorial' and ventured upon 'celebrate'. We rounded out the invitation to communion. We wrote the new middle-way words of administration. We dented Gregory Dix's 'shape' of the liturgy, where before we had tried to conform to it. We raised the profile of the kiss of peace. We incorporated the new Sunday eucharistic lectionary. We experimented briefly with an optional supplementary consecration in silence. We went to town and wrote new 'propers' for more occasions than in the Prayer Book or Series 2. We brought in the David Frost prayers (and Synod threw out two of them, but they are back in appendices to Rite A). We had a field day. The Commission spread itself with reasonable hope of writing what would actually be used. Synod certainly made some assaults, and not only on the Frost stuff. The Commission's decalogue – Moses' originals updated by the Sermon on the Mount – was removed from being mandatory on Sundays in Lent and was dumped as an option in an appendix.[10] Geoffrey had a big hand in those commandments, and revelled in disclosing to the Commission a sixteenth-century precursor, I think from Lincoln cathedral. But Series 3 largely emerged unscathed.

I got my own oar in much more with Series 3, though I suspect my main bequest has been those opening 'Notes', which unobtrusively let each do what is right in his own eyes. One little area I worked at was post-communion sentences – an act of *pietas* towards Edward Ratcliff, as he had proposed such a provision years before. I drafted one set which spoke of eating and drinking, and another which did not, and Geoffrey then fused the two lists into the provision you find after communion in the green booklets. However, he almost overlooked a little artifice of mine. I had not relished the opening sentence for 'Dedication'. Someone – I think Geoffrey – had chosen 'Surely the Lord is in this place? This is the very house of God. This is the gate of heaven.' It is from Jacob's dream at Bethel, but my evangelical suspiciousness was unwilling to dub the church building on the corner 'The House of God'. So I provided a post-communion sentence: 'Even the heaven of heavens cannot contain our God. How much less this house that we have built.' Geoffrey objected that it negated the earlier one, but the Commission accepted it, and published both sentences in mutual con-

[10 Donald Coggan complained at St John's, Nottingham, that the Commission had relegated the Decalogue to an appendix ('I hate appendicitis') – I had gently to remind him that the Commission put them in the main text, and the House of Bishops (no less) had had the appendicitis.]

tradiction between the same covers and no one has ever complained. It is, I think, the only deliberate joke in the text. (For Rite A the Synod Revision Committee provided introductory and post-communion sentences for every occasion which has propers, and I translated on the train from my Greek New Testament many now in the ASB. To my amusement a letter this morning asked me from what version of the Bible they come, for copyright permission to be given for reprints. They are, I suggest, copyright COB in some cases . . .)

I must pass on from these formative years of the present texts. I devote little time to the later 1970s, though they were extra busy for Geoffrey as he represented London University on General Synod from 1975 (on the basis of his one day a week at King's, I believe) and was thus heavily engaged in the synodical infighting of that period.[11] The period is recent in memory, and is treated more fully in my contribution to the Festschrift which will mark Geoffrey's sixty-fifth birthday later this year. Geoffrey laboured particularly over funeral and ordination services (corresponding to Charles Whitaker's labours over the Calendar and Lectionary and initiation services). But he was vigorously employed in the whole enterprise right across the board.

One story will illustrate how things developed and how far they have now gone. It is impossible now to think ourselves back to the presuppositions of the 1960s, so fast have minds moved. But my story here leads on to some more general observations. It concerns Series 3 funeral services in the years 1971 to 1972. Tremendous hassling accompanied petitions for the departed in Series 2 services. The eucharistic text was amended to get agreement. The burial text was referred back from the House of Laity to the Clergy in quest of agreement – but the Clergy (which met separately in those days) declined some amendments which a joint group of catholics and evangelicals had agreed. The Laity, seeking a unitive text, felt snubbed – and, seeing the resultant text as divisive, declined to debate it; and that burial service went to its own special limbo, where it still rests. So what was to be done about a Series 3 funeral service? In part we employed the Doctrine Commission's report (*Prayer and the Departed*); in part we reckoned 'we commend' in the Series 3 eucharist offered a middle position, and could be strengthened without losing its middle position – viz., by rendering it 'we entrust'. But we faced the desire for naked petitions for the departed. I urged that the way to allow such petitions was by a rubric that said '*The*

[11 At this point I recounted the debate he instigated about Rite A as to whether the conjunction 'for' should introduce the narrative of institution (as in Series 3) rather than the relative 'who' – see *Taking the Long View*, p. 76.]

minister may use other suitable prayers', and leave the selection to private manuals, with perhaps a few, wholly agreed, ones in an appendix. Behold, a whole ton of legal bricks fell upon me – no service, said the lawyers, could be authorized unless every word used in it were authorized and printed between the same covers. Well, in the late 1960s individual Commission members had begun writing their own unsolicited memoranda (whereas previously nothing was written unless the chairman commissioned it), and so I addressed this target thus:

(a) the freedom to add free or extemporary prayers within the intercessions in the authorized Series 2 eucharist meant that the law had already established a precedent;

(b) it is nonsense to say you can preach whatever you like in sermons, say whatever you like in notices, sing whatever you like in hymnody, but only pray authorized prayers;

(c) whether the proposals are nonsense or not, once Synod has authorized a service *it is authorized*. No legal tribunal can say Synod has acted *ultra vires*. The lawyers are bluffing to the end of their white-curled wigs. Let us see them off. Synod establishes what is lawful, and the lawyers cannot stop it.

This principle prevailed (for the Commission rallied to it), and we have since been free in new services to provide much more flexibility than the ecclesiastical lawyers would have then allowed.

I now reflect on the whole course of revision leading up to the ASB, and the services for use with the sick currently going through Synod.[12] I raise some largish questions.

First, the Church of England is undoubtedly too hung up on liturgical *texts*. What we are really interested in are liturgical *events* – or, granted a proper sense of time and rhythm, liturgical life in which the events roll on through the year with their basic evenness and yet with seasonal character and a response to special occasions and unexpected great events. I often illustrate this by pointing out that only about ten minutes of an hour's eucharist is composed of official texts – the rest is hymns, sermon, free intercessions, and time taken for notices, kiss of peace (quite extensive in some places), and communion. It is an absurd polarization that the Church of England tithes mint and anise when

---

[12 The Revision Committee was to bring retouched forms for Ministry to the Sick, with two offshoots – the Blessing of Oils and the Reconciliation of a Penitent – to a Synod Revision Stage in July 1982. In the event both offshoots were defeated at Final Approval.]

addressing texts of authorized prayers, but does not care two hoots what gets sung as hymns. Similarly, for ten years the church press – and sometimes the national press – has witnessed arguments about ancient and modern services, both sides presupposing that, when you had cited the text, you had also told others what the *event* was like, and even what the whole liturgical life was like. Nothing could be further from the truth. The history of Uniformity is littered with tens of thousands of instances of people who wanted not just the BCP, but the BCP *as done in my church* – and, without that, trouble. When people have different events in mind – each event a subtle combination of buildings, materials of worship, people and their condition of faith (and bodily vigour etc.) – then they cannot debate in such a way as actually to encounter each other. They miss their targets, and the onlooker is infuriated. To take another illustration of the difference, please consult the titles of the Grove Booklets, now regularly on sale here. There *are* titles about texts, but for each such there are ten more about ethos, presentation, or shape, of rites. The Church of England has by definition no mind on these issues – indeed it has no mind behind its liturgical texts (it is strictly behaviourist about them – when you look at them you are looking at its *mind* – the Bishop of Durham [John Habgood] says so in the ASB Preface). A joy of engaging in textual revision is getting opportunity to advise about the renewal of both liturgical *events* and the liturgical *life* of parishes. And you will recognize that the charismatic movement has played a part, along with Grove Booklets and many other aids, in that mind-forming enterprise.

Second, has not the Church of England at large yet a long way to go in recovering the power of the word of God? We have laid out scripture lavishly in these rites. But that mere two-dimensional provision guarantees nothing about the power in people's lives. Evangelicals are learning to take worship seriously as part of building up the people of God. Yes, but are others expecting the word of God to be powerful in their lives?

Third, we are wise to have regard to the experiential side of worship. Can we express joy, encourage spontaneity, and promote live relationships among our congregations, through our worship? Anglicans have traditionally favoured a most poker-faced style of worship – should not the dawning liberty in our liturgical provision lead to a comparable freedom for the people to be themselves?

Fourth, catholics and evangelicals still enormously need to engage in doctrinal discussion and debate. I am grateful to Geoffrey for insisting that we take the Reformation seriously, and do not kid ourselves we can plan the future simply by invoking 'the early Church' (a wonderful cover phrase), and claiming this enables us to 'get behind the Reformation'. We have to acknowledge our history and work *from* it, not deny it and try to do without it.

Fifth, despite loud noises put up by David Martin and others, we should not run scared about language.[13] There is *not* coming a great nationwide swing back to Cranmer. The Prayer Book Society and the Liturgical Commission are not sparring as equal partners. No, the Commission must be compared to the postman delivering the letters, and the Prayer Book reactionaries to the dog which is determined to bite him. The dog's great aim in life is to disable the postman. But to the postman, the dog is but a passing irritant, distracting briefly from *his* great aim – delivering the letters.

I conclude with three nightmares which have occasionally haunted me – the 'might-have-beens' of our processes of liturgical revision.

Suppose first that the Church of England had had (as Anglicans in Canada, the USA and Ireland have had) an officially authorized *hymn book*. Imagine the doctrine and poetry all being revised line by line in General Synod. Think what the outcome might have been – if any outcome would ever have been a practical possibility . . .

Suppose next that the Welsh dioceses had not departed in 1920 to form a separate province. It is certain that, if they were represented on our General Synod, with all the latter-day resurgence of pride in the Welsh language, they would have demanded that the whole revision process be done *bilingually*. Revision Committees would have been assaulted by outcries that nuances in the English texts had been lost – or exaggerated – in the Welsh. The procedures needed to assist a Synod where perhaps 4 per cent of its members were Welsh-speaking to vote intelligently on Welsh texts would have been enormous, and the resultant aggro worse still.

My third nightmare was, just suppose Gregory Dix had lived. He was younger than some members of the Commission were when I joined it; he was an exact contemporary of Arthur Couratin. Indeed he would be only just 80 today. But just imagine the dance his maverick, mischievous, learned perversity would have led us. The whole course of liturgical revision would have been different. A nightmare indeed.

Those are the 'might-have-been' nightmares. But I offer you now a different nightmare. Suppose there had *not* been a Geoffrey Cuming. Contemplating that dreadful contingency makes me very grateful that he *has* been there at the heart of the revising throughout. Geoffrey, we salute you.

[13 David Martin was a leader of the 'return to the Book of Common Prayer' reaction.]

POSTSCRIPT

Geoffrey Cuming remained a friend. There duly came Kenneth Stevenson's tribute to him, The Liturgy Reshaped *(SPCK, London, 1982). In this I wrote 'Liturgical Revision in Retrospect'. In 1985, Geoffrey led the Alcuin Club to approach the Group for Renewal of Worship (GROW) to inaugurate the Joint Liturgical Studies which run to this day. In 1987 as Bishop of Aston I assisted Geoffrey's son Mark, who had previously withdrawn from ministry, to be restored to it in the Birmingham diocese. So, when Geoffrey died suddenly in March 1988 in the USA, Mark asked my help both in compiling a memorial service (which, from my files, we did largely with Geoffrey's own liturgical drafting) and in preaching at it. In 1991 Kenneth Stevenson and Bryan Spinks edited* The Identity of Anglican Worship *(Mowbray, London), as a tribute to Geoffrey's memory. Donald Gray added a brief sketch of Geoffrey's life in a chapter in Christopher Irvine (ed.),* They Shaped Our Worship: Essays on Anglican Liturgists *(Alcuin/SPCK, 1998).*

In 1998, preaching at the London memorial service for Michael Vasey, I compared him to Geoffrey Cuming. I could conceive no higher comparison. For both Geoffrey and Michael I took the sermon text, 'He, being dead, yet speaks' (Hebrews 11.4) – without realizing that Isaac Basire had used it at the funeral of Geoffrey's hero, John Cosin, Bishop of Durham 1660–63. Geoffrey's Introduction to The Durham Book *closed with that text, his own verdict also on Cosin. And when we worship with Common Worship today, Geoffrey too, being dead, yet speaks.*

Initiation

Initiation

Chapter 3

Infant baptism – the atomized sacrament

FOREWORD

Baptism has been a major theological preoccupation in my life, both in justifying infant baptism on biblical grounds to evangelicals, and in striving against indiscriminate infant baptism to make the biblical justification credible in practice. Early Grove Booklets dealt with both these two thrusts. The latter led to my being invited in 1988 to become honorary president of the Movement for the Reform of Infant Baptism (MORIB), now Baptismal Integrity (BI), a position I still hold. In 1990 Clifford Owen edited a book for MORIB including two essays from me. The one reprinted here typifies my general approach.

The church in the New Testament practised a baptism of initiation which was fundamentally missionary. Enquirers were instructed to submit to baptism as submission to the gospel and were then reckoned to have been converted in the waters of baptism, and the gospel's claims on people's obedience were spread through this use of the sacrament.[1] Similarly at baptism the candidate was incorporated into a missionary fellowship; having confessed the faith of Christ for the first time at baptism, he or she was then expected to confess the same Jesus before the world thereafter.[2] The mission of God in which the candidate was

---

1 Water baptism is not recorded in every case of conversion in the Acts of the Apostles, but it was clearly part of the *kerygma*, and was given at the point of conversion (cf. Acts 2; 10; 16 etc.); similarly in Paul's letters to the young churches, it is taken for granted that all to whom the letters are addressed had received it (cf. Rom. 6.3–6; 1 Cor. 10.1; 12.13; Gal. 3.27 etc.). Thus we conclude it was always given at conversion – and sooner rather than later (cf. Acts 8.36–39; 10.47–48 etc.).
2 The present tendency is to think converts need breaking into active ministry slowly – in the New Testament they were expected to testify on the spot!

now participant was exercised by a missionary *fellowship* into which the person was converted. In the fellowship the newcomer became a participant at the communal meals, and put his or her own home and goods at the disposal of the church. Infant baptism was practised, but it was a component of household baptisms, in which parents (and perhaps heads of extended families) brought their children and other dependants into the fellowship also, for them also to grow in faith and knowledge of Christ.[3] It is no part of my task here to argue a case for infant baptism, which I have endeavoured to do elsewhere, but only to point out that a minority community – whether in Jewish Jerusalem or pagan Philippi – needed to ensure that their children were fully participant with them in the sacramental and believing missionary fellowship.

Our problem today in the Church of England, and to a lesser extent in the other fairly traditionalist churches, is that baptism has in popular understanding lost its missionary and incorporative character, and has lodged in the folklore (and thus in the nation's subconscious) as a dollop of personal benefit which infants ought to receive after birth – just as fairly recently in England they used to receive free, state benefit, orange juice. It is the task of this essay to trace how popular belief over the centuries forgot the missionary role of baptism and almost lost its incorporative character also. This may help us to suggest ways of bringing both practice and rationale back to some approximation to the New Testament emphases.

DEVELOPMENTS OF THE FIRST MILLENNIUM

In the pre-Nicene church, it looks as though this approach to baptism remained fairly constant. By the time of Hippolytus there was a lengthy catechumenate, finishing with a build-up through Lent to the night vigil, and baptisms at dawn on Easter morning. The new converts, whilst baptized in a private baptistery away from the assembly (perhaps because they were baptized naked), were then brought into the community, and were enabled to share the prayers, the kiss of peace (an important point of incorporation), and finally the eucharistic meal.[4]

---

3 'Bring them up in the nurture and admonition of the Lord' (Eph. 6.4) is very much part of the argument for infant baptism – children are to grow up 'in' it, not 'unto' it. For a fullish biblical case see my *A Case for Infant Baptism* (Grove Books, Bramcote, 1973), 4/1990, pp. 18–21. [2009 edition, pp. 20–22.]
4 Hippolytus, *Apostolic Tradition*, chapter 21, in G. J. Cuming (ed.), *Hippolytus: A Text for Students* (Grove Books, Bramcote, 1976), 4/1987, pp. 18–21.

Persecution was still in the air, so that, quite apart from the rigours of the catechumenate, there was a great seriousness about the decision to undergo baptism, and thus to align oneself with this semi-underground religious society. So the sense of incorporation into that society was very strong at the baptism itself, and the only known way to be a Christian was through the gate of baptism into the context of that society.

Infants and children, we are told, were being baptized with the adults, and, whilst they may have been excused a three-year catechumenate, they too were in baptism becoming identified with the Christian community. It looks as though they too passed from the waters into the assembly, and concluded with the reception of communion, at however young an age.

The only early hint we have of a different approach is in Tertullian's famous deprecation of infant baptism. Here he seems to write solely of the moral responsibilities lying upon the baptized (and, by their sponsorship, upon the sponsors of infant candidates) – and the individual is considered alone (in a rather latterday way), without any sense of the sustaining power of the community, or of the context of a believing home, or of the eucharistic rhythm of the fellowship.[5] But then, if we read between the lines, we can perhaps detect that the infants and young children who are receiving baptism in Tertullian's account, against whose baptism he is protesting, are not from believing families at all. Some motivation, which we cannot easily penetrate, has led pagan parents to let their offspring be baptized. In the process, the weight of responsibility has passed from family and community to individual sponsors who often, being outside the family, cannot discharge their task effectively. Thus the incredibility of the particular rationale with which Tertullian is grappling (i.e. that the church can rely upon godparents to do a good job) has become self-evident. Tertullian then becomes an almost classic model for baptismal reformers today – his only mistake being that he has come to believe that all godparents and sponsors are morally answerable towards God for the behaviour of those whom they sponsor. He therefore rejects infant baptism because of that very rationale – as we would have to do also, if we could ground infant baptism nowhere but on that rationale. We differ in that we wish to *retain* infant baptism, rejecting Tertullian's rationale altogether, and pointing out that his account differs from the New Testament basis for infant baptism which we would rather advocate. From Tertullian's own

---

5 Tertullian, *De Baptismo*, chapter 18, in E. Evans (ed.), *Tertullian's Homily on Baptism* (SPCK, London, 1964), pp. 36–41.

account we must judge both that the rationale for infant baptism had changed, and that the practice had become distorted accordingly.[6]

If we go back to the Hippolytan account, there are some elements of contrast with Tertullian: the 'responding' looks to be more like 'articulating vows' which *truly belong to the candidate* and are voiced by the proxy without the same moral hostages given to fortune as in Tertullian; there is a primary expectation that in fact parents are themselves bringing their own infants (i.e. this is within Christian families); and the infants are, we must presume, incorporated fully into the life of the sacramental fellowship – for from then on they follow the same route through baptism as their elders, being similarly greeted with the kiss of peace, being similarly incorporated into the prayers, and being similarly apportioned a share in the eucharistic bread and cup. It all looks much healthier than in the Tertullian account.

However, the trends were to prove to be misleading. In the fourth century Christianity came by stages to be first *licita*, then favoured, then almost mandatory. Thousands flocked into the church, and whilst many deferred their baptism – and deferred it also for their children – in principle the flocking in of first-generation adults spelled the future end of adult initiation, and the corresponding growth in infant baptism. The situation came to pass quite quickly as, in the years from AD 400 to AD 600, the teaching of St Augustine (364–430) bit deep into the Western church's practice. Augustine taught that a child who dies unbaptized cannot catch the Beatific Vision, but at best ends up in a nebulous limbo. Thus the pressure was on – infant mortality rates were high, and baptisms could not be saved up till a bishop came by (or at least not in the large missionary dioceses North of the Alps), and in the last analysis in the Dark Ages and Middle Ages infants did not even have to be saved up till the following Sunday when the parish priest might give baptism in the context of the mass. No – the pressures were so great so quickly upon birth that midwives were learning that they could themselves administer a minimal baptism, and very generally did so to the new-born.[7] Thus

---

6 The alternative explanation is that infant baptism itself was an innovation in Tertullian's time. This view can *just* be propounded, through the paucity of other earlier specific evidence. But, in days when innovation was self-condemned, and tradition had to be sustained and maintained, it is almost unthinkable that, if infant baptism had started during Tertullian's own lifetime, he would not have denounced it simply on that basis. A slowly shifting rationale for an apostolic rite is a hundred times easier to believe than a latterday invention of infant baptism itself.

7 I confess I have never checked this, but rely upon the *obiter dicta* of George Every when he was teaching at Kelham – 'In the Middle Ages, the majority of baptisms in England were done by midwives.'

incorporation into a missionary fellowship was hardly now the question – much more it was the individual dollop of grace (or preservative) which was in view, and this was administered on an individualistic basis.

Not only were baptisms usually not done at the mass in the Middle Ages, but, whether they were or not, the reception of communion was generally not part of the rite. If the baptism was in church, the priest alone offered the mass, and he alone communicated. The people assisted – that is, they stood around. Whereas in Hippolytus' day the members bound themselves to each other by the prayers, the kiss, and the sharing one bread – and thus the newly baptized, adult or infant belonged in the fellowship (cf. 1 Corinthians 10.17) – now the baptism had become detached from the eucharist and incorporation was not visibly enacted. Finally, the cup was withdrawn from the laity from the thirteenth century onwards and, without the cup, infants could not be communicated at all, or at least not until weaned, which might be well into their second or even third year. And once this 'admission to communion' had been separated from baptism and came at an older age, then other pressures pushed the age up to 'first confession' at the age of seven. The eucharist itself in the Middle Ages did not look or feel like a fellowship meal, even at Easter when a general communion was ordered – but how much less did baptism speak of a fellowship. It was a private benefit, conveyed by a kind of tradesperson (though sometimes no doubt by the priest), with no clear corporate implications and no visible connection with eucharistic fellowship at all. If ever a rite were in line to become mumbo-jumbo – and, we insist, individualistic mumbo-jumbo – then that rite was infant baptism.

The universal character of medieval Western Christendom heightened this emphasis. To join a club of limited numbers – perhaps even a secret society, like Freemasonry – gives the entrance rite some significance as the initiate passes into the privileges and perhaps duties of membership. That is how baptism was, even for infants, in the ante-Nicene church. But to receive baptism simply because the whole country receives it at birth, as a standard post-natal ceremony, is to lose sight of its incorporating role. We may compare it with the receiving of an inoculation after birth today – the child does not thereby enter any club. That child has simply received the standard prescribed health-giving dollop which, as an individual, he or she needs. So it was that infant baptism was experienced in the medieval West. It still had that element of being the background to the rest of life, but it was a very shadowy background, to which value largely got attached through the occasional rush to give it to a dying child. Its meaning to the living remained very much at the level of the subconscious – and what meaning it had was that of a preservative for the individual.

THE REFORMATION INHERITANCE

The Reformers argued about infant baptism. But in the 'mainstream' churches – Anglican, Lutheran, or Reformed – they retained it, and retained it believing it to be not only inherited but justifiable from the scriptures. However, they were well caught in the medieval traps, for:

1   they gave it to all the children, and
2   they argued its benefits largely in terms of the Lord's goodwill towards the individual children, and
3   they did nothing about restoring communion to baptized children, and therefore left the newly baptized still not admitted to communion – and indeed delayed admission to an older age than the medievalists had practised.[8]

The Reformed churches deprecated 'private' baptisms of children in danger of death and instead ordered that children should be brought to church as quickly as possible. This was not only because they minded about the presence of the congregation, but also because they did not believe lay people should administer baptism. The minister held the power of the keys, and the responsibility for the administration of the sacraments, and he alone should preside at the rite. The Anglican Prayer Books from 1549 to 1662 reflect a tension between the medieval inheritance and the full Reformed principles on this very point, for private or

---

8 Baptizing all children was part of the *cuius regio, eius religio* doctrine which in England found its expression in the nationalization or 'establishing' of the Church of England. Because they still had no 'missionary' church – and because they were rediscovering 'justification through faith' – individual benefits were as far as they could usually get. (But note the opening of Article XXIV of the XLII Articles of 1553: 'Our Lord Jesus Christ hath knit together a company of new people with sacraments, most few in number, most easy to be kept, most excellent in signification, as is Baptism, and the Lord's Supper'.) And although the Hussites had been keen to restore child communion (cf. David Holeton, *Infant Communion Then and Now,* Grove Liturgical Study 27 (Grove Books, Bramcote, 1981)), the more general Reformation view was that the ability to answer catechetical questions correctly was crucial for admission to communion (cf. my *Anglican Confirmation*, Grove Liturgical Study 48 (Grove Books, Bramcote, 1986), pp. 19–22).

'clinical' baptism at home is still permitted, whilst the propriety of a lay administrant is disputed.[9]

On the other hand, the rationale as to *why* baptisms should be conducted in public was stated clearly – and yet was arguably also misleading. Baptisms were to come after the second lesson at Morning or Evening Prayer on Sundays, and were to be done so that '*the congregation . . . may testify the receiving of them that be newly baptized into the number of Christ's Church*' and also so that '*every man present may be put in remembrance of his own profession to God made in his baptism*'. Now, once private or 'clinical' baptism is acknowledged to *be* baptism, then a congregation cannot be indispensable for a baptism to be a baptism. So the rationale for baptism being public is bound to be slightly oblique or even cosmetic. Apparently the congregation are to be witnesses (i.e. they can 'testify') and to be personally stirred (i.e. they are to be 'put in remembrance'). But they do not seem to have any role in 'being the church' which receives the infant by baptism. They are not in fact there to be the body of Christ into which the person is received at baptism.[10] The strictly 'churchly' angle is missing from these baptisms – the stage is set, the people are to be there, but they are individuals and the church, *qua* church, is missing.

CLERICALIST CENTURIES

To this it might be replied that the very role of the clergyman was to represent the church, even to 'be' the church to the parents and infant candidate. Representation is easy to understand as a principle, but when it is practised exhaustively it becomes something else – substitution. That is how medieval clericalism and sacerdotalism arose. It was purged of its more priestly assumptions at the Reformation, but the ministerial usurpation of all churchly roles continued not only unabated, but with a fresh Protestant ideology to energize the inherited traditions. Thus, from the Reformation until within living memory, in virtually every

---

9 1549, 1552 and 1559 permitted lay persons to give baptism when there was '*great need*'. The Puritans objected at the Hampton Court Conference ('baptism not to be administered by women'), and the titles of the rite and the rubric were altered. Now '*the minister of the parish*' or '*any other lawful minister that can be procured*' is to officiate (all italics my emphasis).

10 To put it at its most paradoxical – an unbeliever would do as a witness, and an excommunicate would benefit by being put in remembrance of his own baptism. Indeed, we might add, even a believer in good standing needs to be put in remembrance of his or her own baptism on a regular basis, and not simply in accord with the unpredictable fertility rate of the parish.

parish in the land, admission to baptism, preparation of the parents, and the arranging of the ritual event all lay entirely within the responsibility of the clergyman. If there were questions about the godparents (one of whom in the 1604 Canons was supposed to be a communicant), or about the name, or about the speed with which it could be arranged, or even (though this was rare till recently) as to whether the child should be baptized at all – then these questions lay entirely between parents and clergyman. There was no organ of 'the church' which could be invoked, or could express an interest – the issue was an arrangement between parents and clergyman for the benefit of the child: not unlike an arrangement made by parents with a bank manager for the benefit of a child. Because the interviewing and arranging only involved these two parties, the concept of a corporate 'church', even if it was articulated in words, was never modelled in experience, and thus never took root in people's minds. It is astonishing that in many parishes this still continues – a clergy person (as we must now say) may have a high or a low doctrine of baptism, and a high or a low set of criteria for admitting the candidate to the sacrament – but as long as one individual alone wields the 'keys', so long will an individualized benefit to the candidate run strong in the tradition and the folklore. The outsider never meets the church in any corporate way, but only has to deal with the official who dispenses the benefit.

THE CURRENT OUTCOME

I need hardly stay on this point for its relevance today to stand out. Once the church is defined not as the whole nation (as in Henry VIII's day), nor even as all the baptized (as, say, in the first half of the present century), but essentially as those who actually meet, then the church has not only become more defined in its membership, but it is also changed in its role. It is now a church *with a mission* – a mission which logically begins with the fringe, and goes on to the baptized who are beyond the fringe, and finally to the whole nation. The candidate for baptism today is to be incorporated into a missionary church. He or she is to belong to a body, the members of which *love* one another and share a common role and purpose and sense of God's calling. *That,* I submit, cannot be explained by a ministerial interview or teaching session alone – it has to be 'felt' by encounter with the living worshipping church. The one-to-one interview between minister and parent, or the teaching session by a minister to a class of parents, cannot by definition convey the nature of the church. Thus ministers, even when talking about the church to enquiring parents, may actually connive by their own structure of interview at a wholly individualistic and static concept of what baptism means.

OTHER INDIVIDUALIZING

If this pattern of individualistic understanding is one which the church has willy-nilly conveyed to the world by its processes, there is another misconception with the same outcome at work within the church's own borders. This theological fifth column I sweepingly dub as 'Baptist'.[11] We shall see that it is not confined to Baptists, it does not always arise from Baptists, and certainly not all Baptists embrace it, but it is typically Baptist, and it flows strongly from outside into Anglican congregations. To what do I refer? Why, to the teaching that baptism is a step in individual discipleship, to be undertaken as a personal response of obedience to Christ, at whatever point in life the inner conviction 'I ought to be baptized' comes to the individual believer. Because it is an individual response, many Baptist believers have gone all the way through adulthood without receiving it at all, and, in the most consistently individualistic circles, it would hardly be appropriate to urge another believer to receive baptism, as the church as such has no stakes in an individual's response except to confer baptism if asked. In many 'Open' Baptist circles neither participation in communion, nor church membership, nor even the holding of responsible office, has traditionally been confined to the baptized. Baptism as an individual testimony to what God has done in one's life, even though done in the presence of the church, has had little or no churchly reference.

Now it is my contention that at the evangelical end of the Church of England (and possibly at all sorts of other points on the spectrum) this 'Baptist' outlook has affected even Anglican understanding of the sacrament. Christians have come to the issue with a wholly individualistic question in their minds: 'What does baptism do for this or that person?' Often, no doubt, it has led to a flight from infant baptism, leading to either a tension within, or a parting from, Anglican churchmanship. But, even where infant baptism has been retained, it has been retained on an individualistic understanding – the rationale again becomes not what in baptism the church is doing, but what in baptism the individual gains. I was myself once curate in a parish where the

---

11 'Baptist' is a tricky word, but I use it not to mean members of a particular denomination, but to cover all those opposed to infant baptism. It will be clear upon reflection that a highly 'voluntarist' doctrine of the church marches alongside their position on baptism, and the two [positions] reinforce each other.

answer to this latter question was clearly: 'the individual gains nothing and loses nothing, so the church can safely give it to all who ask without any awkwardness, and *without the issue touching at all upon our (wholly different) task of preaching the gospel*'! But my point is equally valid if a parish concludes that, in particular cases, as the individuals gain nothing, and are possibly inoculated against the gospel, baptism should *not* be administered. It does not matter which of these two opposite results emerges, nor even which in the economy of God is 'right' or 'wrong'; if it emerges on the basis of questions confined to the individual, then even the 'right' result runs the risk of doing theological evil that good may come.

Evangelicals in the Church of England have had around a century and a half of semi-conscious anti-sacramentalism. Ever since the days of Pusey and Philpotts, they have feared the teaching that men and women receive grace virtually in proportion to their frequency in receiving sacraments. The more they have been driven into a minority complex, the more they have been moulded by these outside forces into a distorted shape, awry from their biblical birthright. Their context has not helped them – conniving until the 1960s in the baptism of all infants born in the land, they have known in experience that the gospel of conversion had nothing to do with the practice of baptism! It has been important to deny that 'baptism makes you a Christian'. Equally, holding a very lightweight doctrine of the visible church, they have been unable to give any ecclesial significance to baptism; and working in undenominational ways to preach an individualistic gospel (as especially exemplified in the great evangelistic campaigns from Moody to Billy Graham), they have been unable also to give much churchly significance to conversion. To be baptized, to be converted, and to 'join a church' have not only been three separate activities, which in the New Testament are one – they have also been three separate activities without any logical links between them. No wonder then that the anti-sacramentalists were as often to be found in indiscriminate practices as were the super-sacramentalists – not because such practices were connected to a wrong doctrine of the church, but because they were connected to no Christian doctrine whatsoever.

The discovery of a conscience about which infants are proper candidates for baptism can be particularly documented over the last three decades. In part the Parish and People movement of the 1950s gave the lead. Ernie Southcott at Halton brought baptisms into the Parish Communion, and took strong steps to incorporate parents and children into the active life of the church. The leaders of the movement stood away from the legal establishment of religion and cried: 'Let the church be the church.' There is little evidence that they went further and attempted to give realistic baptismal boundaries to the church, but they certainly affected the atmosphere.[12]

A further stage had to come. A policy which takes infant baptism as both a gospel sacrament and a churchly sacrament must provide for the serious possibility (whether by parental withdrawal or churchly refusal) of any infant *not* being baptized. The first well-documented policies were to be found in the 1960s amongst evangelicals, and their rise must be related to the concerns expressed by evangelicals at the Keele Congress in 1967 that they should have a high doctrine of the visible church, a positive valuing of the sacraments (including a good conscience biblically about the *principle* of baptizing infants), and a full-orbed internally consistent pastoral ministry.[13] It is not part of this essay to trace the slow recovery of a doctrine of the church by evangelicals – and there is still a long way to go – but that is the head of steam which produced movement on the baptismal front. That is not to say that others were not getting there also, and since the 1960s there have been ever-growing signs of the unease in the church on the issue of indiscriminate baptism.[14]

TRANSITION TO MISSION

It is clear that this growing unease of clergy and laity has related to the steady secularization of English society over the last three decades. It has become more and more clear that many families seeking baptism are

---

12 Some of the tension of trying to make the church credible *as* the church, without giving it credible baptismal boundaries, can be found in the Swanwick Conference papers, Basil Moss (ed.), *Crisis for Baptism* (SCM Press, London, 1965). There were, of course, some who resolved the tension – compare the over-reaction of Christopher Wansey (who gave up all baptizing of infants, and invented – for Anglicans – the post-natal dry run).

13 See P. A. Crowe (ed.), *Keele '67* (Falcon, London, 1967), *passim*.

14 Part of my own experience of this was in writing *Baptismal Discipline* (Grove Booklet on Ministry and Worship no. 3, published in March 1972 originally, and now succeeded by no. 98, *Policies for Infant Baptism*, January 1987). Then came the diocesan debates responding to the Ely Report in the years 1974–6, at the end of which I successfully moved in General Synod the Southwell diocesan motion, affirming the form of vows in Series 2 infant baptism and (draft) Series 3 infant baptism rites, and asking for a re-consideration of the terms on which infants were accepted for baptism. This was followed by almost total inaction – see Roger Godin's chapter [i.e. here in *Reforming Infant Baptism*] for an account of it. The form of the baptismal vows I discuss in my own chapter ['A Ghost in the Grove', also in *Reforming Infant Baptism*] on Mark Dalby's book.

not even minimally Christian, and the conscience of the church has grown accordingly. It has simultaneously taken aboard 'mission' as a priority in England, whereas in 1960 it is doubtful if more than a handful saw 'mission' as meaning other than evangelism in Africa.

However, both the folklore and the establishment problems remain. As long as the folklore teaches that 'the child will never do well till it's christened', so long will the demand be there (though this is, of course, now dying slowly of attrition).[15] The 'establishment' factor then comes into play: if there is any reason to think that parishioners have by sheer birth a part and stake under the law in their local Anglican parish church, so long will an untheological or opportunist clergy prefer to bend to the folklore, rather than engage their congregation in modelling the loving missionary fellowship to the enquirers. For the establishment itself has become the thickest of fogs to obscure the mission of the church. If all the baptized are vaguely members of the church, or puta-tively born again, then there are no boundaries to the fellowship, and no grounds for being even cautious about a 'child's right to baptism'. Where establishment rules, ecclesiality departs. Where there are no boundaries, there is no one outside them – and no meaning to being inside either. But if God has set his church on earth, as a gathered company with a true mission to the world, then for the gospel's sake we must bury the establishment and let infant baptism be seen in its true missionary and corporate perspective.[16]

And then there is the positive side to the sharpening of the issues. Children are to be baptized in believing families, and then to be brought up in an admittedly minority cult to share with their parents in this unpopular faith. The smaller the minority, the higher the gospel profile – and the more sure it is that the church will be wholeheartedly missionary. It is to *that* that the baptismally incorporated children of

---

15 Even as I write this, Michael Saward has published figures showing that in London diocese now, only 11 per cent of children born live receive infant baptism from the Church of England. Whilst some of the decline is no doubt due to parish policies (he shows a widespread desire among the clergy for a tightening of policies), the larger part is almost certainly due to the multi-religious and wholly irreligious character of so many Londoners, and the 'folklore' instinct towards baptism is fading from the urban scene. (At that, if even 11 per cent of live births represented active future church membership, well, the kingdom would be showing signs of coming in London.)

16 There are of course other demanding reasons why the establishment should be ended – not least in relation to the political factors involved in the choosing of our chief pastors.

believing homes will be brought up. It is a most demanding task for parents in a secularized or religiously indifferentist atmosphere. But that is what infant baptism is about.

POSTSCRIPT

Later work in this field came in my Infant Baptism and the Gospel *(Darton, Longman & Todd, London, 1993), in my longer book of ecclesiology,* Is the Church of England Biblical? *(Darton, Longman & Todd, London, 1998), in work on the revision of Common Worship* Initiation Services, *in my Grove Worship Series 163,* Infant Baptism in Common Worship, *and in two books from GROW corporately: Mark Earey and Gilly Myers (eds),* Common Worship Today *(HarperCollins, London, 2001, and St John's College Extension Studies, Nottingham, 2007), and Mark Earey, Trevor Lloyd and Ian Tarrant (eds),* Connecting with Baptism *(Church House Publishing, London, 2007).*

Chapter 4

Confirmation

FOREWORD

I was a founder member of the International Anglican Liturgical Consultations in 1985, and soon after published my Anglican Confirmation, *Grove Liturgical Study 48 (Grove Books, Bramcote, 1986). So I was asked in 1991 to do a preparatory paper on confirmation for the Fourth International Anglican Liturgical Consultation, tackling Christian Initiation, which led to the Toronto Statement. After the Consultation various papers were edited for the volume of essays from Toronto. My essay stops the clock in 1991 on what has internationally been a developing Anglican situation.*

INTRODUCTION

Confirmation is either centre-stage or only slightly off-stage throughout modern Anglican discussions of initiation. Even the decisive removal of confirmation from the sphere of initiation, of which the Toronto Statement is but one example, nevertheless requires a careful consideration of the nature of sacramental initiation. Moreover, the Toronto Statement offers one or two further unexpected twists about confirmation.

I have written elsewhere an ordered account of the development of the rite of confirmation, both as it emerged before the Reformation and as it was shaped by the Reformation and subsequently by the Anglican liturgical tradition.[1] In preparing this paper for the Toronto Consultation, then, I had to ask myself: at what point should I pick up the story in order to provide sufficient background for this discussion? In answer I found a convenient centenary being completed in 1991: the publica-

---

1 Colin Buchanan, *Anglican Confirmation*, Grove Liturgical Study 48 (Grove Books, Bramcote, 1986).

46

tion of the second and definitive edition of A. J. Mason's *The Relation of Confirmation to Baptism*. This will serve to mark the beginning of the paper.

TWO-STAGING: ITS RISE

Mason's book is a landmark in the history of Anglican writings on confirmation. There is no doubt about the theological stance of its author: he is the archetypical 'two-stager'. To be accurate, we ought to call him the 'two-stages-in-one-rite-er', but I hope the simpler 'two-stager' will suffice. The proper expansion should be borne in mind, however, when the shorthand version is used.

Mason was not actually first in the field. Indeed, if you follow his argument, you must agree that the apostles themselves were the first in the field, and it was the *denial* of two-staging which was a later innovation.[2] But even if you do not accept his argument, you can see his antecedents. They derive in the West from Tertullian and Hippolytus and in the East (though less certainly) from the post-baptismal anointing in the *Apostolic Constitutions* and Cyril of Jerusalem's *Catechesis*.

Mason's Anglican predecessors were relatively few, though Jeremy Taylor and his *Chrisis Teleiotike* are usually listed among them.[3] The antecedents which led more immediately to Mason's 1891 publication were:

1 The provision in 1662 that those baptized in 'Riper Years' should also be confirmed as soon as possible afterwards. This gave a framework in which episcopal confirmation was in principle required of all, whether they had received baptism in infancy or in adulthood.

---

2 This is, of course, a wildly perverse view; neither the scriptures nor the authorities writing about the scriptures give any substantial ground for taking such a view. It is almost as though Anglican writers who value confirmation for extra-biblical reasons then go looking for any shred of evidence that might be alleged to point towards it in the scriptures.

3 In *Anglican Confirmation*, I had reason to comment on S. L. Ollard's essay 'Confirmation in the Anglican Communion' in *Confirmation: 1. Historical and Doctrinal* (SPCK, London, 1926). Ollard was trying to establish from sixteenth-century precedents a somewhat twentieth-century 'two-staging' view. My comment was that 'he has to dub author after author exceptional – and his normative authors live in nooks and crannies' (p. 19, n2).

2   The general *tendenz* of the high sacramental teaching of the Tractar-
    ians. This, in itself was, however, for the first fifty years, somewhat
    thin on confirmation.[4]

3   The ever greater availability of confirmation in practice (in England
    – I dare not make statements here about New Zealand or the USA
    in the nineteenth century, let alone about PNG or Central Africa).
    During the years from 1830 to 1891, four different factors made
    for this greater availability in England:
    (a)   the division of dioceses, giving diocesans a smaller area;
    (b)   the provision for the retirement of bishops, giving diocesans a
          way of escape when they could no longer cope physically;
    (c)   the addition of suffragans, giving extra chance of providing an
          itinerant, confirming, episcopal ministry;
    (d)   the spread of the railways, giving quick and easy access to
          distant corners of a diocese.[5]

Thus 'Soapy Sam' Wilberforce was (incorrectly) credited with pioneering 'pastoral' confirmation services when he was Bishop of
Oxford, 1845–69. By 'pastoral' was meant services with hymns and
preaching, and a controllable number of candidates. Several centres
were nominated in a diocese and the bishop started to appear at
them annually. And so, from the mid-century onwards, the sheer
possibility of *getting* confirmed provided a context in which a very
'high' view of the rite could begin to flourish. The reverse had
certainly been true previously: where confirmation could *not* be had,
it had been difficult to view it as an integral necessity for full initiation. That in itself sets the silence of the early Tractarians into
context. Correspondingly, the nineteenth-century change in pastoral
practice was a natural preparation for Mason and his school.

---

4 Thus Pusey, for instance, made virtually no mention of it (cf. *Anglican Confirmation*, p. 31), and we may add here R. M. Benson, whose undated but presumably
mid-century definition of 'Puseyism' began as follows:
  1 High thoughts of the two sacraments.
  2 High estimate of episcopacy as God's ordinance.
  3 High estimate of the visible Church as the body where we are made and
    continue to be members of Christ.
  4 Regard for ordinances . . . such as daily public prayers . . .
(quoted in David Edwards, *Christian England* (Fount, Collins, London, 1989), vol.
III, p. 181).
  Clearly, if confirmation ranked *anywhere* in the basic sacramental system of the
Puseyites, it would have received mention in this list. If it had been part of sacramental initiation, surely it would have had to have been mentioned?
5 See P. Jagger, *Clouded Witness: Initiation in the Church of England in the mid-
Victorian Period 1850–1875* (Pickwick, Allison Park, PA, 1982), pp. 101ff.

4   In the 1870s the anglo-catholic movement sorted out to its own satisfaction the absolute requirement of confirmation as the basis for admission to communion (a basis virtually unknown in Anglicanism before).[6]

This clarification of minds was precipitated by the 'Revisers' Communion' at Westminster Abbey in 1870, a date which neatly coincided with a sensing by anglo-catholics that they could now make the running in the Church of England. They did so make the running that within 50 years or so it was almost entirely gone from common memory that dissenters had once received communion in the Church of England without benefit of confirmation. This pressing of the 'confirmation rubric' inevitably pushed minds towards a high understanding of confirmation as integral to sacramental initiation. The role of confirmation was ceasing to be a kind of certificate of having been catechized and thus of being *prepared* to receive communion, and was becoming a non-negotiable completion of sacramental initiation, totally requisite ritually for admission to communion.

5   Mason was, in the event, preceded by Fr Puller, whose *What is the Distinctive Grace of Confirmation?* was published in 1880 (the advance herald of the major thrust to come – the 'Mason-Dix' line!).

In *Anglican Confirmation* I stated that, in broad terms, the two-stagers were in the ascendancy for 80 years, from 1890 to 1970. Here it will be helpful to see the characteristics of that school of thought, note its deflation, and trace out its continuing effects.

TWO-STAGING: ITS CHARACTERISTICS

Doctrinally the heart of the two-staging position is that there are two *inward* stages in initiation, denominated, represented and conveyed by the two outward stages: a re-birth in water, and a baptism with the Holy Spirit. This reference to baptism in the Holy Spirit was not a phenomenological statement, however; anglo-catholics never traditionally expected confirmation candidates to speak in strange tongues or otherwise go ecstatic. So the assertion of either re-birth or the coming of the Holy

---

6 Of course the American colonies in the seventeenth and eighteenth centuries, and many other parts of the Empire in the nineteenth, had no bishops. Anglican incumbents in those parts had perforce to do what rural clergy very often did in England at that time, that is, admit to communion without episcopal confirmation.

Spirit, more or less without visible effect in the candidates' lives (even without anything much in the way of faith), was a problem to evangelicals. The assertion that the two effects came *separately* in two different stages of a rite, whose parts might be divided by a period of ten, 15 or even 50 years, only compounded the problem. Though I am not going to explore it at this point, that side of the issue must be understood and noted, for it is part of the backdrop to other sacramental disputes.

Biblically, there is little to be said for the two-staging view. The two-stagers, however, had four great strings to their bows:

1 they went to town on the Samaritan episode in Acts 8;
2 they asserted that references in the scriptures generally to *baptisma* referred to a complex of initiation which included the laying on of hands;
3 they laid great weight on the tradition of the church, in which the *Apostolic Tradition* of Hippolytus in Dix's hands underscored and reinforced the case of Mason (who had not had the benefit of it);
4 they were unopposed by evangelicals as there was virtually no evangelical scholarship worthy of the name in the first half of this century (the biggest querying of them came rather from Pusey-like anglo-catholics such as Wirgman and Darwell Stone).[7]

Liturgically the 1662 rite looked fairly denuded if it were to be taken seriously as a main service in this period (1890–1970).[8] Accordingly

---

7 As a check on this I referred to the only evangelical exceptions I could easily identify. W. H. Griffith Thomas, in *The Principles of Theology: An Introduction to the Thirty-Nine Articles* (Church Book Room Press, London, 1930), gives a page and a half of his 540 pages to 'those five commonly called sacraments'. In a few lines only he expounds confirmation more or less as Cranmer would have done, simply to make the (not very easy) point that Anglican confirmation is 'a state of life allowed in the scriptures', whereas Roman Catholic confirmation is 'the corrupt following of the apostles' (3rd edn, 1945, pp. 353–5). He nowhere even mentions Mason (nor, of course, Dix). The same author, in his *The Catholic Faith* (1920 edn), gives a pastoral interpretation of the rite. On 'after the example of thy holy apostles' he comments (without biblical reference): 'We thus retain the exact form of the apostolic action, but with a different purpose' (p. 181).

8 It *was* a main service, of course, though one without scripture, hymnody, sermon, presentation, welcome, or communion, as it stood in its 1662 form. The great English precedent was for it to happen mid-week and to be followed by a special 'first communion', as likely as not at 8 a.m. on the Sunday following. (It must be remembered that large parts of the Anglican Communion observed fasting for communion until about 1970 – the Pope relaxed *his* rules in the 1950s, but it took some time to get through!)

most attempts at revision tried to incorporate the Acts 8 passage into the preface, whilst the 1922 Canadian book even added Acts 19 *and* Hebrews 6 as well. These passages, if they were relevant at all, taught almost too much: Acts 8 appears to record the initial (indeed Pentecostal) coming of the Holy Spirit, whereas the [liturgical] texts only wanted to say that a 'special gift' of the Holy Spirit was imparted. Other liturgical touching up of 1662 was that the renewal of baptismal vows tended to get articulated in full in this period, and there was a strong tendency to sing *Veni, Creator Spiritus*, all kneeling, before the bishop's confirmation prayer.

Later liturgical priorities do not obtrude into the pre-1970 rites. Confirmation, as noted in an earlier footnote, is, in these rites, still a separate service from baptism and still admits to communion. First communion is still a separate event on the first Sunday following confirmation.[9] In England the popular tendency still brought considerable numbers of 12-year-old children from unbelieving homes to join confirmation classes in the pre-1970s.

Psychologically, confirmation looked important, demanding, and even promising (Acts 8, if read on such occasions, is full of misdirected, if not actually spurious, promise of experiential results). But the importance came as much as anything from the sheer pomposity of an episcopal occasion. Episcopacy has a religious romanticism woven around it (a romanticism from which the occupants of the office are not always themselves immune), and the very scarcity value of a bishop seems to give great significance to the occasion. It will be recalled that

---

9 A marginal exception to this would be the coming of fully 'two-stage' rites in the Church of England's experimental series near the end of the period. The mind of Dix can be seen here. Draft services were produced in 1959 and, in a heavily amended shape, these were then authorized as 'Series 2' services in 1967 and 1968. They originated from the Mason-Dix theory that water and the laying on of hands *together* make up sacramental initiation. The groundwork for them had been done in the various Convocation reports (sometimes in minority reports) on initiation in the period 1944 to 1954 (see *Anglican Confirmation*, p. 23, including n4). They also included the celebration of the eucharist (and thus first communion) as a norm, and in this too they were pioneering (though *permission* for the eucharistic context had been provided in the Church of South India in the late 1950s). It is somewhat anomalous that the ASB rites today run on in this 1950s mould, and the difficulty of breaking the mould in England is enormous. Apart from the Church of England, I cannot find any pre-1970 provision for uniting baptism and confirmation in one rite except in the Canadian 1959 book, and that makes no provision for the eucharist.

the Puritans objected at Savoy, that the provision that only a bishop could confirm 'seemeth to put a higher value upon confirmation than upon baptism or the Lord's supper; for . . . every deacon may baptize, and every minister consecrate and administer the Lord's supper, but the bishop only may confirm.'[10] To this the bishops replied:

> The reserving of confirmation to the bishop doth argue the dignity of the bishops above presbyters, who are not allowed to confirm, but does not argue any excellency in confirmation above the sacraments. St. Hierom argues the quite contrary . . .[11]

I offer as a contemporary English analogy the suggestion that this is like comparing Maundy money with ordinary currency. From the point of view of scarcity, and of the royal occasion at the presentation of it, Maundy money has enormous value. No one, however, could live on Maundy money or hope to exist on dole-outs from the Queen; the necessities of life come in ordinary currency terms. This analogy, I think, preserves the emphasis in what the bishops were saying, though whether their answer was accurate or credible others must judge. What is clear is that the importation of a bishop (cope, staff, mitre, outriders and all) for the event threatens to turn it into a royal debutantes' ball (and, traditionally, the girls were dressed accordingly). If to that pomp is added the Acts 8 passage, let alone a sermon from a bishop schooled in the two-staging era, then the recipients can be forgiven if their expectations are pitched very high – and if they feel let down when 'nothing happens'.

On the other hand, the bishop is far from let down. Confirmation is his special outing and feeds his wanting to be needed. Whether he holds to a two-staging view or not, he becomes very sure of the necessity of episcopal confirmation in the life of the church and, indeed, the necessity of it looking and *feeling* in accordance with existing expectations. There is an episcopal conservatism in relation to episcopal services which corresponds to the much-vaunted lay person's conservatism in relation to great festivals. I retain a strong suspicion that, just as all biblical hermeneutics must take into account the context of the reader as well as that of the writer, so attempts to evaluate (and perhaps

---

10 Edward Cardwell, *Conferences on the Book of Common Prayer* (Oxford, 2nd edn, 1841), p. 329.
11 Cardwell, *Conferences*, p. 359.

to restructure) existing Anglican confirmation patterns are up against the experiential loading of the evaluation made by existing bishops.[12]

Ecumenically, the upshot of a two-stage view of confirmation is that Christians in denominations which do not practise episcopal confirmation have been viewed by Anglicans as only half-initiated.[13] So the pressure is often upon other denominations to insist on a laying on of hands as well as water baptism for 'full' sacramental initiation. Meanwhile, the matter may be relieved marginally by rites in some of the new prayer books of the Anglican Communion for receiving Christians from other denominations, rites which are avowedly not to be

---

12 For instance the present Bishop of Coventry (Simon Barrington-Ward), in his speech in the General Synod of the Church of England in July 1991, said:

> I would like to speak very much from experience . . . [In] the whole discussion of this issue there has been a gross undervaluing of confirmation itself as an aspect of initiation, yet this is one of the things I have come to value enormously in my experience as a bishop . . . I have had a very different sense [from that of the Bishop of St Edmundsbury and Ipswich], from my own experience of confirmation . . . My experience has certainly illustrated that sentence in 1 Corinthians chapter 6 verse 11 . . . That experience has become meaningful to me in confirming and in experiencing this as a gift of the Spirit, and as the true completion of baptism and entry to communion for many, many people . . .' (General Synod, *Report of Proceedings*, July 1991, p. 319)

This was a statement of enormous sincerity, springing from services which had been most carefully planned and conducted under the most careful and sensitive episcopal leadership; this is a statement by a bishop I hold in high esteem. I officiate in such confirmations myself, so I both thrill to them and honour all that the speaker is investing in these rites. And yet I still believe we should not give confirmation a higher place in the economy of the Holy Spirit than scripture would warrant. No amount of high experience – even for bishops – should distort our hermeneutics.

13 The same is of course true of the view taken of others (including Anglicans) by the Orthodox, and sometimes by Roman Catholics. The Orthodox give the 'seal' to Protestants who become Orthodox, and are irretrievably two-staging themselves. In the very course of writing this paper I came across the essay on 'chrismation' by the Orthodox writer Cyrille Argenti in Max Thurian (ed.), *Ecumenical Perspectives on Baptism, Eucharist and Ministry* (World Council of Churches, Geneva, 1983). Argenti's article includes a solemn citation of the Acts 8 and Acts 19 passages, though even he reveals that crucial lacuna when he goes on to say: 'anointing or chrismation administered immediately after emerging from the waters of baptism, and conferring the gift of the Holy Spirit, is solidly attested in the Universal Church from the third century of our era' (p. 53). This is a sharp-edged (and probably non-negotiable) view, and makes it astonishingly clear that [on this view] the coming of the Holy Spirit is sacramentally distinct from baptism in water. [I am uncertain whether 'that crucial lacuna' was as between the two 'stages' or as between the scriptures and the third century – both qualify!]

called 'confirmation', though they confer the same canonical status as confirmation.[14]

THE COLLAPSING OF THE VIEW

Those who propounded a two-stage view might have had some difficulties in the New Testament texts but, in accordance with their own principles, they had at least to locate the view in the practice of the early church. Indeed, the plea was that they were driven by the practice of the early church. In recent years, however, they have run into problems on both fronts, that is, in both the New Testament and the early post-apostolic church; it is these problems which expose their methodologies as special pleading with the evidence.[15]

I have offered 1970 as a symbolic date for the ending of the two-staging ascendancy. One major factor was the passing from the scene of the heavyweight two-staging scholars which, in England in the post-war years, included Gregory Dix, Arthur Couratin, Edward Ratcliff, J. D. C. Fisher and Michael Ramsey.[16] Fisher was still writing in the

---

14 These are the American *Book of Common Prayer* (1979), the Canadian *Book of Alternative Services* (1985), *A South African Prayer Book* (1989) (though the rite in this book appears to be giving episcopal confirmation *de novo* to those from non-episcopal denominations), and *A New Zealand Prayer Book* (1989). Such rites do *not* appear in the Church of England's *Alternative Service Book 1980*, nor in the Church of Ireland's *Alternative Prayer Book* (1984). They are, however, in view in the Church of England and the Liturgical Commission has done some initial work on them (thus the General Synod asked in July 1991 for such rites to be produced). At Toronto, the section handling 'Renewal of Baptismal Faith' said clearly that drawing a distinction between those who have previously received episcopal confirmation and those who have not 'is no longer appropriate' (para. 3.22).

15 See the Toronto Statement, 1.15–16; 3.1–2; 3.15–18.

16 I include Michael Ramsey, referring to his famous *The Gospel and the Catholic Church* (Longmans Green, London, 1936). In the course of a major discussion of baptism in Chapter V, he simply lets slip, in passing, his two-staging view: 'Baptism, therefore (with the laying-on-of-hands as its normal completion*) is the first significant fact about a Christian' (2nd edn, p. 59). The asterisk in the quotation refers to a footnote: 'Cf. Acts 8.14–17, 19.1–7, Titus 3.5, and probably 2 Tim. 1.6.' This almost passing comment suggests, however, that the covert implication of all his references to baptism is that they need the 'completion'. Curiously, when, forty years later, Ramsey in retirement wrote a book entitled *Holy Spirit*, I could find no reference in it to the 'completion' of baptism, or to the coming of the Holy Spirit through the laying on of hands or anointing. Had Michael Ramsey himself emerged from the pre-1970 era? (Certainly the conversation the authors of *Growing into Union* had with him in May 1970 suggested he was well aware of a changing question in the church.)

1970s whilst Couratin and Ramsey lived into the 1980s, but the impetus was gone. No new 'Mason-Dix' authors have appeared, and this theological oddity has perished at the age of fourscore years. Certainly, it simply ran out of steam, but this was hastened by a series of 'one-stage' findings which helped to bring its era to an end.

First came Geoffrey Lampe's *The Seal of the Spirit* (Longmans Green, London, 1951). This established, at the very least, that the two-stage case could be contested historically, and undertook the task from the very patristic evidence that was supposed to teach the two-staging position.[17]

There was then, in June 1966, a slight advance shock in an area where the Church of England authorities had not even realized there was a problem. The House of Laity, which had been elected in Autumn 1965, denied to the 1928 confirmation service the two-thirds majority it needed if it were to be authorized as 'Series 1', making it clear that it was the citing of Acts 8 which was central to the objection.[18]

Then came in 1970: (a) J. D. G. Dunn, *Baptism in the Holy Spirit*; (b) E. C. Whitaker (ed.), *Documents of the Baptismal Liturgy* (second edition, but with a new introductory essay); (c) the beginning of the admission of unconfirmed children to communion in New Zealand; (d) *Prayer Book Studies 18* in the USA (though it was equivocal on this issue); (e) and a tiny extra weight added by the above-mentioned *Growing into Union*. Immediately after came the 'Ely Report', *Christian Initiation: Birth and Growth in the Christian Society* (Church Information Office, London, 1971). This affirmed the central principle that 'sacramental initiation is complete in baptism', and recommended not only that unconfirmed children should be admitted to communion on the basis of their baptism, but also that confirmation should not be required for all those baptized as adults. In 1971–2 in England, there was also a change made by General Synod in the canons which

---

17 It is fascinating now to read the review comment of Cyril Pocknee (a lesser 'Mason-Dix' man) on *The Seal of the Spirit*. Pocknee termed it: 'the last and most skilful rearguard action on the part of the more conservative element of the Church of England who are now in retreat' (quoted in Leonel Mitchell, *Baptismal Anointing* (Alcuin/SPCK, London, 1966), p. 188).

18 I was myself helping out on the Church of England Liturgical Commission at the time, as we were engaged in re-touching the aborted 1959 proposals for a new attempt at authorization. Acts 8 was not being cited; but other suggestions that the laying on of hands is the candidate's Pentecost were. The Series 2 services were much improved in the process, and, when they were completed, I included merely a note of dislike (see my *Liturgy for Initiation: The Series 3 Services*, Grove Booklet on Ministry and Worship 65 (Grove Books, Bramcote, 1979)).

thereafter gladly and unambiguously welcomed baptized communicants of other denominations to receive the sacrament at our eucharistic celebrations.

Since the early 1970s, the practice that would allow (sometimes only just allow) the continuance of a two-stage theology has continued on previously acquired momentum (sustained virtually till the present day by an episcopate 'formed' prior to 1970), but its momentum has been slowed by various braking forces. Among them, I draw attention to the following:

1   The growth of treating baptism as the sole sacramental prerequisite for receiving communion, along with statements on the subject such as the Boston Statement (1985) and the 'Knaresborough Report' in England (1985). Even in the month before I originally drafted this chapter, both the Church in Wales Governing Body and the Church of Ireland General Synod had been showing a lively interest in this practice.

2   Similarly, episcopal confirmation has generally not been required of guests at Anglican eucharists, over which the post-1870, anglo-catholic reading of the 'confirmation rubric' had previously run rampant (cf. the row over the 'Kikuyu Communion' in 1913).

3   Whilst the finally authorized American Episcopal *BCP* in 1979 (following the 'Zebra Book' of 1973) retained the laying on of hands on all at baptism (even on infants), the separate 'confirmation' service was placed not with initiation but instead in the section entitled 'Pastoral Offices'.

4   In the Canadian *Book of Alternative Services* of 1985, the laying on of hands was not required of those being baptized as adults, they being admitted to communion without this ceremony.[19] The separate service of confirmation for those baptized as infants was placed not in with baptism but in the section entitled 'Episcopal Offices'.[20]

5   The Lima text (1982) is ambivalent (and actually not fully entitled to all the praise heaped on it). Under 'II', 'III' and part of 'IV' (paras 2–13) the whole discussion is based upon baptism *being*

---

19 See the Toronto Statement, 1.18: 'the administration of confirmation at or following adult baptism is unnecessary and misleading, and should be discontinued'; also the 'Ely' recommendations cited previously.

20 See the Toronto Statement, 1.18: 'Confirmation therefore stands as a pastoral office in its own right, and not as part of the initiatory process.' (Note the contrast with the Church of England's texts and proposals.)

baptism, a single, once-for-all act. All the discussion of faith, conversion, of the gift of the Spirit, apparently relates to such a single
act; and all the references to the scriptures are of baptismal and
'one-staging' passages. So all thus far appears univocal and clear on
that particular issue. But it is all contradicted in paragraph 14.
Suddenly the text lapses into 'Christians differ in their understanding of where the sign of the gift of the Spirit is to be found.
Different actions have become associated with the giving of the
Spirit . . .' And in paragraph 20 there appears worse still: 'Some
churches consider that Christian initiation is not complete without
the sealing of the baptized with the gift of the Holy Spirit . . .' This
kind of inflation of a post-baptismal ceremony in turn casts doubt
upon everything said in such an unqualified way about baptism
itself in paragraphs 2–13.[21]

6   The first International Anglican Liturgical Consultation in Boston
in 1985 (the findings of which were re-endorsed by the Toronto
Consultation in 1991) included in its recommendations: 'vii. That
each Province clearly affirm that confirmation is not a rite of
admission to communion, a principle affirmed by the bishops at
Lambeth in 1968.'[22] In this, as in various other reports, the centre
of attention is baptism, and admission to communion springing
from baptism. Once these landmarks have been established, confirmation becomes something handled more or less in passing. It is
treated not as something vitally important to a scriptural and prin-
cipled ordering of the church, but more as something which has a
negotiable pastoral role within the life of the church; it is not of
commandment, and ranks as important *only in the sense that it must*

---

21 In *Ecumenical Perspectives on Baptism, Eucharist and Ministry*, David Holeton
contributed a learned, panoramic, pastoral and phenomenological essay on confirmation. For what it does, it is marvellous. This reader could not help wishing,
however, that (a) he had been more dogmatic about what positions were credible
and what not, and (b) he had addressed himself to the Lima text in relation to confirmation, which as far as I can see, he did not do, and thus it escaped his dissectory
processes. (It is perhaps unfair to complain of Homer nodding, and it is certainly
the more notable for being so rare. But how his scalpel might have exposed the
fudge on this occasion!)

22 For the Boston recommendations, see Colin Buchanan (ed.), *Nurturing
Children in Communion,* Grove Liturgical Study 44 (Grove Books, Bramcote,
1985), p. 49. These are repeated in *Christian Initiation in the Anglican Communion,*
Grove Worship Series 118 (Grove Books, Bramcote, 1992), p. 25. The Boston
Statement itself wrote an epitaph on 'Mason-Dix': 'The foundation upon which the
"Mason-Dix" approach was ostensibly based, historical enquiry, proved to be its
weakest dimension.'

not be allowed to become too important. The emphasis is, therefore, often upon what confirmation cannot and must not do or be thought to secure, as a corrective to the appalling over-bidding of the 'Mason-Dix' era.

7   Also in 1985 came the Church of England's report, *Communion before Confirmation?* (Church Information Office, London, 1985). This working party, under the chairmanship of the then Bishop of Knaresborough, unanimously found that baptism alone is the basis for admission to communion. Its treatment of confirmation closely paralleled the Boston findings. It expressed, moreover, a broad hope that, if its provisions for admission to communion long before the existing age of confirmation were brought into use, then the age of confirmation would move upwards and the rite would become a genuine occasion for mature decision, and that it would be by confirmation that Anglican Christians would be enfranchised within the church structures. The General Synod 'took note' of the report in November 1985, and it then lay with the House of Bishops until July 1991.

8   The 1988 Lambeth Conference Report included a statement on liturgy in its 'Mission and Ministry' section, and I was myself secretary of the group which compiled the statement. In paragraph 192 we said: 'Baptism by water is the scriptural sacrament of once-for-all initiation into Christ and into his Body.'[23] Later paragraphs reassert this uniqueness and completeness of baptism whilst not wholly escaping, though certainly minimizing, a fudge in relation to confirmation. In particular the group was pressured by the Ministry and Mission sub-plenary section not to air the Canadian *BAS* pattern of adult initiation. (Some bishops in the Section who were not on our Group did not want to know what was actually happening in Canada, and it had to be suppressed.[24])

---

23 See *The Truth Shall Make You Free* (Anglican Consultative Council, London, 1989), p. 70.

24 The 'experiential' factor was again at work. Bishops show extreme nervousness about anything which might appear to touch confirmation, and it was easy in the Section, which was surveying drafts from our Group very summarily, to appeal to that nervousness. The Conference revealed a triple difficulty about making points which might vary or alter confirmation when bishops are running the discussion: (a) bishops are usually over 50 (or over 60) and so have imbibed some 'Mason-Dix' in their own training; (b) the 'experiential' factor is week by week reinforcing their position about confirmation; (c) they are rarely reading the literature on the subject as the teachers of liturgy must (and few liturgists ever become bishops – and no one was ever made bishop *because* of his liturgical knowledge).

9   The Toronto Consultation itself became the next major place of inter-Anglican theological proclamation about Christian initiation, and it is extensively surveyed and portrayed in this volume of essays. It consciously echoed the findings of the Boston Consultation of six years earlier. It will suffice here to collect a *catena* of materials relating to confirmation.

The Recommendations

(only two of the seven mentioned confirmation)

(c) Baptism is complete sacramental initiation and leads to participation in the eucharist. Confirmation and other rites of affirmation have a continuing role in the renewal of faith among the baptized but are in no way to be seen as a completion of baptism or as necessary for admission to communion.[25]

(g) The pastoral rite of confirmation may be delegated by the bishop to a presbyter.

The Statement

. . . There is little warrant in Scripture, the Reformers, or in the Prayer Book tradition itself, to support the notion that the imposition of hands somehow completes baptism and concludes the process of Christian initiation . . . (1.16)

. . . With this . . . understanding of baptism [that it admits to communion], the pressure for early confirmation is relieved so that the rite may actually express a *mature* ratification of baptismal faith. (1.17)

. . . Given this understanding of the rite [that those baptized as infants may ratify their baptismal faith as adults], the administration of confirmation at or following adult baptism is unnecessary and misleading, and should be discontinued . . . (1.18)

---

25 Four members of the Consultation dissented from this recommendation, and their names are recorded in the published edition. They proposed an alternative text which would have kept the substance of the recommendation finally approved. The Consultation voted this out by a majority, however, and the four were left to dissent. But they had very nearly got there.

Confirmation therefore stands as a pastoral office in its own right, and not as part of the initiatory process. If the title 'confirmation' is retained, the status of the rite as a pastoral office must nevertheless be clearly understood. (1.19)

(In addition there is a brief historical outline in 3.1 to 3.5, largely clearing away misapprehensions, a survey of the whole spectrum of possible current views in 3.15 to 3.18, and a mention of confirmation in connection with reception from other denominations in 3.22.)

Whilst much assimilation is still to come and some division of opinion still clearly exists, and whilst Anglican ecclesiastical inertia remains most awesome, yet the directions appear well set. Indeed, if this were another field of reform, it is likely that the term 'reception' would be invoked; that is, that we (undefined) *know* what is right, and we are sure that, as others come to a right mind also, so the doctrine will be duly 'received'. It is distrust of the mischievously altered use of the term 'reception' which inhibits me from using it (here and elsewhere), and not any lack of conviction as to the direction in which we are going.

RESIDUAL (AND VIRULENT) TWO-STAGE ELEMENTS

The present situation, however, still involves division; consequently, we must address the continuing two-stage features. The momentum acquired in those 80 years of theological ascendancy has not all disappeared in one breath. In some places, in fact, two-staging has acquired some minor, new impetus, even whilst its old momentum was running down. I list a series of influences upon the situation:

1   The first is the power of the concept of an originally 'integrated rite' which in later years 'disintegrated' and is now being 'reintegrated'.[26] This concept (which was not popularized much earlier than Dix, and reached its zenith well after Dix's time) still runs strong. *In the beginning it was not so*, however, and the first and second centuries

---

26 The historical assertion being made here is open to investigation and, of course, tends to fall at the first fence (see *Anglican Confirmation*, pp. 6–17, and the Toronto Statement 3.1–3). But the terminology of 'disintegrated' and 'reintegrated' has had a further subtle effect, for there is a subliminal moral judgement conveyed by these words. 'Integrated' tends to be seen as a positive word, 'disintegrated' as a negative one. (The reverse effect is achieved if we discuss how baptism during the early centuries became 'cluttered' with other ceremonies [negative], and later became 'uncluttered' [positive], before being 'recluttered' in Anglican history.)

must be viewed as the *primitive* church, not the early third century.[27]

2   A second influence is the persistence of ceremonial which is less-than-a-sacrament. Not only do Anglicans generally still expect those baptized as adults also to be confirmed (though for what purpose is wholly unclear, unless it be 'Mason-Dix' ideology), some also show signs of wanting to add anointing to both baptism and confirmation.[28] This situation can quickly bring us back to the old problems with the signing of the cross after baptism. The Puritan issue (met in the American *BCP* of 1789) was that a secondary ceremony which was *of commandment* purported to be part of the dominical sacrament, which it is not. It is well attested that since then many have thought that the sign of the cross *is* the sacramental sign in baptism; and a rationale which teaches that a ceremony is not requisite before God, but is enforced by the church, gives out a very uncertain sound.[29]

3   This effect is increased where vast claims are made for the chrism of confirmation. In the Church of England such chrismation is allowed by an opening note in the rite, but that small gap has since had to accommodate a coach and horses. There are prayers around the dioceses for use at the Maundy Thursday rite for new oils

---

27 See, for instance, the citation from Argenti in an earlier footnote [n13], where he claims '. . . from the third century of our era'. That to an Orthodox (if it is true history, and there are some muddy spots here) is decisive as autonomous tradition. To an Anglican, however, that is not so.

28 I confess I am also astonished to encounter rites, such as have just been approved in Wales, where an ecumenical provision includes a *mandatory* imposition of hands immediately after baptism.

29 It was delightful to me at Boston and Toronto to probe a little at the position of Leonel Mitchell, who some time ago wrote the major work *Baptismal Anointing*. To this day, he strongly advocates anointing at and with baptism, but limits his advocacy and argues that: (a) baptism is baptism, even without anointing (his illustration is that a eucharist even without a reading of the gospel is a eucharist, though he does not like to think of such a defective rite); (b) such anointing belongs in, with and to baptism itself, and is the lesser part of a single rite which cannot be separated from it to become a kind of confirmation, nor be treated as a second half of baptism giving 'completion' to an otherwise incomplete sacrament. Mitchell is therefore a signatory of the Boston and Toronto recommendations and Statements. I stick to my own caution about rubrics which require ceremonies which scripture and sound theology do not require, however. Such rubrics easily become the basis of a changed theology by those less sophisticated than Leonel Mitchell (as, for instance, happened with the 1662 requirement of confirmation for those baptized in 'Riper Years').

(largely drawn from Rome) which apparently teach that the anointing at confirmation is *the* great time of the coming of the Holy Spirit. Yet the use of chrism only occurs in about one parish in 20, and when it is used it has no liturgical accompanying prayer or declaratory formula whatsoever. The congregation in general, therefore, would hardly know it is there. (The Canadian *BAS* makes a slight and slightly ambiguous bow in the direction of chrism in the provision for blessing oils, but allows for its use at baptism alone.)

4   The matter is not helped by the episcopal concern about 'the bishop's role in initiation'. I would urge that Anglicans, and especially bishops, look hard at this, and see whether there is anything of substance in it.[30] In biblical terms it is very doubtful, and a new convert would only think episcopally if told to do so by those receiving him or her. To enter into the life of the church through one sacrament of baptism, and to become, thereby, participants in the other sacrament at the Lord's table, *is* to be fully in communion with the church and, *ipso facto*, with the bishop.

The Toronto Statement examines closely (in section 3, paras 33–40) the claims being made, and concludes in broad terms that the role of the chief pastor is in no way endangered if functions are delegated by him or her. Hence it is that Recommendation (g) can open the idea of confirmation itself being exercised by presbyters, a practice well established in the Roman Catholic Church but sufficient to cause the sky to fall in the Anglican.

5   I suspect also that we may be in some danger from the RCIA lobby (though I write with the greatest of admiration for the pastoral concerns of the philo-catechumenate school). The 'stepped' approach to adult initiation runs risks in its liturgical drafting and the message of its structuring of not only ascribing separate, further, post-baptismal benefits to confirmation (which the Roman Catholic Church does attempt to do), but also of doing so in a

---

30 Quite apart from anything else, it is in many situations highly inconvenient. There are two alternative ways of administering adult initiation in a consistent way. One is to give baptism 'on the spot', wherever a new convert is found (but bishops are not usually ready to drop everything in their schedules and come up to 1000 miles to give baptism); the other way is to move towards Easter baptisms everywhere (but, again, the bishop is not able to be in many places at one time). Either of these possibilities, then, is self-defeating. It is clear that, if bishops are persuaded that their touch, given either at or after baptism, is somehow crucial to the standing of young Christians within the life of the church, then we are very nearly back at a covert 'two-staging' rite.

'polarized' way where (as in that *fons et origo* in Acts 8) the two stages are far separated from each other.

6 There are also problems to work through in the growing notion that the laying on of hands may not be a once-for-all-life ceremony, but may be repeatable. That is fully in line with the flexibility of scripture in this area, but it will be no gain if *either* one of the times of laying on of hands proves on inspection to be the 'seal of the Spirit' *or*, alternatively, if it is not defined which one is vital. However, it is certain that a minimum of one such administration is necessary for the recognition that confirmation has somewhere been given. A *programme* of theoretically repeatable rites will do nothing but confuse if its proponents or chief practitioners still use once-for-all-for-life sacramental terminology. If the once-for-all-for-life concept is abandoned (along with 'character' etc. terminology), then it will be no longer possible to describe any Christian as 'confirmed' (any more than it would currently be possible or desirable to distinguish the 'anointed' or even the 'blessed' from the 'unanointed' or 'unblessed'). And, conversely, whilst the status of 'confirmed' remains, then some once-for-all-for-life rite must bear that title.

7 Next we have the old rite with yet a further rationale. Aidan Kavanagh has propounded a theory that the laying on of an episcopal hand is in fact the 'coming to the bishop's hand' of the newly baptized, or, to use his more rigorous term, a 'dismissal'. Thus, it is a ceremony illustrative of baptism and properly going with it – not the locus for the illapse of the Spirit but a liminal ceremony ushering the newly baptized from the fountain to the table. Kavanagh writes that, if we restored the ancient significance, 'it might then become possible for people to hear what confirmation has to say, namely that baptism and eucharist are the premier sacraments of Christian initiation, and confirmation itself nothing more nor less than the Roman Catholic Church's way of linking the two'.[31] This appears to be very close to declaring the rite to be contingent, domestic and negotiable. However the effect is to bind confirmation more closely into the baptismal initiatory process, and Kavanagh can even suggest that first communion should *never* be allowed to precede confirmation.[32] Thus whilst he evades any

---

31 A. Kavanagh, *Confirmation: Origins and Reform* (Pueblo, New York, 1988), p. 111.
32 Kavanagh (*Confirmation*, p. 110) is drawing out a parallel with the Orthodox 'seal'. This is, of course, very unlike the developed Roman Catholic practice of the last one thousand years.

historical connection between the laying on of the hand and the coming of the Spirit,[33] he appears to fall back into the trap of a *necessary*, secondary ceremony following baptism. His thesis has had a certain appeal for those romantics who, nevertheless, recognize that a full-blown 'Mason-Dix' is no longer sustainable, but want confirmation to be around and to mean at least something.[34]

8   The last bastion of resistance to change is to be found in the Church of England and most notoriously in the public response of the House of Bishops to the Knaresborough proposal. Whilst diocesan synods were passing resolutions calling for the implementation of the so-long-delayed Knaresborough proposals, the House of Bishops finally compiled the following resolutions to bring to the General Synod in July 1991:

That this Synod

(a)   affirm the traditional sequence of baptism–confirmation–admission to communion as normative in the Church of England;

(b)   accept that within this sequence confirmation can take place at an early age when this is deemed appropriate by the parish priest and the bishop;

(c)   agree that experiments of admission to communion before confirmation should be discontinued at a rate which gives due regard to the pastoral difficulties in the individual dioceses and parishes;

(d)   ask the Liturgical Commission to prepare a series of rites . . . for the renewal of baptismal vows, for the reception of members of another Church, and for reconciliation and healing;

(e)   [this concerned patterns of nurture.]

---

33 Whilst fully aware of Tertullian, for instance, he nevertheless finds a propaganda purpose behind Innocent I's citation of Acts 8.14–17, the first recorded dependence upon Acts 8 for episcopal handlaying (Kavanagh, *Confirmation*, p. 57). But *why* did Tertullian associate the handlaying with the illapse of the Spirit? I am sure there is a reason which will easily allow us to treat Tertullian's account as historically conditioned and therefore not binding. Kavanagh, however, is so determinedly unpneumatic in relation to the handlaying that he does not even discuss the significance of an allegedly pneumatic instance.

34 See, for instance, David Stancliffe in his chapter on confirmation in the recent *Liturgy for a New Century* (Alcuin/SPCK, London, 1991). The Kavanagh view gets aired, with attribution, in the Toronto Statement at 15.6, thus completing the spectrum of views (likely and unlikely) from which, if there is to be confirmation, the best candidate must be chosen.

Whilst the House of Bishops was not corporately bound by this composite motion, the Synod was somewhat thrown by it. The House of Bishops had done a full reverse turn, disregarding recent scholarship, diocesan motions, the Boston findings, overseas experience, Knaresborough, and the lot. In the event, the Synod did three things of consequence: (i) it removed the back-tracking clause (c) from the motion; (ii) it added a new clause after (d) above to 'ask the Liturgical Commission to prepare a rite of Adult Commitment . . .'; (iii) having then passed the composite motion, it voted on the Rochester diocesan 'following' motion:

> That this Synod request the House of Bishops to prepare draft regulations that enable children to be admitted to Holy Communion before confirmation, so that discussion can take place within the Church and conditions for such admission, if any, can be considered.

This motion went to a count by Houses (see Table 1).

Table 1: Voting by Houses

	Ayes	*Noes*
Bishops	7	34
Clergy	112	105
Laity	116	102

It was thus defeated heavily in the House of Bishops and, as a result, fell just short of an overall majority. Perhaps a marker had been put down.

So how fares confirmation itself in all this? A large part of the debate seemed to be handling the question: how can confirmation as we know it be defended?[35] Indeed, the Knaresborough proposals have been treated by the House of Bishops as first and foremost an attack on confirmation. It is clear in (a) and (b) of the main motion that the bishops of the Church of England did not particularly object to lowering the age at which baptized children would be first receiving communion, so long

---

35 This was more or less explicit in the speech of the Bishop of Coventry quoted in a previous footnote [n12], and in various other episcopal speeches. But no scriptural or patristic evidence was adduced for that which was being defended.

as they could still confirm such children as a means of admitting them. The upshot is, of course, that the minimum age of confirmation might well go down to seven or some such age. The concept of confirmation as a mature ratification of baptismal faith would be further off than ever, and the amendment to bring in a 'Rite of Adult Commitment' was openly intended as a corrective or supplement to an immature confirmation.

The complexities of all this defy the imagination, and, as a way of preserving the common traditional discipline (which is how it was presented), it is wholly absurd. In addition there was a cheerful ignoring of all the rest of the Anglican Communion.[36] The crucial conclusion (very obvious in the voting on the Rochester diocesan motion) is that the House of Bishops must have confirmation. Yet the Synod debate did not close the door entirely to reform, and particularly the excision of that clause to end all 'children in communion before confirmation' parish projects was significant. The great hope must be that the Toronto Statement will itself be taken seriously in England, particularly as it was signed by so many official members of the Church of England Commission.

So there are many obstacles to progress in England, and quite a confused undergrowth of ideologies, policies, and practices to encounter in order to effect change. The big hope must be that the Toronto Statement will itself facilitate the process. If it provokes Anglicans to have a worldwide view and thus to escape from a provincial parochialism, then clearing the undergrowth will at least come onto the agenda.

---

36 It was of course alleged that confirmation of 12-year-olds and of older teenagers also had almost ceased in some parts of the world where they had been admitted to communion early. To that extent it *might* be said that the pastoral role for confirmation envisaged in Knaresborough and Toronto would not work out. Certainly we need more surveys of the sort the Archbishop of New Zealand is providing. But meanwhile the Church of England has to ask itself: (a) how many children of 12 years and under are coming to confirmation nowadays? (b) how many of them are still regular communicants at age 16 or 17? (c) if teenagers are going to lapse, is it better that they should have been confirmed prior to lapsing or not? And (d) are we in fact *sure* we ourselves have a pastorally successful (as well as biblically impeccable) discipline in place? We might ask ourselves whether, if there do happen to be those in New Zealand or the United States who grow up baptized, believing and communicant, but do not, as it happens, ever get confirmed, there is any great loss to the individual or the church. *Does* confirmation have any revealed and commanded status or not?

On the worldwide scene itself, despite all the contrary factors listed above which slow down the process, the direction is clearly set. The theological changes since 1970 move on securely, and Toronto takes its place in that ongoing march, setting signposts for confirmation which the practice of the provinces will surely follow in due course.

SUMMARY

I conclude that the XXXIX Articles and the 1604 Catechism had it right: that there are *two* sacraments of the gospel – baptism and the Lord's Supper – and the outward sacramental sign in baptism is solely the administration of water (in the appropriate liturgical context). Toronto (and I) would want to go further and then assert that admission to baptism in principle *is* admission to the Lord's table, and that infants and children can qualify for admission to both sacraments as members of the body of Christ in believing homes.

Where, then, is confirmation? It is excluded, or excluded at least as being a requisite component of initiation or a completion of baptism, or as in any way the necessary door of admission to communion. It cannot have these initiatory roles; to create them is to place upon it a weight it cannot sustain.

There is a case for a pastoral ceremony (even an episcopal one) for the candidate's ratifying and the church's recognizing baptismal faith at the age of discretion for those who have been baptized and become communicant in younger years. The laying on of hands would be wholly appropriate here. There may also well be a case for restoring the lapsed, renewing baptismal vows, and even welcoming the newcomer who is 'joining' the Anglican church with a similar ceremony. But such ceremonies have no standing as scriptural and catholic sacraments; they have no promise of 'inward grace'; they must not be a necessary (as opposed to illustrative) part of sacramental initiation; they must not be wished on those who do not need them (particularly on those baptized as adults); and they must not be made a *sine qua non* in reunion negotiations. And at each and every point in this conclusion, the Toronto Statement points in the right direction.

There is in this Statement a very explicit programme for hard reform. It has been part of the glory of Anglicanism to be able to reform its traditions in each generation, and often to be able to do so country by country as the vision has grasped bolder spirits in one land than it has so far done in another. The Toronto Statement at large, and its handling of confirmation in particular, provides a good instance of this capability. The thin end of the wedge had been driven far into the practice of some provinces since 1970, and Toronto now furthers the reform by driving a theological wedge into the thinking of us all. Certainly, much existing Anglicanism is characterized by a soft-headed romanticism, mindless conservatism, theological muddling, or knee-jerk defensiveness, and our confirmation inheritance is no exception. Yet the Toronto Statement is urging us into hard-headed, clear-eyed, critical engagement with this received traditional inheritance. Province by province, step by step, there should be a God-given critical response.[37]

POSTSCRIPT

In England it was terribly hard to get official attention paid to the Toronto Statement (see my Taking the Long View, *chapters 4 and 5). The Synod authorities declined to circulate it to the members. Progress came in the late 1990s. This essay reads very much as of its own time. Yet even today the Anglican Communion presents a very mixed picture of the role of confirmation, and of the admission of baptized children to communion.*

[37 The original Toronto Statement, *Walk in Newness of Life*, is in print simply as the Statement in David R. Holeton (ed.), *Christian Initiation in the Anglican Communion* (Grove Worship Series 118, Grove Books, Bramcote, 1992). The volume of accompanying essays, to which the above chapter belongs, is David R. Holeton (ed.), *Growing in Newness of Life: Christian Initiation in Anglicanism Today* (Anglican Book Centre, Toronto, 1993). There have also been over the last three decades IALC Statements on Children in Communion, on Inculturation of the Liturgy, on the Eucharist, on Ordination, and on Anglican Liturgical Identity. Each of these has similarly existed in Statement-only form and also in a larger volume of essays. Details are available through the Anglican Consultative Council, and the story is told in the account I wrote with David Holeton, *A History of the International Anglican Liturgical Consultations 1983–2007* (Joint Liturgical Study no. 63, SCM-Canterbury Press, London, 2007).]

Eucharist

Chapter 5

What did Cranmer think he was doing?

FOREWORD

This exploration of the 1548, 1549 and 1552 eucharistic texts was origi-nally written to replace Arthur Couratin's SPCK booklet which had gone out of print. In preparing it I studied the entire five books of Thomas Cranmer's Answer to the Crafty and Sophistical Cavillation of Stephen Gardiner, *specifically to enable liturgical text and doctrinal writing from the same hand to explain and reinforce each other.*[1] *It became Grove Litur-gical Study 7 in 1976 and, minimally revised in 1982, has remained in print for 32 years. The 1982 text is reprinted here. I am unaware of its accuracy being challenged.*

CRANMER'S DOCTRINE OF THE EUCHARIST

In Cranmer the disputing theologian[2] and the writer of new liturgy are bound together in the one person. He was still the theologian when he was the writer of the liturgy, and students may properly look for the hand of the one in the work of the other. What then were Cranmer's eucharistic beliefs at the time when he was writing his Communion services?

[1 Quotations from Cranmer's writings are always made from the Parker Society volumes (Cambridge, vol. I, 1844, and vol. II, 1846). They are cited as follows: vol. I – *On the Lord's Supper*; vol. II – *Miscellaneous Writings and Letters.* Where necessary, the distinction between *The Defence, The Answer,* and *The Answer to Smith's Preface* in volume I has also been noted, but only where necessary. Gardiner is also always quoted from *On the Lord's Supper.* The then newly issued publication edited by A. H. Couratin and D. H. Tripp, *E. C. Ratcliff: Liturgical Studies* (SPCK, London, 1976), is always quoted as *Ratcliff.*]

2 'Theologian' is here used to denote a writer on theology without any implication that he has to be reckoned an outstanding theological thinker.

Undoubtedly his doctrine was now reformed, and akin to the 'Swiss' position.[3] It had not always been so. He himself writes:

> But this I confess of myself, that not long before I wrote the said catechism,[4] I was in that error of the real presence, as I was in years past in divers other errors: as of transubstantiation, of the sacrifice propitiatory of the priests in the mass, of pilgrimages, purgatory, pardons . . .[5]

As the 'said catechism' was published in 1548, and as Cranmer's coming to a decided mind is usually attributed to the influence of Ridley,[6] who became his chaplain in 1546, it looks as though the origin of his fully reformed stance was virtually synchronous with the accession of Edward VI, and with the opportunity (under Somerset's influence) for a reform of the worship of the Church of England. There is little need here to stay upon the interesting question as to whether Cranmer held an intermediate position, perhaps undefined, but akin to Lutheranism, in the years from 1538 onwards.[7]

---

3 The term 'Swiss' is used to characterize a general doctrine of the sacrament, not the provenance of each and every theologian approximating to this view.

4 The catechism is that of Justus Jonas, published in August 1548, and in its original Latin of a clearly Lutheran cast. Cranmer translated it into English, though, in the words of one author, 'taking a somewhat unfair advantage of translator's licence' (P. N. Brooks, *Thomas Cranmer's Doctrine of the Eucharist* (Macmillan, London, 1965), p. 43). A new emphasis is laid upon reception, and less upon what in the original was 'quando . . . dicit hoc est corpus meum, tum mox ibi est corpus Domini' (ibid.). Gardiner, however, constantly refers to Cranmer's translation of Justus Jonas as though it were an Achilles' heel in Cranmer's position (see *On the Lord's Supper*, pp. 19–20, 55, 106, 188, 227 – though in the last reference Gardiner cites the original, knowing it has been doctored by Cranmer!). It remains an interesting question why, if Cranmer wished to disavow Lutheranism, he took a Lutheran catechism as his source, running considerable risk of being misunderstood by his reformed friends, especially those in France and Switzerland who had no English.

5 *The Answer to Smith's Preface* (*On the Lord's Supper*, p. 374).

6 '. . . doctor Ridley did confer with me, and . . . drew me quite from my opinion' (*Miscellaneous Writings and Letters*, p. 218).

7 The great argument *against* an intermediate position is the well-known outburst at his examination in September 1555. Dr Martin claims Cranmer has taught 'in this high sacrament of the altar three contrary doctrines'. Cranmer replies, 'Nay, I taught but two contrary doctrines in the same' (*Miscellaneous Writings and Letters*, pp. 217–18). Dix calls this Cranmer's 'own repeated and passionate claim' (G. Dix, *The Shape of the Liturgy* (Dacre/Black, London, 1945), p. 646), but it must be noted

From his writings we can detect several main strands of thought which both align him with the reformed 'Swiss' views of the continent, and also give several clues to interpreting his liturgical work. The following recurrent themes are to be found:

1   Those who eat the body of Christ inevitably have everlasting life (so John 6.53), but those who eat 'this bread' unworthily are under condemnation (1 Corinthians 11.29). Therefore only the 'worthy' eat the body of Christ in the sacrament, and the wicked receive the sacramental sign, but *not* the thing signified.[8] This position sets him apart from both Romans and Lutherans.

2   There is a common understanding needed for both sacraments, baptism and communion. As it is agreed on all sides that there is nothing 'in' or 'under' the water, but that the Holy Spirit works through the administration of it, so it is clear that there is nothing 'in' or 'under' the bread and wine independently of reception, but that God works through the actual administration of it ('in usu sacramenti').[9] This position undermines both transubstantiation and any Lutheran [doctrine of] objective presence.

---

that Dix's footnote references do not add to the one instance. Brooks' careful study suggests there *was* an undefined phase of belief in a 'real presence', and he gets round Cranmer's answer to Martin thus: 'It is surely foolhardy to regard the answer of Cranmer, at a moment when he was submitted to all the anxieties of a sixteenth century heresy trial, as being a well-nigh infallible and authoritative comment on his own doctrinal position' (*Cranmer's Doctrine*, p. 12). The very speculative thought occurs to me that Cranmer was in fact exhibiting himself as the don, that the emphasis in the answer is not on 'two' as against 'three', but is on 'contrary'. The logician in him would admit that his first and last positions were 'contraries' – i.e. they inevitably excluded each other. But he could not view his intermediate position, lacking firm edges, as logically 'contrary' to either. On this view he is *scrupulously* exact about the nature of his earlier views, as he himself had lived with them, and he is at the same time showing that scholarly logical precision which so often marks his disputatious writings. Far from showing his anxieties, it would reveal him as in the coolest possible possession of himself! This would make Brooks' position even more self-consistent.

8   *On the Lord's Supper*, pp. 207–11 *et passim*. The famous quotation from Augustine's treatment of John 6, which later was incorporated into Article XXIX of 1571, is part of his evidence here (Augustine, *In Joannem* De Cap. vi Par ix).

9   The use of the parallel from baptism by Cranmer has the recurrence of a drumbeat. See *On the Lord's Supper*, pp. 17, 25, 41, 45, 64, 69, 92, 122, 134, 146, 150, 155–6, 161, 174, 183, 199, 205–6, 221, 226, 254, 271, 273, 305, 308, 310, 315, 320, 341, 356–7, 404, 406, 411. See also G. W. Bromiley, *Baptism and the Anglican Reformers* (Lutterworth, London, 1953). Gardiner has to wriggle in opposing this – see, e.g., *On the Lord's Supper*, pp. 155, 174, 184, 309, 340.

3 The meaning (for the 'worthy') of eating the body and drinking the blood of Christ has two different but interlocked expositions by Cranmer. He is clear (again from John 6) that eating is believing.[10] He sees the very strong reference in the supper to the cross of Christ,[11] and so is inclined to expound the eating and drinking as believing that Christ died for us. 'This saying of Christ [from John 6] . . . is a figure, commanding us to be partakers of Christ's passion, keeping in our minds, to our great comfort and profit, that his flesh was crucified and wounded for us.'[12] This trusting in the past event is, of course, a way of life, rather than a weekly event, and it is that which leads Cranmer to say that we eat Christ's body and drink his blood just as the patriarchs did,[13] and on other occasions to say that the presence of Christ is in the recipients, not in the elements.[14] The difficulty about this is that it produces a static concept of the sacrament. It speaks to an already existing situation, perhaps to confirm or reinforce it, but hardly to be a means of grace. It is exactly the position which Dix cartoons: 'This was what it all came to in the end – the bread had nothing to do with the Body – That was what he was dying for –'.[15] But it does not seem to be exhaustive of Cranmer's position. There is another strand in his thought which is more truly dynamic. The whole comparison with

10 As, e.g., in *On the Lord's Supper*, p. 36 *et passim*.

11 A It is frequently said (e.g. by Dix, *The Shape*, pp. 606–7) that Cranmer simply inherited a medieval emphasis on Calvary, and remodelled his rite round this. His writings suggest rather that the New Testament was his source.

12 This actual quotation is from Augustine, *De Doctrina Christiana* Lib.III, Cap. xv.xvi (*On the Lord's Supper*, p. 115, translated slightly differently by Cranmer on p. 212). But it is repeated in dozens of ways by Cranmer as his own understanding of the supper.

13 As, e.g., in *On the Lord's Supper*, pp. 74–8, 111, 296 etc. The first of these instances is interesting as including (p. 78) a citation from 'Bertram' (Ratramnus) teaching the same doctrine. The concept is from one point of view a good test case concerning the theological divide at the Reformation, but from another it is hardly one which would quickly occur to us. Dix scorns it (*The Shape*, p. 649).

14 'They [the papists] teach, that Christ is in the bread and wine; but we say (according to the truth), that he is in them that worthily eat and drink the bread and wine' (*On the Lord's Supper*, p. 52). Wording of the sort abounds – see, e.g., pp. 54, 57 etc. It hardly differs from Hooker's famous statement (which Dix, *The Shape*, p. 677, calls 'receptionism' and, in a footnote, 'Hooker's new heresy'): 'The real presence of Christ's most blessed body and blood is not therefore to be sought for in the sacrament, but in the worthy receiver of the sacrament' (*Eccl. Pol.* V.67.6).

15 Dix, *The Shape*, p. 674. Cartooning was easy for Gardiner also: '[Cranmer] speaketh of a jolly easy way, without any mystery, or marvel at all' (*On the Lord's Supper*, p. 63).

baptism entailed a communicating of grace by the Spirit to the recipients. The whole locus for this communicating was the point of reception,[16] but a true communicating it was. The point which Dix consistently (and deliberately?) overlooks is the actual encounter by faith not just with a past event but with a living person. Thus to feed on Christ is to strengthen that relationship. Thus 'it is my constant faith and belief that we receive Christ in the sacrament verily and truly'.[17]

4 This last point is undergirded by Cranmer's frequent discussion of *where* Christ is today. 'But all that love and believe Christ himself, let them not think that Christ is corporately in the bread; but let them lift up their hearts unto heaven, and worship him, sitting there at the right hand of his Father.' He then continues: 'Let them worship him in themselves, whose temples they be, in whom he dwelleth and liveth spiritually . . .'[18] True biblical faith encounters the living Christ, and the doctrine of Cranmer includes the mediation of the living Christ to his people in the administration of the sacrament. The difficulty is how to express any *distinctive* mediation of Christ to his people in the sacrament, but there the Scylla of finding no distinctive sacramental mediation of Christ is probably better, at least in Cranmer's polarized situation, than the Charybdis of actually finding it!

5 Once the points above have been grasped, it is clear that Cranmer has no objection to any 'realist' language, *so long as it is concerned with what is received by the faithful.* Gardiner three times probes him about the rubric in the 1548 *Order* and the 1549 rite that says '*Men must not think less to be received in part than in the whole, but in each of them the whole body of our saviour Jesus Christ*'.[19] But it is no problem to Cranmer, because the very strong language is all in

---

16 'Cranmer after 1548 maintained that Christ's body is present, not in the sacraments, but in the administration of the sacraments, and is spiritually received by all who receive him worthily, that is, by those in whom Christ is already spiritually present' (C. H. Smyth, *Cranmer and the Reformation under Edward VI* (SPCK, London, 1926, 1973), p. 66). The dynamic feeding is expressed in the first part of this quotation, the more static being in Christ in the second. Both do justice to the oscillating presentation in Cranmer's writings, and neither should be treated on its own as *the* single summary of his position. Smyth treats them here as identical, but that they are not.

17 *On the Lord's Supper*, pp. 184–5.

18 *On the Lord's Supper*, p. 238.

19 The probes are in *On the Lord's Supper*, pp. 63, 142 and 325.

the context of receiving.[20] What he will not stand is any objective location of the presence of Christ in the elements independently of reception. Thus there can be no worshipping of consecrated wafers, no reservation, no processions or other activity which would tend towards such worship.

6 There remains the question of eucharistic sacrifice. Even prior to any quoting from his fifth book, of which this question is the theme, we can already see that there is in his understanding no such presence of Christ in the eucharist as would enable us to offer him to the Father, and no instituted action to be fulfilled with the elements except the eating and drinking of them. This position is then reinforced in his fifth book by an exposition of the Epistle to the Hebrews, which makes it clear that we have no propitiatory sacrifice to offer today at all, and no earthly priest who could possibly be a candidate for that task. He handles the question of sacrifice in the eucharist very explicitly:

> Another kind of sacrifice there is [i.e. apart from Christ's propitiatory sacrifice] which . . . is made of them that be reconciled by Christ, to testify our duties unto God, and to shew ourselves thankful unto him. And therefore they be called sacrifices of laud, praise and thanksgiving. The first kind of sacrifice Christ offered to God for us; the second kind we ourselves offer to God by Christ. And by the first kind of sacrifice Christ offered also us unto his Father; and by the second we offer ourselves and all that we have unto him and his Father.[21]

Cranmer therefore accepts much *language* of offering, but all the medieval understanding and use of it is, on his view, in great need of remodelling. Moderns might also care to note that both Cranmer and Gardiner agree that the Greek *anamnesis* means

---

20 As we shall see below, he will nevertheless change it in 1552! He could apparently stomach even stronger language, so long as it concerned reception, as is evidenced by the note at the end of the First Book of Homilies [in 1547]: '*Hereafter shall follow Sermons . . . of the due receiving of his [Christ's] blessed body and blood under the form of bread and wine.*' I do not think the phrase '*under the form*' occurs in his writings against Gardiner in this acceptable sense, but it could have done. It is defended as consonant with Cranmer's doctrine by N. Dimock, *Papers on the Eucharistic Presence* (Macintosh, London, n.d., but around 1910), pp. 224–64. But if it was drafted by Cranmer before (or even around) the time of Edward's accession [January 1547] it does not *have* to be exactly in accord with his later determined mind in any case.

21 *On the Lord's Supper*, p. 346.

'remembering' – the frequent use of 'remembrance' and its cognates never seems to include the idea popularized in the twentieth century that a 'memorial' is a recalling objectively into the present of the sacrifice of Christ, or a pleading of that sacrifice before the Father.[22] Argument about eucharistic sacrifice (and in fact Gardiner is much milder than, e.g., the position opposed in Article XXXI[23]) is conducted on different lines.

With that brief doctrinal sketch set out, we turn to consider the historical processes by which Cranmer's theology was turned into liturgy, and

---

22 It will be recalled that 'memorialism' was a hostile description of Swiss sacramental theology – characterized by its opponents as being a 'nuda commemoratio'. The term 'memorial' is used not only (in the agreed sense set out above) in the disputations, but also in the text of the 1549 rite. It does give rise to the interesting speculation that Cranmer could probably have signed the 1971 Anglican–Roman Catholic Agreement on the Eucharist, whereas his opponents could probably not have. But that Statement stops short of saying that the sacrament recalls into the present an event from past time, and simply says that it makes 'effective in the present' that event in the past – i.e. that the sacrament is an effectual means of grace. This Cranmer could have accepted. The later statements in paragraphs 8 and 9 about the presence of Christ in the sacrament go very much with his use of language, and the footnote explaining away transubstantiation without committing anyone to it would have made him chortle. Indeed, because there are imprecise points in it, the Statement stands near to 1549 (or to Cranmer's understanding of 1549). In the sixteenth century the opponents could not agree even on forms of words. See *The Anglican–Roman Catholic Agreement on the Eucharist* by Julian Charley, Grove Booklet on Ministry and Worship 1 (Grove Books, Bramcote, 2nd edn, 1972, 1973 and 1975). Some blunt criticisms of 'actualizing' theories are raised by David Gregg in *Anamnesis in the Eucharist*, Grove Liturgical Study 5 (Grove Books, Bramcote, 1976).

23 'Wherefore the sacrifices of the Masses, in the which it was commonly said, that the Priest did offer Christ for the quick and dead, to have remission of pain or guilt, were blasphemous fables and dangerous deceits.' The text is Cranmer's no. XXX of 1553. Although Gardiner can say, '[In Lombard's view] this daily offering by the priest is daily offered for sin' (*On the Lord's Supper*, p. 358), it is more typical of him to say, 'The catholic doctrine teacheth not the daily sacrifice of Christ's most precious body and blood to be an iteration of the once perfected sacrifice on the cross, but a sacrifice that representeth that sacrifice, and sheweth it also before the faithful eyes, and refresheth the effectual memory of it; so as in the daily sacrifice, without shedding of blood, we may see with the eye of faith the very body and blood of Christ by God's mighty power, without division distinctly exhibit' (*On the Lord's Supper*, p. 360). The emphasis here is more on showing the propitiation to us than on propitiating God. Trent of course was far stronger, and it is that which Article XXXI opposes. The arguments of Cranmer's fifth book would also completely undercut Trent, whilst demolishing Gardiner en route.

the curious close interplay between politics, doctrine and the eucharistic rite which the brief years of Edward's reign exhibit. There are three main points to consider.

1 The doctrinal position of Cranmer, first publicly revealed in its full Swiss vigour in the great Parliamentary debate in December 1548, was unchanged through the period of liturgical revision. It is arguable that 1552 gives more consistent and explicit expression to it than 1549, but it is hardly arguable *either* that Cranmer's own doctrinal position moved between 1549 and 1552, *or* that 1552, although it was drafted by him, went beyond the goals for reform he had set himself, and exhibited him drafting (under pressure) a more 'Zwinglian' rite than he himself could easily have advocated.[24]

2 The liturgical programme of Cranmer was designed from the first to be a stepped one. In the Royal Proclamation preceding *The Order of the Communion* of 1548,[25] the King is made to say:

> [We will our subjects] . . . also with such obedience and conformity to receive this our ordinance, and Godly direction, that we may be encouraged from time to time, further to travail for the reformation and setting forth of such Godly orders as may be most to God's glory, the edifying of our subjects, and for the advancement of true religion. Which thing we (by the help of God) most earnestly intend to bring to effect . . . We would not have our subjects, so much to mislike our judgment, so much to mistrust our zeal, as though we either could not discern what were to be done, or would not do all things in due time . . .[26]

There is therefore every reason to reckon not only that the 1549 Book of Common Prayer was already in an advanced state of

---

24 Dugmore argues it: 'It is obvious that Cranmer had to allow very substantial concessions to be made to the radical Reformers, but it does not follow that he interpreted the rite of 1552 in exactly the same sense as they did, or that he welcomed all the changes made' (*The Mass and the English Reformers* (Macmillan, London, 1958), p. 171). Dugmore's thesis is generally regarded as implausible.

25 Hereafter often called the '*Order*' or 'the 1548 *Order*' or '1548'.

26 The text of this is to be found in the Parker Society edition of the liturgies of the reign of Edward VI, in H. A. Wilson's edition of the 1548 *Order* in the Henry Bradshaw Society series (1908), and in G. A. Michell, *Landmarks in Liturgy* (Darton, Longman & Todd, London, 1961), pp. 232–3. [Also in Colin Buchanan (ed.), *Background Documents to Liturgical Revision 1547–1549*, Grove Liturgical Study 35 (Grove Books, Bramcote, 1983).]

drafting before the *Order* came into force at Easter 1548 (and not only that the 1550 Ordinal was being drafted whilst the 1549 material was itself being printed and distributed), but also that the drafting of 1549 was itself avowedly interim, and that Cranmer was involved, perhaps even as early as 1548,[27] in sketching in for himself what the next step would be. The whole concept contained in the Royal Proclamation above is that the work will involve revision 'from time to time' – the exact opposite of a promise that 1549 would be the final and definitive piece of work.

This in turn means that of the events which succeeded the imposition of the 1549 Book – whether the Cornish rebellion, or the willingness of Gardiner to use the Book,[28] or Bucer's *Censura*, or criticisms from Geneva, or complaints from English puritans – none of them in the strictest sense shook Cranmer's planning, and although they may have affected the *timing* of the next step in revision, they probably necessitated only peripheral trimming of the draft contents of the 1552 Book, as the plan for the next stage was already implicit within the 1549 Book itself before it ever started its period of currency.[29]

It follows, of course, that the three stages of liturgical revision in 1548, 1549 and 1552 represent no change whatsoever in Cranmer's own theology, but rather constitute a carefully conceived plan for weaning the country progressively from Henrician Catholicism.

---

27 See below p. 88 for the suggestion that the very drafting of 1549 was designed to lead on to an *already known* next step. See also Dix, *The Shape*, p. 658.

28 Cranmer somewhat ironically applauds Gardiner's acceptance of the Book: 'But yet glad I am to hear that the said book liketh you so well, as no man can mislike it, that hath any godliness in him joined with knowledge' (*On the Lord's Supper*, p. 56). It was of course no real pleasure to Cranmer, as Gardiner's acceptance of it was on the basis of his 'Crafty and Sophistical Cavillation' (as it is called in the title of Cranmer's *Answer*). For the actual citing of the Book by Gardiner see p. 111 below.

29 There was also a suggestion (connected to the suggestion in the previous paragraph) that the 1549 rite tended to move on (as if of its own accord?) when it was out of the public arena. Thus Thirlby complained that the rite to be brought before Parliament in December 1548 was not quite as it had been when he had put his hand to it in Chertsey in September (*Ratcliff*, pp. 193–4; F. Gasquet and E. Bishop, *Edward VI and the Book of Common Prayer* (Sheed & Ward, London, 2nd edn, 1928), p. 144). J. T. Tomlinson, in a tract entitled *The Great Parliamentary Debate*, apparently argued that Thirlby's complaint about the omission of 'oblation' was not about the 1549 communion rite at all, but some other book. I have not seen Tomlinson's book, but a complaint of this sort in December 1548 by a bishop who had been at Chertsey is most probably about the communion rite! See pp. 88 and 92 (n65) below.

3   Because Cranmer the theologian and Cranmer the liturgist were one and the same person (and perhaps because Cranmer the master of English prose encompassed them both), there are strong verbal resemblances between his theological and his liturgical writings. Behind this we can see that he must have frequently been required to explain the concepts he was using, as much in private conversation as in public disputes or books, and it is hardly surprising that he came to use certain turns of phrase which recur in both of his literary fields. The best-known instance of this is his exposition in his *Answer* to Gardiner of the meaning of 'that they may be unto us the body and blood of . . . Jesus Christ' in the 1549 rite:

> . . . we do not pray absolutely that the bread and wine may be made the body and blood of Christ, but that unto us in that holy mystery they may be so; that is to say, that we may so worthily receive the same, that we may be partakers of Christ's body and blood, and that therewith in spirit and in truth we may be spiritually nourished.[30]

This wording is very close to the 1552 phraseology which replaced 'may be unto us'. It does not matter for the moment whether the *Answer* preceded the writing of the 1552 text, or whether a 1552 text in draft lay open on Cranmer's desk when he was refuting Gardiner[31] – for it is likely on our present premises that *both* documents simply represent the standard exposition of 'may be unto us' which Cranmer had been using since 1549 had been published, or even before.

Some further instances of this 'common currency' phenomenon will assist the argument.

---

30   *On the Lord's Supper*, p. 79.
31   Arthur Couratin (*The Service of Holy Communion 1549–1662* (SPCK, London, 1963) p. 4) half suggests that 'the book of 1552 was already taking shape as early as 1550', because Cranmer was quoting from it here. But notice that, although the suggestion is probably true, this citation does not help it very much. Indeed Couratin here (and again on p. 9) dates Cranmer's interpretation as 1550, which is impossible, as, being in his *Answer*, it must be 1551.

From 1549 and 1552	From *On the Lord's Supper*
. . . Jesus Christ to suffer death upon the cross for our redemption, who made there (by his one oblation of himself once offered) a full, perfect, and sufficient sacrifice, oblation and satisfaction for the sins of the whole world . . . (1549 Canon)	And to perform the same he made a sacrifice and oblation of his own body on the cross, which was a full redemption, satisfaction, and propitiation for the sins of the whole world. (p. 5)
And as concerning the natural body and blood of our Saviour Christ, they are in heaven and not here. For it is against the truth of Christ's true natural body to be in more places than in one, at one time. (1552 'Black Rubric')	And forasmuch as it is against the nature and truth of a natural body to be in two places at the one time, therefore you seem to speak against the truth of Christ's natural body, when you teach that his body is in heaven naturally, and also naturally in the sacrament. (p. 186)
Take and eat this in remembrance that Christ died for thee . . . Drink this in remembrance that Christ's blood was shed for thee . . . (1552 Words of Administration)	Do not the words of Christ's supper learn us to eat the bread and drink the wine in remembrance of his death? (p. 264)
. . . we . . . do celebrate, and make here before thy divine Majesty, with these thy holy gifts, the memorial which thy Son hath willed us to make, having in remembrance his blessed passion, mighty resurrection, and glorious ascension, rendering unto thee most hearty thanks . . . entirely desiring thy fatherly goodness mercifully to accept this our sacrifice of praise and thanksgiving. (1549 Canon)	[the Council of Ephesus] spake of no propitiatory sacrifice in the mass, but a sacrifice of laud and thanks, which Christian people give unto God at the holy communion by remembrance of the death, resurrection and ascension of his Son Jesus Christ, and by confessing and setting forth of the same. (p. 369)

If we add to the random instances above the unconscious employing of 'Lift up your hearts'[32] and the more deliberate 'that we receiving' already noted, then the picture starts to fill out. There was but one man at work. He thought, talked, taught and wrote in a consistent way over the years from 1548 to 1553. And in the midst of debate, the literary liturgical genius was never far away. Particularly notable are his crescendos:

> [Christ] paid the ransom for the sins of the whole world: who is before us, entered into heaven, and sitteth at the right hand of his Father, as a patron, mediator, and intercessor for us, and there hath prepared for all them that be lively members of his body, to reign with him for ever, in the glory of his Father; to whom with him and the Holy Ghost, be glory, honour and praise for ever and ever. Amen.[33]

> From this your obscure, perplex, uncertain, uncomfortable, devilish, and papalistic doctrine, Christ defend all his; and grant that we may come often and worthily to Christ's holy table, to comfort our feeble and weak faith by remembrance of his death, who is our only satisfaction and propitiation of our sins, and our meat, drink, and food of everlasting life. Amen.[34]

If, in the middle of fierce, acrimonious, and often metaphysical dispute, he can so easily lapse into the liturgical language of prayer, it is hardly surprising that in the midst of prayer he can so easily slide into polemics!

1548

There was no small stir about the sacrament in 1547. Unofficial, often scurrilous, tracts against the mass started to appear. But the Council, though determined on reform, was also determined on going at its own deliberate speed (no doubt partly related to the speed at which Cranmer was working on texts in his own study, perhaps with Ridley assisting). All was to remain in their control – licence would lead to Anabaptist anarchy. The Royal Injunctions issued in August 1547 required that the Epistle and Gospel be read in English, and also (and the relevance of

---

32 See above p. 75.
33 *On the Lord's Supper,* p. 354.
34 *On the Lord's Supper,* p. 367.

this will appear) that a strong box for alms should be fixed 'near the high altar'. It seems likely that the use of English was from this date seen as inevitable, and the Council winked at the translating of part or whole of the mass or the offices, though no doubt often the translators exercised considerable licence in doing so.[35] It was in 1547 also that Hermann's *Deliberatio* (the reformed Church Order of Cologne[36]) was published anonymously in English, and this presumably added both incentive and actual liturgical material to the unofficial endeavours which occurred.

On 17 December 1547 Parliament passed an Act 'Against such as unreverently speak against the Sacrament of the Altar, and of the receiving thereof under both kinds'. The major part of this hybrid Act is directed to the first aim in its title, and the latter part was tacked on to it at a late stage. Despite the title this latter part of it is perhaps more concerned with ensuring reception[37] than ensuring it occurs in both kinds. It requires the priest to exhort the people the previous day to prepare themselves, and speaks of a 'godly exhortation' to be used on the day itself. It is not absolutely clear that this was to be published by authority, but it is a fair inference in the light of events. There is no mention of English, but exhortations would have to use the vernacular, and it is likely that it was already taken for granted that English would be used in new liturgical texts. The *Order* was duly published on 8 March 1548, and was to be used from Easter onwards. It was clearly interim in character. The mass itself remained untouched and in Latin. The Royal Proclamation[38] was followed by a 'Warning Exhortation'[39] and a 'Long Exhortation' which met the stated requirements of the Act. It is clear that the consecration (and presumably therefore the elevation and adoration) at the heart of the mass were undisturbed, because the

---

35 See F. E. Brightman, *The English Rite* (Rivington's, London, 1915), vol. 1, p. lxx (where sources are mentioned for these scanty materials), and G. J. Cuming, *A History of Anglican Liturgy* (Macmillan, London, 1969), pp. 60–1; 2nd edn, 1982, pp. 39–40.

36 For the text, see Cuming, *A History*, pp. 334–57 (2nd edn, pp. 286–304).

37 '. . . it is more agreeable with the first institution of Christ . . . that the people being present should receive the same with the priest, than that the priest should receive it alone' (H. Gee and W. J. Hardy, *Documents Illustrative of English Church History* (Macmillan, London, 1896), p. 327).

38 For sources see n26 above.

39 This title and 'Long Exhortation' following it will be used hereafter as the natural titles of these particular liturgical pieces. They are both to be distinguished from the 1552 'Exhortation to the Negligent' (though in 1549 the 'Warning Exhortation' is to be addressed to the negligent!). There is some consistency of contents if the exhortations are entitled this way, though the order of them changes. Neither capitals nor quotation marks will be used hereafter.

priest was now (according to the rubric after the warning exhortation) to consecrate enough of both elements for the people to receive. The rubric then directs that the mass be unvaried until after the priest's own reception, and that he then turn to the people and deliver the long exhortation. Then followed the familiar material, all in English also, of the short exhortation, confession, absolution, comfortable words, prayer of humble access [hereafter 'humble access'], words of administration, and blessing. Continental influences can be seen in these materials, but the matter of interest to us is not so much their origin, but their later continuance, almost unchanged, through successive rounds of liturgical revision. Cranmer had put down his sheet-anchor – a devotional approach to the Lord's table, designed to provoke self-examination, reliance upon Christ for forgiveness, thankful remembrance of his death for us, and thus fruitful reception.

The final rubrics of the *Order* are significant. The first ordered the breaking of the wafers which were distributed, and assured the recipients that '*the whole body*' was received in each.[40] The second prescribed a supplementary consecration of wine if the supply ran out,[41] and this was to be done with the requisite part of the narrative of institution in the Latin mass, but '*without any levation or lifting up*'. Here is a hint of changes to come.

The mass had previously had, from the worshippers' point of view, one great 'moment' – the consecration, marked by ringing of bells, elevation, genuflection by the priest, and adoration by the people. This 'moment' remained. But a new great 'moment' was added, admittedly looking at this stage like an afterthought. If in the diagram following it is ranked lower than the consecration, that is because it is certain that few people actually received with the frequency the Act desired. To most worshippers the mass acquired a tailpiece with a definite climax, but one which left them personally unaffected (see Figure 1).

The history books are infuriatingly silent about the use of the 1548 *Order*. We do not know if the priest was expected to use it once a week, once a month, or whether it was entirely at his own discretion. We do

---

40 For a discussion of this, see pp. 75–6 above. See also p. 95 below.

41 The supply was triply like to run out: (1) despite the rubrics urging cups in place of the (minute) medieval chalices, the particular cups might be too small; (2) through inexperience the priest might have failed to consecrate enough; (3) through the sheer novelty of the practice the individual communicant might consume too much. There was no provision for supplementary consecration of the bread, not only because it was easy to provide the right number of wafers (remembering each had now to be broken) but also because the reserved sacrament was still available.

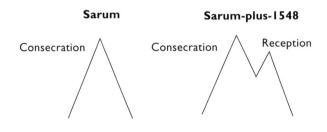

Figure 1

not know how serious an effort he was supposed to make if no parishioners signified their desire to receive. The Act said *he* was not to refuse *them*, but what was to happen if they refused him? What is certain is that the *Order* did not lead to a great rise in the number of communicants, and, as we shall see, this probably affected the drafting of the 1549 eucharistic rite, which must have been occupying Cranmer's attention (along with Jonas' Catechism!) during the late Spring and early Summer of 1548.

1549

The rubric early in the 1548 *Order* which stipulated '*without the varying of any other rite or ceremony*' added immediately '(*until other order shall be provided*)', and it is that 'other order' – the 1549 rite – which now occupies the scene. It was, of course, to be in English throughout,[42] and was thus the first ever English Book of Common Prayer, and that point is taken for granted from now on. But it was Cranmer's treatment of the

---

42 The actual impact of this is forgotten by those who only read the Latin materials in translation, and up to a point any discussion of verbal similarities between Sarum and 1549 helps to obscure this fundamental difference. Despite anything said anywhere else in this Study about 1549 sounding like the Sarum rite, in use it obviously did not. Indeed the canon had previously been silent, so that a further great difference between reading the Sarum in the dry and encountering it in an actual celebration was set up. The point is probably a great difference between Gardiner and the West Country rebels. *He* could move happily from Latin to English and back, and hence see (however perversely!) sufficient points of continuity for the rite to be 'not distant from the catholic faith' (*On the Lord's Supper*, p. 92). *They* were involved in advanced transcultural shock.

canon of the mass which gives 1549 its major place in history. There are some minor or consequential matters to be noted also.

The general pattern of the ante-communion follows the Sarum rite, though there are now no private conversations between the priest and his assistants, no multiplicity of collects,[43] and no gradual,[44] and there is provision for a sermon or homily.[45] The setting of the service is as before (the priest is *'standing humbly afore the midst of the altar'*), and the vesture is unchanged. The 'clerks' are still to sing an introit, Kyries, Gloria in Excelsis, and Creed.

It is after this that the surprises start. The priest is to read the long exhortation from 1548[46] (unless the sermon or homily has covered that ground), and the warning exhortation is printed after it. There is a significant rubric preceding this: *'And if. . . the people be negligent to come to the Communion; Then shall the Priest earnestly exhort his parishioners . . .'* There had been no hint of such 'negligence' in the 1548 *Order*, but it recurs constantly thereafter. It must have been the immediate experience after Easter in 1548 which dictated the retreat from the hope of regular communion into a series of shifts to try to keep *some* coming to communion, with ante-communion on its own for when they still obdurately refused.[47]

The *shape* of the service thereafter follows the shape of Sarum-plus-1548 almost exactly. The *terminology* too is often close to Sarum. But the appearance is deceptive, and probably deliberately so. The stepped programme for reform meant that changes in the *meaning* (and those themselves not quite explicit enough to exclude Gardiner) could appear in a familiar outward dress. It is the meaning which must attract attention.

---

43 Two collects would be used on Good Friday, and possibly on Saints' Days (this was undecided), and the collect of the day was always followed by one of two collects for the King.

44 In Sarum the gradual had been used for the first ceremonial introduction of the elements, so it is not only dropped in 1549, it is explicitly banned! *'Immediately after the Epistle ended . . .* [the Gospel follows].' *'Immediately'* spells volumes.

45 The First Book of Homilies, originally commissioned in 1542, had been published and authorized in 1547. The Second Book dates from Elizabeth's reign. They were intended for clergy who either could not preach, or needed to be prevented from preaching heresy. 1549 permits 'part' of a homily to be read.

46 The 'warning to the wicked', which in 1548 followed after the long exhortation, is now incorporated into the middle of the text. There are other very small verbal changes.

47 See the fuller discussion on p. 94 below.

The 'Offertory' follows the exhortations. But this 'offertory' is nothing to do with the sacrament, a far cry from the ornate ceremonial of preparing the elements in the Sarum use. Cranmer's offertory is a collection of money. Sentences of scripture sung by the clerks are to provoke generous giving of money. The people offer to '*the poor men's box*' and, if they are to receive communion, they are then (by a further rubric) '*to tarry still in the quire*'. It is clear that the poor men's box is still 'near the high altar' where the 1547 Injunctions located it,[48] and after two years there is now provision for money to be put in it! But the significant provision is (in the closing rubrics of the service) that if there are no communicants then the service ends '*after the Offertory*'. Cranmer's offertory belongs entirely to the ante-communion.[49]

When the intending communicants are properly segregated and settled in the quire, then the priest places the elements on the altar, the only hint of ceremonial being the mixing of the wine with water, and the sacramental part of the service starts.

The canon is the chief centre of attention. Cranmer leaves the Sursum Corda, Preface and Sanctus (which last again the clerks are to sing) as they had been before. He then groups the intercessions for the living and departed (which were separate before) in a single prayer introduced by 'Let us pray for the whole state of Christ's church'. The intercession is only loosely based on its predecessor, and is interesting for three reasons:

1 It exhibits the verbal sleight of hand of 1549 very typically. Previously the church offered 'oblations' on behalf of the living and the dead – now it still offers, but offers prayers only. This means that the whole section of intercession is now unrelated to the sacrament, for all that it occurs within the canon.[50]

2 Not only is this section verbally and substantially unrelated to the sacrament and the sacramental action, it is also an entity on its own account. It concludes 'grant this, O Father, for Jesus Christ's sake, our only mediator and advocate'. This cries out for an 'Amen'

---

48 See pp. 82–3 above.

49 For a further discussion, see my *The End of the Offertory: An Anglican Study*, Grove Liturgical Study 14 (Grove Books, Bramcote, 1978). [This is provided here in shortened form in the next chapter below – see especially pp. 130–3.]

50 Admittedly there is one sentence where prayer for 'this congregation' includes mention 'which is here assembled . . . to celebrate the commemoration of the most glorious death of thy Son'. This is almost additional proof of the main point above – it is the self-evidently temporary adhesive which just serves to keep the intercession from falling out of the canon, until it is deliberately moved!

following – no strange idea in Sarum, but apparently contrary to Cranmer's remodelling of Sarum. Ratcliff conjectures that it was from here that Cranmer removed reference to 'oblation' between September and December 1548,[51] and that it was because of the excision that the end of the intercession was left unrelated to the material which followed. This seems to me to be highly unlikely. The material following would not join well to a reference to 'our oblations' here (as inspection will show), and some other point would have to be sought as the setting for Thirlby's missing treasure. A far more cogent explanation would be that Cranmer was already preparing for 1552! If he intended later, that is, in 1552, to move the intercession into the ante-communion, what could be a better preparation for that move in 1549 than to ensure that the intercession was already free of its seating, unanchored, and ready to travel? Why not move it in 1549 itself then? Surely because in 1549 the material had to retain its 'Sarum-plus-1548' setting, on Cranmer's own principles of revision?

Why then should he want to move it away at the next revision? Could he have foreseen Gardiner's unreformed reasoning?[52] Or was he genuinely trying to be primitive – for example, finding Justin's position for the intercession?[53] Or was he already in 1548, through those few months' experience of the 1548 *Order*, realizing that if he banned non-communicating communions (as he clearly reckoned to, for very good reasons), then there would usually be no communion at all? This would entail, on the 1549 pattern, where the intercession was in the canon, that there would be no intercession when there was no communion, and the people's service which was left would be correspondingly defective. Certainly the continental services included the intercession in the ante-communion, following the sermon. So Cranmer may have had good reason, when preparing the 1549 rite in 1548, to 'tee it up' for the later move of the intercession in 1552.

---

51 *Ratcliff*, pp. 193–4. See also Gasquet and Bishop, *Edward VI*, p. 144. See also n29 on p. 79 above and n65 on p. 92.

52 Gardiner seems to say that the intercessions in the canon are recommended to the Father by the sacrifice of Christ, with which the church is joining itself in that same canon (*On the Lord's Supper*, p. 84). See also p. 111 below.

53 Cranmer well knew Justin's account, though he cites it very little (see *On the Lord's Supper*, pp. 143, 263 and (at his trial with reference to his earlier use) p. 420), and then never discusses the 'shape' of the liturgy. But what did he make of Justin's position for intercession?

3   The final point about the intercession is the retention of petitions for the departed. Naturally, there was no longer any offering of 'oblations' on behalf of the departed, but there was prayer for them. The general tenor of reformed thinking on this issue was to discard petitions for the departed as unbiblical.[54]

After the intercession came Cranmer's most typical masterpiece, the commemoration of Christ's death, serving devotional, didactic and polemical purposes simultaneously.[55] This insertion of 'salvation-history', even if concentrated wholly on the cross, was more like to primitive models than to the medieval canon – even if by accident.[56] The 'epiclesis' or 'petition for consecration', corresponding to the previous *Quam oblationem*, has strong echoes of the Latin 'ut nobis Corpus et Sanguis fiat' though with the softening to 'be unto us' and the apparently novel invocation calling for God to work by his Holy Spirit and word.[57] It immediately raises the question as to what sort of 'consecration' the canon intends to effect.

---

54 It is no part of this Study to pursue this particular point. It is certain that modern attempts to commend petitions for the departed without grounding them on purgatory would have won little sympathy from the reformers. It is far more probable that Cranmer, knowing that he is conducting a stepped programme of reform, is content to take one step at a time, without necessarily seeing that step as a good place to stop. Sadly, Gardiner fails to glory in these particular sentences, else we might have had Cranmer's own (and no doubt loaded towards 1552) interpretation of them!

55 Devotional, to stir the worshippers' hearts; didactic, to instruct their minds; polemical, to exclude any possible Roman error about the sufficiency of Calvary. This is an instance of the theologian and the liturgist intermingling – see pp. 71 and 82 above.

56 Cranmer obviously had no access to Hippolytus, where a christological preface leads directly into the narrative of institution, but such Eastern patterns as he knew linked the Sanctus to the narrative by reference to salvation-history, whether of enormous length as in the Clementine liturgy, or very brief as in the Liturgy of St Chrysostom. There was no dependence. The independence of Cranmer's drafting is proved by his inclusion of 'until his coming again'. This is derived direct from 1 Cor. 11.26, and was included not because the point was controversial, but because it was biblical.

57 This is discussed by all authors, some seeing the Eastern sources as the model, some the Western tradition of writing about the sacrament. It has appealed to those who have reverted to 1549 for their models, and is found today in several Anglican rites (particularly in America, which got it from the Scottish 1764 rite, and in Madagascar and Japan). It was a *very* long arm of coincidence which three centuries later turned up the rite of Sarapion, Bishop of Thmuis in the fourth century, and found that he had called for the 'word' to come upon the elements, rather as other Eastern texts call for the Father to send the Spirit upon them.

Without prejudice to the later problems about 1552, we may ask what evidence there is within 1549 itself for a 'consecration'. At first sight the answer is easy – the *Quam oblationem* paragraph, in the western position looking forward to the narrative of institution, is distinguished by the two black crosses at 'bless and sanctify'. In the narrative of institution itself the dominical words are marked out with indented rubrics, instructing the priest to take the bread and cup in turn into his hands. With the ceremonial stripped down almost to a bare functional minimum, nevertheless the medieval 'moment' of consecration remains. Cranmer's concept of consecration has also changed – 'Consecration is the separation of any thing from a profane and worldly use into a spiritual and godly use.'[58] And in those terms a 'moment' of consecration in the 1549 rite would be wholly in line with Cranmer's understanding of his own rite.

On the other hand, there is a move away from even that concept. The term 'consecration' with its cognates is never used. The 1548 provision for supplementary consecration is omitted, so that there is no guidance given as to procedure if the elements prove insufficient.[59] And Cranmer's own interpretation of his own *Quam oblationem* looks forward to reception rather than to the narrative.

On balance, the indented rubrics which provide for the picking up of the elements, at least to designate them for the new use, seem to justify the retention of the description. Ratcliff points out also that in the first of the two final rubrics in 1548 *'bless and consecrate'* are used with identical meanings. This would mean not only that 'bless and sanctify' in the 1549 *Quam oblationem* would have the same meaning, but also that the addition in the narrative of 'when he had blessed and given thanks' probably also confirms this view.[60] But it must be remembered that it is a 'consecration' which looks wholly to reception – the priest is to remain standing between the people and the altar, and must not lift

---

58 *On the Lord's Supper*, p. 177.

59 *Ratcliff*, pp. 205–6, says that, as the priest would know the number of communicants in advance, 'no need for additional consecration could be expected to arise'. This does less than justice to the problems, concerning which see n41 on p. 84 above. It is more likely, in my view, that Cranmer expected that supplementary consecration would continue where it was needed, but he was not going to advertise his own mind on the matter too strongly at this stage. Supplementary consecration focuses the understanding of the original consecration very closely indeed, and to have included it here would also have made the later transition to 1552 (which, again, surely he was planning?) too abrupt. See pp. 98–102 below.

60 *Ratcliff*, pp. 206–7.

up the elements for the people to see, for fear lest the people adore them (still having unreformed ideas of consecration).[61]

The form of the narrative, carefully revised after continental and scriptural models, need not detain us. But the following paragraph, the anamnesis, must. Traditionally, the anamnesis responds to Jesus' command 'Do this in remembrance of me'. 'In memoriam mei' finds its response in 'Unde et memores'. But the crucial question is '*What* do we do in remembrance of Jesus?' The Latin rite said, 'we . . . offer to thy most excellent majesty . . . the pure victim, the holy victim . . .' It is probable that this originated in the second-century assertion that the eucharist was the prophesied 'pure sacrifice' of Malachi 1.11. It did not at that point need to be more than bread and wine, or praise and thanksgiving, and it was certainly vague.[62] But the medieval doctrine of consecration meant that it was now Christ himself whom the priest, with and on behalf of the church, offered to the Father. And this, as we have seen, Cranmer did not believe. His own understanding of 'Do this' is clear – we are to eat the bread and drink the cup.[63] But his cosmetic exercise holds him back from the full volte-face this would involve – he has his eye still on 1552, and can be patient in the meantime. He therefore writes a high-sounding and involved anamnesis,[64] and at the heart of it he makes our response to Jesus' command, 'we . . . celebrate and make here . . . the memorial which thy Son hath willed us to make'. When this in turn is unpacked, it appears to mean 'Whatever form of remembrance Jesus intended by his words, that is the form we intend in our celebration.' It is a refusal to unpack further. It has gone a hundred miles from the Roman position, but it does not

---

61 The rubric follows the narrative and reads: '*These words before rehearsed are to be said, turning still to the altar, without any elevation, or shewing the Sacrament to the people.*' It is to be feared that many of the old way had already done all their elevating during the narrative before they reached Cranmer's prohibition.

62 Its original rationale was to provide an Old Testament proof text showing the superiority of Christians to Jews in God's economy. Its second-century exposition varied enormously, but never, ever included an offering of the Son (or his sacrifice) to the Father. Nevertheless the slide into the Latin 'puram hostiam' obviously opened the door to the later understanding that it was a very personal and particular *victim* who was being offered, not an impersonal and somewhat vague sacrifice.

63 '". . . do this in remembrance of me" – admonishing us . . . that whensoever we do eat the bread in his holy supper, and drink of that cup, we should remember . . .' (*On the Lord's Supper*, p. 136).

64 It is an extraordinarily long sentence, and must have called out for revision by anyone who had ever tried saying it aloud! It offends against purist standards for the anamnesis by keeping its responsive echo of 'in remembrance of me' to the second half of the sentence, instead of beginning like the Latin *Unde et memores*. Part of the text of this is on p. 81 above.

quite assert Cranmer's own position distinctly. Again, we are left asking ourselves whether he did not then have a fairly clear idea where he would go at the next revision.[65]

The last main item of the canon is the section now broadly called the 'prayer of oblation'. It is in fact a working out of Cranmer's doctrine of sacrifice,[66] suggesting that the contents of his fifth book were clear in his mind in 1548. He canvasses every form of responsive sacrifice we can possibly offer (using fairly cultic language), but all the time there are for him two absolutely separable categories of sacrifice never to be confounded with each other. Couratin tellingly illustrates this by putting together the words 'there . . . here . . . here' from Cranmer's new writing of 1549.[67] What Jesus did 'there' is wholly different from what we do 'here'. Thus the oblations offered by the church in the Sarum canon in *Supplices* with a view to obtaining 'heavenly blessing and grace' could not be repeated in 1549. Rather there is in their place simple prayer for 'grace and heavenly benediction' and it is not connected with the 'oblation' we make (of ourselves, our souls and bodies, etc.) which has *no* impetratory (let alone propitiatory) virtue whatsoever. The nearest to a medievalism which survives is the request that our prayers may be brought by the ministry of the angels to the holy tabernacle into God's presence – but this, whilst odd, also represents a careful trimming of the Sarum request for the angel to bring the offerings to the altar on high. Sarum is echoed in every line of this section of the canon, and an echo is exactly what it is – it *sounds* like the original, but does not have the same substance behind it, and in fact comes from exactly the opposite direction. It has been an extraordinary feature of twentieth-century Anglicanism to think that 1549 presented a doctrine and a practice of eucharistic sacrifice wholly at variance with the more obviously protestant tradition of 1552 and 1662.[68]

---

65 It seems to me more likely that Thirlby's lost 'oblation' (see p. 88 above) had been here than near the end of the intercession. Suppose that the first draft had read '. . . do make here the oblation which thy Son hath willed us to make . . .', or some such wording. This would be just more than Cranmer could stand, just enough to keep Thirlby's support. But after Chertsey had Cranmer reworked it? This would account for the unusual word 'memorial' perhaps, and the small bone tossed Thirlby (who declined to catch it) in the words 'before thy divine Majesty'. From his point of view it was all window-dressing – he could tell a 'nuda commemoratio' when he saw one! But this is the merest speculation.

66 See pp. 76–7 above, and especially the quotation on p. 81.

67 Couratin, *Holy Communion 1549–1662*, p. 11.

68 I have discussed this point at greater length in my chapter 'Series 3 in the Setting of the Anglican Communion' in R. C. D. Jasper (ed.), *The Eucharist Today: Studies on Series 3* (SPCK, London, 1974), pp. 10–12.

After the canon the service takes a predictable course. The Lord's Prayer survives from Sarum whilst the embolism (and fraction) disappear.[69] The peace remains, and the new and lovely 'Christ our Paschal Lamb . . .' is added after it. Then comes the whole of the devotional material from the 1548 *Order*, from the short exhortation to humble access, leading into the communion of the priest and people.[70] If we concede that the canon does include a 'moment' of consecration, yet the movement of the rite towards reception as *the* great 'moment' stands out very strongly. The diagram of the 'moments' of climax will now look as in Figure 2.

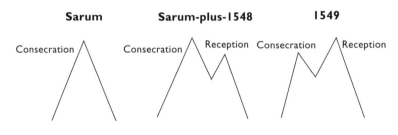

Figure 2

After communion there is some new material. Sentences of scripture about discipleship (called the 'post-communion' – and sung by the clerks) lead into a single prayer of thanksgiving. Its most notable features are its understanding that the sacrament, or rather the inward 'feeding', is to 'assure' us we are members of Christ's body, 'the blessed company of all faithful people', and its further emphasis on our response as disciples. The blessing follows – 'The peace of God . . .', the simple 1548 form, is now succeeded by a trinitarian blessing.

---

69 A fraction was of course required at the distribution (see pp. 84 above and 107 below), but there was no ceremonial fraction. It is not surprising that Cranmer (who did think the 'broken' bread helped symbolize Christ's death) would want all communicants both to receive it as broken (which the 1548 provision first introduced) and to see the fraction as associated with the reception (which is where the 'visible preaching' of the sacrament is done). Thus the ceremonial (and, from the congregation's point of view, detached) fraction now ceases as misleading and irrelevant.

70 The words of administration, though taken via 1548 from the Sarum communion of the sick, were not a problem to Cranmer. Although they referred to 'body' and 'blood', they did so wholly in the context of reception. See p. 75–6 above.

The closing rubrics are largely concerned with non-communication. There comes through them the cry (from experience with the 1548 *Order*) that the reformers are being impaled on a terrible dilemma they have inadvertently created – communion is to be held every Sunday as the great central service of the church, but there can be no communion without communicants, the people refuse to receive communion except on special occasions, and therefore there can be no communion! Cranmer has to provide somewhat humiliating retreats from both horns of the dilemma. On the one hand, he instructs households to send somebody (anybody!) to each advertised communion service, '*And by this means the minister having always some to communicate with him, may accordingly solemnize so high and holy mysteries, with all the suffrages and due order appointed for the same.*' Thus, whenever the priest reckons to hold a full communion service, he can (which on this 1549 pattern is the only way to ensure the church actually offers its prayers ('*suffrages*'?) to God). But the cost is high. The time of writing this is at most only a few months from the time when Cranmer's first question to the bishops in his enquiry was whether the sacrament could be 'received of one man for another, or to be received of every man for himself?'.[71] Now he stands but a hairsbreadth away from the position he (along with the catholic bishops also) then excluded. The device of a press-gang to provide a communion service was not only bound to be self-defeating, it was also really contrary to Cranmer's own principles which he worked out for a perfect world.[72] The experience of providing the 1548 *Order* and finding it did not lead to the increased and regular communion of the people revealed the imperfections of the real world.[73] The question then descended quickly from principles to panicky pressure.

The other provision, already noted here, is the guidance for when there are no communicants. He acknowledges in both the first and the fifth rubrics that mid-week services may have no communicants, and provides that such services shall end after the offertory. He is fearful of

---

71 *Miscellaneous Writings and Letters*, p. 150.

72 Did he really think that the provision of communion for the people as the purpose of the rite would in fact make the people regular communicants? He *could* have been starry-eyed about it (though he must have had contrary experience from the continent to daunt him). Certain it is that the 1547 Act (mentioned above pp. 83 and 85) only anticipated the clergy being reluctant to give the communion to the people. The 1548 Royal Proclamation was similar. The 1548 *Order* envisaged no problems. But suddenly in the 1549 text, all is changed . . .

73 This was precisely the problem which Calvin faced at Geneva, and it was constantly paralleled elsewhere in the reformed churches also.

private masses in 'Chapels annexed', and gives special mention to them in the second rubric. But the full scale of his provision comes through when, at the end of both first and second rubrics respectively, he embraces '*all other days*' (i.e. including Sundays) and '*all other places*' (i.e. including parish churches) and forbids there to be a communion if there are '*none disposed to communicate with the Priest*'. It is no wonder if he is already wrestling with providing a better ante-communion for 1552.

The other rubrics need not detain us here. The only ones which affect the conduct and meaning of the service provide for a wafer '*something more larger and thicker than it was, so that it may be aptly divided in divers pieces*',[74] and for the delivery of the elements into the communicants' mouths, rather than their hands.[75]

Such then was the rite which Cranmer prepared in 1548. Such was the text which he presumably tabled, and the others perforce agreed, at Chertsey in September 1548. Such was the matter under review when Cranmer declared his doctrinal hand so clearly in the Great Parliamentary Debate in December 1548. Such was the communion service in the Book of Common Prayer imposed by Edward's first Act of Uniformity on 21 January 1549. And such was the service which worshippers on Sunday 9 June 1549, Whitsunday, ought to have both expected and used. The brief use of the 1548 *Order* had itself affected the form of this 1549 rite. However much, therefore, 1552 was already taking shape before Whitsunday 1549, we would still expect the outline plan to be affected by reactions to the publishing and use of the 1549 rite after that date. It may have been – but the amazing thing is that 1552 was already there implicit in the 1549 rite.

1552

1552 was no accident, no afterthought, and no overreaction. We know it to have been assumed in principle in the 1548 Royal Proclamation. We have seen that it was probably assumed in broad outline in the drafting of the 1549 rite. The verbal resemblances between Cranmer's *Defence* (1550) and *Answer* (1551) and the actual 1552 text have

---

74 The rationale of receiving *part* of a wafer is discussed on p. 84 above.

75 Cranmer seems to have feared that, with the end of reservation (which seems to have come in 1549), those who wished to adore the elements would smuggle a piece of wafer home for those purposes. He does not record anywhere that this actually happened, it was simply a difficulty which he tried to anticipate in advance and solve by rubric.

already been mentioned. We attribute the rite to the masterhand of Cranmer, and see it as the fulfilling of his plan.[76]

This does not mean that the post-1549 influences can be ignored. Both Gardiner's reply to Cranmer (which made 1549 all too catholic) and Bucer's *Censura*[77] are met head-on in the 1552 rite. But it is clear on the reasoning above that they neither provoked the 1552 rite into existence, nor greatly affected its contents. It is more that Cranmer, in working out his grand strategy, managed to deal in passing with the particular problems they set him – viz. how Gardiner could be driven into opposition to the rite (!), and Bucer into more full-hearted approval. The ways in which he met their points are summarized in an appendix,[78] and will only otherwise appear below in a casual and piecemeal way. At most they occasioned Cranmer's actions, they very rarely caused them.

1552 itself yields up its secrets best if it is approached from the centre outwards.[79] And that is how it is here treated.

The key to almost the whole set of changes from 1549 is contained in Cranmer's new treatment of the narrative of institution and the anamnesis. We have seen how in 1549 he wrote a lengthy, but ultimately not very explicit, anamnesis to echo our response to the Lord's command, 'Do this in remembrance of me.'[80] He then wrote that what we do is to 'celebrate and make here before thy divine Majesty . . . the memorial which thy Son hath willed us to make . . .'. It is perfectly clear that he himself could only understand that clause to mean 'We eat this

---

76 It might be asked, 'Was there not another rite to come?' Couratin (*Holy Communion 1549–1662*, p. 5) makes much of the Marian Exiles' claim that 'Cranmer Bishop of Canterbury had drawn up a book of prayer a hundred times more perfect than this that we now have'. It is tempting to speculate on what the communion rite could have contained (*was* it the communion rite which they meant anyway?), but imagination boggles once the controversial ceremonies have been deleted. It is prudent to weigh the fact that the more extreme exiles had a very strong interest in there having been such a book, and the claim was by definition incapable of falsification!

77 This seems to have been published in January 1551, and Bucer died on 28 February 1551. The text is in E. C. Whitaker, *Martin Bucer and the Book of Common Prayer* (Mayhew-McCrimmon, Great Wakering, 1974).

78 See pp. 110–12 below.

79 One of the infuriating features of asking students to write a comparison of 1552 with 1549 is their tendency to list 1552 item by item in order of appearance (rather as 1549 can be compared with Sarum-plus-1548). This process normally guarantees that the significance of the 1552 revision is completely lost in a gazetteering exercise. Books too are prone to this approach.

80 See p. 91 above.

bread and we drink this cup.'[81] It is therefore intriguing to wonder whether in 1549 his pen had actually hovered over words like: 'Therefore, O Father, in remembrance of thy Son Jesus Christ, and in thankfulness for his death upon the cross for our sins, we eat this bread and drink this cup.' Whether that were so or not, it was inevitable that 1552 would give expression to this sort of response. But the suggested words above cry out for a further step forward. Why merely *say* we eat and drink, when in fact what we are supposed to *do* is actually to eat and drink? The question is unanswerable. So the eating and drinking itself got moved to follow the narrative – and that is the key to the whole reconstruction.[82] Because the communicants were near the table[83] there was an actual continuity of action between saying '. . . Do this . . . in remembrance of me' and administering the elements. So there was no 'Amen' after the narrative, and the words of administration were changed to be the 'anamnetic' response: 'Take and eat this in remembrance . . .' and 'Drink this in remembrance . . .'. There is no need to look for any doctrinal motivation whatsoever in that change – the liturgical exactness of the words needed in the new position for the administration is ample reason in itself.

In the past it has been conventional to expound this change as though it were designed to bring together the 'consecration' and the reception.[84]

---

81 *On the Lord's Supper*, pp. 136, 352 etc.

82 'His purpose was to give an exact liturgical expression to the fulfilment of the command, "Do this . . ."' (*Ratcliff*, p. 196; cf. Couratin, *Holy Communion 1549–1662*, p. 19). Dugmore comments, 'There is a little more to it than this' (*The Mass*, p. 161, n1), but this seems either a truism or else somewhat too dismissive of this key concept.

83 See the explanation about the setting of the service on pp. 106–7 below. See also G. W. O. Addleshaw and F. Etchells, *The Architectural Setting of Anglican Worship* (Faber and Faber, London, 1948), pp. 26–9.

84 E.g. 'The revisers, accepting the current western and medieval doctrine of consecration, were anxious that the Communion should follow immediately upon it . . .' (F. Procter and W. H. Frere, *A New History of the Book of Common Prayer* (Macmillan, London, 1901), p. 73). Similar understanding is found in Brightman, *The English Rite* (vol. 1, p. cliii); Cuming, *A History* (1st edn, p. 105); T. W. Drury, *How We Got Our Prayer Book* (Nisbet, London, 12th imp., 1957), p. 71; D. E. W. Harrison, *Common Prayer in the Church of England* (SPCK, London, 2nd edn, 1969), p. 53); and most other authors. J. H. Srawley, in W. K. L. Clarke and C. Harris (eds), *Liturgy and Worship* (SPCK, London, 1932), writes of the administration being inserted *into* the consecration prayer (p. 343). Cuming has altered his presentation in his second edition (p. 78). In C. Jones, G. Wainwright and E. Yarnold (eds), *The Study of Liturgy* (SPCK, London, 1978), the writer on Cranmer is R. T. Beckwith, who holds to the 'conventional' position. His views are more fully set out in his earlier work examined on pp. 98–101 below.

But this is to read 1552 through post-1662 eyes. It is far more internally consistent to read 1552 as having no consecration at all. The *only* possible action with the bread and wine is reception. The 'petition for consecration' (*Quam oblationem*) before the narrative now clearly refers only to reception.[85] There are no rubrics whatsoever which mention the bread and wine anywhere in the service at all until the actual administration.[86] There are certainly no instructions for the priest to take them into his hands during the dominical words in the narrative. They are not even 'separated unto a holy use' any more.[87] And not only is there no provision for supplementary consecration, and no use of the words 'consecrate' or 'bless and sanctify'[88] – which there is not – but also there is a new and very significant rubric at the end: '*And if any of the bread or wine remain, the curate shall have it to his own use.*' There is no concept of 'consecration' anywhere in the service at all. The only 'moment' is reception – and the only point where the bread and wine signify the body and blood is at reception. If a point of consecration has to be sought – then it is at reception. Thus by definition any bread or wine left over is mere bread or wine, and by definition the only point in including the narrative of institution at all is to instruct the recipients. If the bread and wine are insufficient, then more can and should be obtained and distributed, but no further instruction about the institution need be given to the recipients.[89] Thus, because there is no original consecration, there can be no supplementary consecration – or, to put it the other way round, the lack of supplementary consecration reinforces the case set out above against an original consecration. We shall then find that the service is designed as a didactic and devotional approach to the table, with the whole point, movement and rationale of it focused on reception. We may illustrate it as in Figure 3.

If this view of the lack of objective consecration in 1552 has been emphasized in the 1950s and 1960s by Ratcliff[90] and Couratin,[91] then

---

85 See the text on the outside front cover. [The original cover had a photo of this page in a first edition of the 1552 Book.]
86 This can be put in the most paradoxical way by saying that, as far as the rubrics are concerned, the bread and wine could still be in the vestry until the administration! This would normally not have been so in practice, of course.
87 The quotation is from the citation of Cranmer on p. 99 opposite.
88 Even the word 'blessed' in the narrative of institution (see p. 90 above) is now omitted.
89 Cf. Whitaker, *Martin Bucer*, p. 60. See also the Robert Johnson case mentioned on p. 108 below and *Ratcliff*, pp. 213–15.
90 *Ratcliff*, pp. 208–10.
91 Couratin, *Holy Communion 1549–1662*, pp. 15–16.

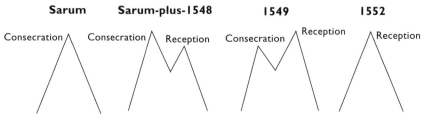

Figure 3

we should also note that it has been deliberately opposed by Beckwith and Tiller in the 1970s.[92] They draw together several lines of argument which certainly deserve refutation:

1 '. . . it was apparently because his own views were akin to transubstantiation that the late E. C. Ratcliff could not see that Cranmer believed in the consecration of the elements . . .' [i.e. Ratcliff would not recognize *as* consecration Cranmer's 'separation . . . unto a spiritual and godly use'].[93]

2 Cranmer makes several statements about consecration, and they quote at length from the major one, in which Cranmer says: '. . . Even so [viz. as with the water in baptism], when common bread and wine be taken and severed from other bread and wine to the use of holy communion, that portion of bread and wine, although it be of the same substance . . . yet it is now called consecrated, or holy bread and wine . . . And there St Dionyse called the bread holy bread . . . But specially they may be called holy and consecrated, when they be separated to that holy use by Christ's own words, which he spake for that purpose, saying of the bread, "This is my body" . . . So that commonly the authors, before those words be spoken, do take the bread and wine but as other common bread . . .'[94]

3 That the manual acts were abolished 'may have been due to a fear of encouraging the continuance of elevation, though it is usually attributed to the objections of Bucer'.[95]

---

92 R. T. Beckwith and J. Tiller, *The Service of Holy Communion and its Revision* (Marcham Manor Press, Appleford, 1972), pp. 40–4.

93 Beckwith and Tiller, *Holy Communion*, p. 41.

94 Beckwith and Tiller, *Holy Communion*, p. 41 from *On the Lord's Supper*, p. 177.

95 Beckwith and Tiller, *Holy Communion*, p. 44.

4   The absence of an 'Amen' after the narrative and before the distrib-
     ution is 'certainly fortuitous'.[96]
5   They still go half-way towards the position set out above by acknowl-
     edging 'the reception is itself in reality a vital consecrating action'.

It is my own view that these arguments do not answer the case. In the
first place, they do not reckon with the close parallel with baptism, where
Cranmer may have argued in the passage above from a 'consecration' of
the font, *but he completely abolished any such thing in his baptismal liturgy
of 1552*. In baptism, from which he so consistently argues, the only
essential action, the only *sine qua non*, is administration.[97] In the second
place they do not follow the logic of the movement on from 1549, where
consecration arguably *had* been retained in the residual sense that they
defend.[98] And in the third place the arguments stated are fairly thin:

1   Ratcliff fully acknowledges a consecration subsequent to 1662,[99]
     when the doctrine of the Church of England (and of the Revisers)
     was no nearer to transubstantiation than in 1552.
2   The passage from Cranmer is a defence of 1549, and an exposition
     of ancient authors. As a defence of 1549 it implies nothing re 1552
     – on the whole he tends to be hostile to consecration,[100] and the
     defence of it here as possible does not entail it as necessary.
3   The 'fear of encouraging the continuance of elevation' would be
     quite anachronistic, both because it had already been stopped by
     rubric in 1549, and also because the priest did not now have his
     back to the people (which therefore made elevation more or less
     unnecessary anyway).[101]

---

96 Beckwith and Tiller, *Holy Communion*, p. 44.
97 See the summary on p. 73 above. In Sarum and 1549 there was an objective
'consecration' of the font (except in emergencies), but in 1552 the wording was
skilfully changed into being a petition for fruitful reception. This exactly parallels
the change in the eucharistic 'petition for consecration' before the narrative.
98 See pp. 90–1 above.
99 *Ratcliff*, pp. 217–18. They are wrong to suggest he was blind. He *could* see what
was there in 1662. Equally he could not see what was not there in 1552.
100 When referring to the narrative Cranmer frequently uses phrases like '"This is
my body": which they [the papists] call the words of consecration' (*On the Lord's
Supper*, p. 242). 'Consecration, as you call it . . .' (p. 288). Much of his discussion
about what remains after consecration is *ad homines* and rather tells against his having
any addiction to the subject. There is no line in his writings which *bound* him to have
a consecration in 1552 – the most the passages do would be to permit it.
101 For the setting see p. 106 below.

4 It goes well beyond the evidence to say that an omission is 'certainly fortuitous' – and even if an 'Amen' had been present it would only have made the liturgical material a prayer (with a beginning and an ending), and would not of itself have made it a 'prayer of consecration'.[102] But it is still worth considering whether the omission was not deliberate.

5 If reception is necessary for complete consecration, well, the 'consecration' defended by Cranmer and quoted by Beckwith and Tiller probably proves too much. At the same time the concession may leave them a very short distance from the position taken here.

Thus the contention stands that Cranmer had no objective consecration whatsoever in 1552, and that his two-stage process via 1549 and 1552 enabled him to remove everything, whether text, rubric or ceremony, which might suggest it. If the narrative itself remained, it did so for didactic purposes to instruct the people, and for liturgical purposes to provide the cue for the anamnesis, which was now the administration.[103]

The rest of the service was bound to be radically affected. In 1549 the narrative and the administration had been separated by the end of the canon (anamnesis, prayer of oblation (including petition for fruitful reception) and doxology); Lord's Prayer; the peace; 'Christ our Paschal Lamb'; short exhortation; confession; absolution; comfortable words; and humble access. All this material (much of it drafted by Cranmer himself and not lightly to be discarded) had to be relocated if it were not to be lost. It is the relocation which gives 1552 so much of its distinctive flavour:

1 Anamnesis. By definition this paragraph had ceased when the administration took its place. On the other hand, the concept of remembrance was incorporated into the new words of administration (and it was also worked into the new petition prior to the narrative).

2 Prayer of oblation (and the doxology). This was moved to become an alternative to the post-communion thanksgiving. Apart from the actual necessity (for reasons already noted) to move this part of the canon, its new place much more fully expressed Cranmer's

---

102 To use a later title. It is of course a problem what to call the prayer (for prayer it undoubtedly is, even without an 'Amen'), but 'sacramental prayer' is the best I know.

103 See pp. 90–1 above.

doctrine of sacrifice. If 'our sacrifice' is to be 'made of them that be reconciled to Christ',[104] then it is responsive to God's grace, and logically follows reception. The prayer was further revised by the excision of all mention of angels and the tabernacle, and its wording about receiving the benefits of communion was slightly altered for its new position also.[105] The most *telling* criticism of Cranmer's treatment of this material is *not* to complain that it belongs in the canon, and should be restored there – though there have been many such critics. It is rather to note that he failed to make this prayer mandatory, and thus allowed the strong possibility that 'our sacrifice' offered 'here' would not figure in the rite as celebrated.[106]

3   The Lord's Prayer. As Cranmer was working in all his services to a pattern whereby the Lord's Prayer was used to introduce a section of prayers, this found its new place naturally. He had already used this pattern in 1549 in matins and evensong, matrimony and burial. He now adopts it in 1552 for baptism, and, quite naturally, for communion too. The Lord's Prayer begins the post-communion, leading into the two alternative post-communion prayers.

4   The peace and 'Christ our Paschal Lamb'. These two short bits could not be fitted in anywhere, and were simply dropped.[107]

5   The short exhortation, confession, absolution, comfortable words. This 1548 material was moved as a single block to precede the Sursum Corda. This had the effect of making the short exhortation follow the long one immediately, which was the original 1548 position, disturbed in 1549. The new position for the material is

---

104   *On the Lord's Supper*, p. 346. See p. 76 above.

105   It is put into very general terms, which only refer to the communion in an adjectival, and as it were historical, way ('. . . that all we which be partakers of this holy Communion may be fulfilled . . .'). It is arguable that the request in the prayer for 'remission of our sins' has become misleading by being placed after communion (for surely the service ought *somewhere* to accept that we *have* remission?), but, as the request is general about life, rather than about the sacramental feeding, it probably just escapes the criticism. On the other hand, it is now just that fraction less relevant.

106   Some of the attempts to put it back into the canon have had this point in mind, but there have also been those who wanted it made mandatory after communion, and the Irish Prayer Book of 1878/1926 allowed both post-communion prayers, to go some of the way towards meeting this desire.

107   The peace was not an action in 1549, only a versicle and response with the (now abolished) 'clerks'. 'Christ our Paschal Lamb' was new in 1549.

satisfying, and there has been little temptation, even amongst those who in other respects idealized 1549, to move this penitential material back to the position just before reception.[108] On the other hand, the prayer of humble access was not kept as part of this single block, but received separate treatment (as set out below) which gave it a role now distinguishable from that of the rest of the penitential material. It has therefore shown a tendency to move back to its 1548 and 1549 position immediately preceding reception.[109]

6 The prayer of humble access. We would have expected this to be moved with the rest of the penitential material, but it was not. Instead it was placed after the Sanctus.[110] Why? This position for it has always been treated as an oddity of Cranmer's work, disturbing the flow of the canon by insertion as much as the breaking off of the second half does by omission.[111] However, as usual, there is an inner logic to Cranmer's work.

Let us suppose that on a first draft he moved all the 1548 penitential material together to before the beginning of the canon. His difficulty then was the transition from humble access to 'The Lord be with you'. Humble access led nowhere: the canon started nowhere. But a slight glance of the eye would show that to omit the *last* item of the 1548 material (viz. humble access) and the *first* item of the old canon (viz. the salutation) would leave a fine transition. Now 'we have an advocate with the Father, Jesus Christ the righteous, and he is the propitiation for our sins' is to be followed

---

108 The Scottish Liturgy of 1764 (with its descendants down to 1929) is the only major Anglican rite to make this transposition. Korea has had something like it (Sarum-based!).

109 This happened in the American rite of 1928 (before which date the Americans still had it in Cranmer's 1552 position), and in most '1549-type' rites from then until 1960. See the rites of South Africa, Canada, India etc. in B. J. Wigan (ed.), *The Liturgy in English* (Oxford University Press, Oxford, 2nd edn, 1964). But the rites of England have not done this. [They have now in *Common Worship*.]

110 The Benedictus Qui Venit had been removed, perhaps because it suggested (from the Triumphal Entry into Jerusalem) all too physical a 'coming' of Christ. But a better explanation is that its deletion may have been inspired by the particular transition from the Sanctus to humble access, which is explored here.

111 The Scottish Liturgy of 1637 first ran on from the Sanctus to the commemoration of Christ's death, but the idea has spread and grown in this century (cf. the point at which it reached America, as noted in n109 above). Frere was one of the first major writers to refer to the 'dislocation' of the canon, and to urge the removal of humble access from its 1552 position (*Some Principles of Liturgical Reform* (John Murray, London, 1911), pp. 186–94). Out of this criticism he constructed his 'Interim Rite'.

by 'Lift up your hearts'. This not only is good in its liturgical flow – it also assisted Cranmer in his concern to emphasize the presence of Christ 'bodily' in heaven, and not here.[112] To achieve this transition Cranmer deleted the salutation.[113] Why did he not simply delete humble access also? The reason may have been Bucer's immoderate attachment to it.[114] But in any case another place for it was dawning on Cranmer. From his point of view there was no necessary *direct* link between the Sanctus and the commemoration of Christ's work. The Sarum canon was intercessory here, and was more than one prayer anyway. In 1549 he had the intercession at this point. For reasons noted above,[115] he now reckoned to move the intercession to the ante-communion. From his point of view therefore there was a yawning gap left behind. What more natural than to see if the spare bit – humble access – would fit into it? And it did. It fitted very well. For another transition was set up, almost as if by accident. The Benedictus Qui Venit was removed from the end of the Sanctus, and the whole biblical order of Isaiah 6 came to light. If we catch the vision of God and sing the angels' song, then, if Isaiah is to be believed, we immediately express our own unworthiness.[116] What could be more natural than the location of humble access at this point? Once we acknowledge that Cranmer was not engaged in trying to salvage some traditionally shaped canon (which he had only retained in 1549 as a matter of tactics), then there is no oddity in his action at all. He was pursuing a service which would primarily give the right approach to the table, and although he might *say* it was consonant with primitive rites, by this he meant that it should express his understanding of scripture, not that it would conform to known ancient rites.

Once the changes consequent upon the move of the administration are grasped, then virtually all else either follows from these changes or coheres closely with them.

The post-communion takes a slightly different shape, through the elimination of the post-communion sentences in order that the Lord's

---

112 See his writings on pp. 75 and 81 above.

113 He showed no enthusiasm for it elsewhere in the Communion service, and deleted also the 1549 uses of it before the collect and before the post-communion thanksgiving. But he kept it in Morning and Evening Prayer etc.

114 Whitaker, *Martin Bucer*, pp. 64ff.

115 See p. 88 above.

116 I am indebted to Professor G. R. Dunstan for this suggestion.

Prayer may head the section. This is then followed by the choice of one of two prayers – oblation or thanksgiving – and, surprisingly, the Gloria in Excelsis. There is a tradition that this was to conform to the biblical account that at the end of the Last Supper they sang a hymn.[117] What is undeniable is that this is the only point left in the service where *anything* may be sung. The '*clerks*' of 1549 have disappeared, and so have all their musical items and bits and pieces.[118] The possibility must therefore be kept open that in this case there was special reason why singing should be allowed – and biblical precedent is far and away the best candidate for 'special reason'. It would account for *both* the transfer of the hymn to the post-communion, *and* the retention of singing for it and it alone. It also acquired an extra clause.[119] The blessing from 1549 concludes the service.

The ante-communion is a deliberate attempt to provide a service of word and prayers for the situation where communion itself was rare. Apart from the excision of any pretext for singing,[120] the major changes are fourfold. Firstly, there is the inclusion of the Decalogue. This enabled Cranmer to work up the Kyries into penitential responses, but the purpose (or at least a very important purpose) was obviously to provide a penitential section for the many occasions when the later penitential material would never be reached. The second change is the removal of the Gloria in Excelsis, discussed above. And the third change is the bringing of the intercession into the ante-communion to follow the offertory. This enabled a mention of the alms to be inserted into the intercession, and further changes in the prayer included omission of any mention of the departed (saints or sinners alike) and the addition of 'militant here in earth' to the heading. The reference to the 'commemoration of the . . . death' of Jesus was also, for obvious reasons, omitted.[121] The fourth change was the manner of taking up the offertory. Gone is the 'poor men's box' near the 'high altar'. Indeed the whole

---

117 The tradition goes back at least to Sparrow's *Rationale* (*ad. loc.*) in 1657.

118 See the discussion in R. A. Leaver, *The Liturgy and Music*, Grove Liturgical Study 6 (Grove Books, Bramcote, 1976), p. 10, showing how singing was systematically eliminated from 1552 under the influence of Zurich.

119 J. Dowden, *The Workmanship of the Prayer Book* (Methuen, London, 1891), p. 81, discusses (and dismisses) Scudamore's suggestion that Cranmer deliberately worked in the substance of the Agnus Dei, which had been omitted from the communion time. It looks a hundred times more likely to be a scribal error.

120 To be fair, it should be noted that a rubric in Morning Prayer allows the singing of the Epistle and Gospel ('*in such places where they do sing*') – presumably by intoning?

121 See n50 on p. 87 above.

setting for this had disappeared.[122] It is possible that the processing up to the box had been the point of the Cornish rebels calling 1549 a 'Christmas game'.[123] The new service provides that the churchwardens or others will 'gather' the alms, and deposit them in the poor men's box themselves. Even if the change in setting had not made the 1549 rubrics anachronistic before 1552, the adding of the intercession to the ante-communion *after* the offertory would also have made it inappropriate to use the offertory for sorting out communicants from non-communicants as 1549 provided.

The setting of the service fully underlined the nature of the protestant service. Altars were broken down by the authority of Order in Council in 1550.[124] Trestle-tables began to be used – often at right angles to the line of the old altars. The 1552 rite prescribes that the table shall stand '*in the body of the church or in the chancel*', and presumably the decision about this was to be taken according to '*where Morning and Evening Prayer be appointed to be said*', but also according to the number of worshippers. Indeed the reference to Morning and Evening Prayer may well be symbolic – that is, indicating that there is no special 'sanctuary' reserved for holy communion, but that there is to be the same space or area used for non-sacramental and sacramental services alike. Probably large numbers would use the nave, smaller the chancel, and in principle the table could be moved from one location to the other.[125] The priest was to stand '*at the North Side of the Table*' which would be in the middle of the long side of a trestle-table turned at 90° from the old altars. The ministers were to wear the same attire as at Morning and Evening Prayer.[126] The people would be placed round the table (on stools or benches in many parishes), and the administration would thus flow immediately on from the end of the narrative of institution in conformity with the sequence Cranmer was employing. A

---

122 See the next paragraph below and p. 107 opposite.

123 This is Dix's suggestion re the 'Christmas game' (*The Shape*, p. 661), and I have never seen a better one.

124 Ridley pioneered this in London in May 1550, and the Council enforced it nationally in November. (See A. G. Dickens, *The English Reformation* (Batsford, London, 1966), p. 247).

125 In some other countries chancels were pulled down, as catering for superstition. Cranmer's concept was different – a two-room church complex. Thus he ordered in the rubrics before Morning Prayer in 1552 '*and the chancels shall remain, as they have done in times past*' (the comma in this rubric fell out in 1662 (or during the intervening century), thus apparently changing its sense).

126 This was ordered by the rubrics before Morning Prayer – the original 'Ornaments Rubric'.

closing rubric prescribes wheaten bread '*such as is usual to be eaten*'. The end of the wafer meant the end of explicit directions that the bread had to be broken into at least two pieces. It was unnatural to break wafers, inevitable that one should break ordinary bread! Thus any explanation about not losing anything by only having half a wafer is now unnecessary. The breaking would still be done during administration. The people were to kneel to receive, and, when Knox objected violently to this, the 'Declaration on Kneeling' was inserted into the rite, whilst the Book was at the printers, by Order in Council.[127]

Finally (and we can imagine Cranmer scanning over his work just before releasing it), verbal consistency was achieved. The title was altered. Wording that spoke of receiving Christ's body and blood 'in these holy mysteries' was changed whenever it occurred.[128] The mention of 'auricular confession' in the warning exhortation was eliminated (as it was also from the direction following the absolution in the Visitation of the Sick). The task was done. The 'mistakers' of 1549 were settled for good and all.[129] And All Saints' Day 1552 dawned bright and fair.

POSTSCRIPT – 1559 AND AFTER

So the story might have finished had Edward lived. This Study is on Cranmer's rite and could well finish there also. But history cries out for the postscript. How did Cranmer's rite become the 1662 on which we were all brought up – or the over-40s among us?

In 1559 three changes were made. The restoration of the 1549 words of administration queered the sequence '. . . do this in remembrance . . .', 'Take and eat this in remembrance . . .', and incidentally gave the Church of England words far too long to say to each communicant. At a guess I would suggest that Queen Elizabeth herself wanted the words added – the words 'body' and 'blood' did not occur at the administration, and she, as a

---

127 It is possible that it had been sheer oversight on Cranmer's part to enforce kneeling for reception in 1552, because it had presumably been generally used with the 1549 book, though not actually mentioned by rubric. Puritans *could* before 1552 cite the closing note in the 1549 book which allowed kneeling to be used or omitted '*as every man's devotion serveth*'. Nevertheless, Cranmer will not yield to Knox's point, and explanation is his *ne plus ultra*. He apparently did allow sitting in his *Reformatio Legum Ecclesiasticarum* in 1553 (I owe this point to Geoffrey Cuming).

128 There were three main places: in the long exhortation, in humble access, and in the post-communion thanksgiving. A comparison of the wording between 1549 and 1552 is instructive in each case.

129 'Mistakers' is a quotation from the preamble to the 1552 Act.

communicant, wanted to hear them.[130] Cranmer would have had no doctrinal objection to them, and they do not represent any doctrinal shift in the service. The 'Declaration on Kneeling' was omitted – probably because the 1559 Act revived the Book annexed to the 1552 Act – and the 'Black Rubric' was not in that! And the 'Ornaments Rubric' dealing with the vesture of ministers lost its plain text of 1552 and became a stamping-ground for controversialists.[131]

The rite suffered another reverse also. Jewel chose to defend it, against the attack of Harding, as having a consecration.[132] He meant 'consecration' in the sense that Cranmer expounded it in relation to 1549 – but 'consecration' it was. Thus when Robert Johnson, the Puritan, failed to recite the dominical words when he added supplementary bread and wine, he gave the game away. Despite the plain sense of Cranmer's rite, he was found guilty, and jailed – a matter of policy rather than rubrics![133] The possibility of this happening in a later generation was prevented when Canon XXI of the 1604 Canons required a second recitation of the words of institution.

The early Stuart period saw another reversal for Cranmer's project. The Laudians removed the communion tables back to the east wall, and placed them there 'altarwise'.[134] Rails were put round them, and though

---

130 One recalls her famous rhyme ending 'and what his word doth make it, that I believe and take it'. This sort of fancy (whilst not necessarily doctrinally different) would be unhappy with 'Take . . . *this* . . .'! She was a queen, and could get her way. And is it possible that the long words were now to be said to each communicant? Again a queen could expect this for herself, but ministers would probably not have wanted to have to say it. It should be noted that a more conventional guess is Bishop Guest.

131 There are whole libraries of books on this issue. The paradox begins with the (illegal) rubrical enforcing of 1549 vestments, when in fact in the country it was the enforcing of the surplice which preoccupied the authorities. And it continues through the Savoy Conference, and the 1662 changes, into the court cases of the nineteenth century, and even then does not stop.

132 J. Jewel, *Works* (Parker Society, Cambridge, 1845), First Portion, pp. 122–3.

133 See *Ratcliff*, pp. 213–15.

134 Perhaps it is worth noting that they (like many Elizabethans before them, who had the table parallel with the east wall, even if at the west end of the chancel or in the nave) still understood the rubric about 'North Side' to mean 'northwards from the table'. Thus there arose the 'perched at one end' (or, if an assistant were present, the 'ping-pong') position, which ruled from the seventeenth to the nineteenth century (and was prized as a true indication of evangelical purity till the 1970s). But to escape the charge of Laudianism (unfavoured by evangelicals) men ought to concentrate on how to bring people and table into relation, rather than worry about where the minister is standing round a table far-distant from the people.

this was defended as keeping dogs from fouling them, it also provided the place where the worshippers received communion. The ministers were at the table in the chancel, the people in the nave, and they now had to be summonsed 'up' to receive communion. This meant there was now no continuity between 'consecration' and reception.

This state of affairs was further canonized by the Scottish liturgy of 1637. There the position of the table was prescribed against the east wall,[135] and the (1549-type) canon was entitled 'The Prayer of Consecration'. Manual acts were ordered by indented rubrics in the narrative of institution, the canon ended with 'Amen', and it was followed by the Lord's Prayer and humble access. Provision was made for consuming any consecrated remains, and for supplementary consecration if the bread or wine ran out. Other rubrics prescribed the 'offering up' and placing on the table of the elements before the prayer for the church militant, and for covering any consecrated remains to await consumption after the service.

Although 1662 did not adopt the 1637 shape, but kept Cranmer's text (as opposed to rubrics) almost unchanged, yet the seventeenth century was finally riveted onto that text. The opening rubrics were surprisingly left unchanged,[136] but thereafter the Laudian picture emerged. After the offertory, bread and wine were to be placed on the table.[137] Before the 'Prayer of Consecration' (so dubbed) the priest has to 'order' the bread and wine. In the narrative of institution there are *five* indented rubrics (1637 had two), including a 'fraction'. The narrative is followed by 'Amen', sealing the division between consecration and reception. After the administration comes provision for supplementary consecration, and for the covering of any consecrated remains. After the service comes consumption of any consecrated remains (but the curate can take home any unconsecrated).

---

135 The opening rubrics pulled out all the stops: '*The holy Table, having at the Communion time a carpet and a fair white linen cloth upon it, with other decent furniture meet for the high mysteries there to be celebrated, shall stand at the uppermost part of the Chancel or Church, where the presbyter, standing at the north side or end . . .*'
136 Surprisingly, because the 1552 setting envisaged had long since passed, and the 1637 sort of wording (see footnote above) lay before the revisers.
137 It is perhaps worth noting that this did *not* constitute any part of the offertory, which was still only money, and did *not* itself give rise to the addition of 'and oblations' in the prayer for the church militant, which Dowden has conclusively shown to be offerings of money for the minister (*Further Studies in the Prayer Book* (Methuen, London, 1908), pp. 172–222).

What are we to say to these things? In wording (and thus in explicit doctrine), the service stands where it stood in 1552. And yet the 'feel' of it is subtly changed. The priest functions 'up there'. The consecration is a priestly event. The consecrated elements have a special character independently of reception. The rite has now moved to a 1549-type diagram – it has two 'moments' (see Figure 4).

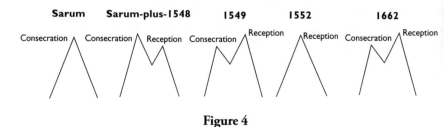

Figure 4

APPENDIX: GARDINER, BUCER AND CRANMER'S CHANGES IN 1552

The points at which Gardiner cited 1549 as teaching unreformed doctrine (and therefore commended it), and those at which Bucer cited it as teaching insufficiently reformed doctrine (and therefore wanted it changed), are here gathered together and tabulated along with a list of the ways in which Cranmer met their points in 1552 (see Table 2). It is the contention of this Study that almost all of the changes would have happened in any case (see pp. 88 and 91–2 above), and that rarely can Gardiner or Bucer be held to have caused or provoked those changes.[138] Nevertheless there is a certain thoroughness with which, even if incidentally, Cranmer in 1552 removed the basis for their respective comments. Points where Bucer liked 1549 (as, e.g., his raptures over humble access (see p. 104 above)) or where his objections were not directly against its text and rubrics (as, e.g., his complaints about low standards of preaching) are omitted here.

Page numbers for Gardiner are from Cranmer, *On the Lord's Supper* and for Bucer are from Whitaker, *Martin Bucer and the Book of Common Prayer* (the even numbers of the pages, i.e. those of the English translation, are given). The points are arranged in each case in the order in which they come in the 1549 rite.

---

138 It is anybody's guess which of the changes were directly inspired by Gardiner or Bucer. My own guess would be that the only ones where this causation appears really plausible are nos (iii) and (x) in the Bucer list. Everything else was a natural next step (on Cranmer's presuppositions) in any case.

Table 2: Comparison of 1549 and 1552 in respect of issues raised by Gardiner and Bucer

Points re 1549	Action taken in 1552
(a) GARDINER	
(i) The intercession is effective because it comes in the canon. (p. 84)	It is removed from the canon into the ante-communion.
(ii) The 'petition for consecration' is our trust in God to make the body of Christ present. (pp. 79, 83)	'. . . may be unto us . . .' is changed to 'that we, receiving . . .'.
(iii) The prayer of humble access is addressed to Christ present in the sacrament to be adored. (p. 229)	Humble access is removed to a point well before the narrative of institution.
(iv) The words of administration teach 'the body and blood of Christ to be under the form of bread and wine' (p. 51, cf. p. 55)	The words of administration are altered and omit the terms 'body' and 'blood'.
(v) The closing rubric says that Christ's whole body is present in each part of the consecrated bread. (pp. 63, 142, 325)	Any such closing rubric is omitted.
(b) BUCER	
(i) Vestments are a 'source of superstitious belief'. (p. 18)	Vestments reduced to surplice only.
(ii) Tables should not be at east end. (p. 40, referring to p. 16)	New rubric orders table to stand in body of church.
(iii) Homilies should not be cut into pieces. (p. 46)	Rubric altered to omit mention of 'portion of homily'.
(iv) There should not be provision that only sufficient bread and wine for communion should be prepared (as it gives rise to superstition that remains must be consumed after communion). (p. 40)	Rubric about preparing elements omitted, and provision made for any left over to be taken home for the curate's own use.
(v) Sanctus and Agnus Dei should not be sung whilst the minister is praying. (p. 48)	Sanctus not now to be sung by the clerks, and Agnus Dei omitted.
(vi) We should not pray for the dead. (pp. 50, 52)	Prayer for the dead excised.

Table 2: continued

Points re 1549	Action taken in 1552
(vii) Prayer that God should bless and sanctify the gifts (and the use of black crosses and manual acts) ill-advised. (pp. 54, 56, 58, 60)	Prayer changed, and crosses and manual acts omitted.
(viii) We should not ask that the angels should take our prayers to the tabernacle. (pp. 60, 62)	Angels and tabernacle omitted.
(ix) There should be no 'half-mass'; but, if there are no communicants, there should be no pretence at a mass (this is mostly against vestments for ante-communion, but is slightly obscure). (pp. 20, 22)	Vestments are abolished, and surplices worn for all services. Ante-communion is retained, and built up into more of a service in its own right.
(x) No encouragement should be given (by mention of 'chapels annexed') to rich people giving themselves superior airs. (p. 22)	Chapels annexed not mentioned in rubrics.
(xi) Wafers (and the explanation about receiving part of a wafer) possibly undesirable. (pp. 22, 24)	Wafers are abolished, and explanations made unnecessary.
(xii) Frequent communion should be restored 'by constant teaching'. Non-communication should not be recognized. Sending one of the household in place of the others should cease. (pp. 26, 28, 30)	The minimum of one communicant is increased to a 'goodly number' (or three or four in tiny parishes). Exhortation to the negligent is added. 'Vicarious' communion is not now mentioned.
(xiii) The minimum of once a year (as requirement for receiving communion) should be removed. (p. 30)	The rubric is changed to make the minimum thrice a year.
(xiv) Bread should be delivered into communicants' hands, not their mouths. (pp. 34, 36)	Rubric at the administration provides that communion shall be given 'in their hands'.

POSTSCRIPT

As this was a purely historical enquiry it has run on without becoming dated. I added to it in 1983 as relevant texts both Eucharistic Liturgies of Edward VI, *Grove Liturgical Study 34, and* Background Documents to Liturgical Revision 1547–1549, *Grove Liturgical Study 35 – both of which have also remained in print.*

I have had further opportunity to work on the development of the historic Church of England 1662 rite. In 2002 I edited The Savoy Conference Revisited *(Alcuin/GROW Joint Liturgical Study 54, Grove Books, Cambridge), and, as the present volume goes to press, I am preparing for publication in Autumn 2009* The Hampton Court Conference and the 1604 Book of Common Prayer *(Alcuin/GROW Joint Liturgical Study 68, SCM-Canterbury, London). Meanwhile the original Cranmer Study has been through four printings, and, as far as I know, has still remained relatively unchallenged in both its main thesis and its detailed argument. I have been encouraged to keep it in print from passing commendations of it by two heavyweight scholars who have written on Cranmer in recent years, Diarmaid MacCulloch in* Thomas Cranmer: A Life *(Yale University Press, 1996), and Gordon Jeanes in* Signs of God's Promise: Thomas Cranmer's Sacramental Theology and the Book of Common Prayer *(T & T Clark, London, 2008).*

Chapter 6

The end of the offertory

FOREWORD

The End of the Offertory, *Grove Liturgical Study 14 (1978), was originally drafted alongside actual issues in the revision of Series 3 Communion (but it generally supported the Commission's main thesis). On page 2 I wrote: 'I have always thought the case of Dix and the parish communion people was overstated, but it has been my actual reading of many of the sources which they cite which has shown me how much this was so'. The present essay compresses that Study to little over half its length without losing crucial features of the evidence or the argument deployed in 1978.*

THE BEGINNING

The disciples did as Jesus had directed them, and they prepared the passover . . . (Matthew 26.19)

When it was evening . . . as they were eating, Jesus took bread . . . (Matthew 26.26)

Here is where it all begins. The simplicity of this description readily solves the questions that surround the 'offertory'. If we handle the questions of church history, we are wise to keep the Matthean account in view. We start by examining the terms we need in place of that elusive 'offertory'.

The preparation of the elements

The first action is the preparation of the table before Jesus reached the Upper Room. Whether it was a passover or not, when Jesus came to 'take' the bread, his 'taking' was wholly separate from this earlier preparation of the table by his disciples. For his 'sacramental action' no further functional preliminaries needed to be observed. And in the preparation we learn nothing about how the bread and wine got to the table. That was clearly wholly irrelevant to the Gospel writers a generation later; and, if it was irrelevant to their accounts of the Last Supper, it was perhaps of little interest to them in their own contemporary Sunday eucharists.

The same is true of the Jewish blessing (or 'grace') said over the bread and cup at the passover. Such prayers acknowledge that God has provided the elements for the participants, but have no mention of their harvesting, processing, or being brought to the table. Any human role in their provision is simply not in sight.

The 'taking' of the bread and cup

The second action is Jesus' 'taking' of the bread and cup, each in turn, before giving thanks over them. This 'taking' was the lifting up from the table (by a handsbreadth) of each element, identifying it as that to which the blessing referred. Such lifting in Jewish ritual was functional, leading into the blessing, and was not an offering, nor a manipulation, nor even a separable event on its own. Its rationale is summed up in the term 'designatory'. At the Last Supper Jesus was still only designating the bread and cup to which the thanksgivings referred, and his lifting up was not only not symbolic, it was also not consecratory.[1]

Conclusion

At this stage we conclude from both the Jewish background and the actual accounts of Jesus' institution (hereafter simply the 'narrative') that neither of these two actions would naturally attract the title 'offertory'. The two are wholly separable from each other, are not easily confused with each other, and at root are both merely functional, and of little weight compared with Jesus' main actions in giving thanks and

---

1 Whether or not the Last Supper was a passover, we have no reason in what we read to attribute 'consecratory' significance to either the taking or the thanksgiving, as we are not told of special interpretation at those stages. The words 'This is my body' etc. came *at the distribution*. At that Supper, prior to the distribution what inference could the disciples have drawn from the ritual that Jesus was intending to feed them with his body and blood?

distributing.[2] There is a difference between them, however. Bringing the elements to the table is wholly separate from the 'eucharistic action' of Jesus, whereas 'taking' bread and wine is (in whatever small way) integral to that action. An unexpected witness is E. L. Mascall:

> The first of the four 'actions' of which the eucharist is composed – the 'taking' – does not occur until after the elements have been brought up.[3]

In broad terms that is the thesis of this Study.

THE SECOND AND THIRD CENTURIES

Before inspecting individual second- and third-century authors, we note some common eucharistic trends among them:

1   Any 'agape-context' seems to have gone by Justin's time in the 150s. The only food and drink then needed was for sharing in the sacramental elements. The meal began at the point where the sacramental liturgy began, and the table was laid up then, and not earlier. The preceding liturgical sequence – the 'synaxis' – was strictly prior to the meal.
2   Without a fuller meal context the participation in the bread and wine became one event, rather than two separated ones. So a single thanksgiving indicated that they had come together, and were going to be received together.
3   The early writers regularly refer to the eucharist as *in some sense* a 'sacrifice'. Probably the use of the term began unreflectively, but was institutionalized as Gentile Christians saw in the eucharist a fulfilment of the prophecy of Malachi 1.11:

> From the rising of the sun to its setting my name is great among the Gentiles, and in every place incense is offered to my name and a pure sacrifice . . .[4]

---

2   There can well be a recognizable eucharist without a clear 'taking' or 'breaking', but not without a clear thanksgiving and distribution. Even a Dix-related modern author can acknowledge this (see G. A. Michell, *Landmarks in Liturgy* (Darton, Longman & Todd, London, 1961), p. 41), and the Liturgical Commission in the 1970s was getting near to it.

3   In an article, 'The Offertory in the Eucharist', *Parish and People*, no. 21, Autumn 1957, p. 15.

4   R. P. C. Hanson, in his *Eucharistic Offering in the Pre-Nicene Fathers* (Royal Irish

The New Testament gives no hint that the eucharist is a sacrifice or that it fulfils this prophecy. Second-century Christians, however, used it specifically to promote their dispensation over that of the Jews;[5] but in the process they ingested the notion that the eucharist is a sacrifice. They each then expounded the notion differently.[6] But, as the notion passed into their eucharistic prayers, so some language of sacrifice attached to the bread and wine. They became 'oblations'.

4   An authorized officer presided at the eucharistic action.[7] While obviously true of the Last Supper, this is not evident in other New Testament references. However, a hierarchical structuring soon develops.[8]

These things noted, we turn to the individual authors.

Clement of Rome

In *1 Clement* 44 the bishops (or presbyters) are 'those who have offered the gifts of the bishop's office'. This is hardly a *preliminary* offering, but is a central act of the bishop. It may testify that the eucharist was called an offering, but it is irrelevant to any discussion of 'offertory'.

Pliny the Younger

Pliny reports to Trajan that the Christians whom he had interrogated had admitted they had met 'to take food, but ordinary harmless food'. It sounds like an agape, presumably with the eucharist within a shared meal. The participants no doubt brought their food with them.[9]

Academy, Dublin, 1976) [later repeated within his *Eucharistic Sacrifice in the Early Church*, Grove Liturgical Study 19 (Grove Books, Bramcote, 1979)] cites *Didache*, Justin, Irenaeus, Tertullian and Cyprian, but further instances could be added and the influence of the quotation upon liturgical texts should not be ignored.

5 The original Malachi context set up the Christian authors (e.g Justin, *Dial.* 41 and Irenaeus, *Adv. Haer.* IV.17) to exploit the anti-Jewish possibilities in the text.

6 In *Didache* 14 it is simply 'your sacrifice'; in Justin, *Dial.* 41, it is the meal-offering of the cleansed leper; in Irenaeus it is a sort of harvest thanksgiving.

7 This is found first in Ignatius of Antioch, and it appears usual thereafter for it to be the bishop.

8 Michell (*Landmarks*, pp. 86–9) suggests a parallel between the Apocalypse and Ignatius *Magn.* 6 where the bishop presides 'in the place of God', i.e. enthroned centrally in the apse of a basilica. A president and a table are prerequisites of any discussion of who carries what whither!

9 The Corinthians apparently brought their food but *did not share it*. So the naturalness of each bringing food in order to share it underlies both the disorder in Corinth and the hints of an agape in later authors.

Ignatius of Antioch

Ignatius mentions the eucharist at intervals (e.g. *Eph.* 5, 20; *Rom.* 7; *Phil.* 4; *Smyrn.* 6, 8). In *Letter to the Smyrnaeans* 8 he says 'agape' where we would have expected 'eucharist' (cf. the Pliny point above). But he neither identifies the point of origin of the eucharistic elements, nor any significance of them prior to their being called the body and blood of Christ.[10]

The *Didache*

Didache 9 and 10 present a puzzle. If they relate to our subject, they describe a meal-plus-eucharist – that is, an agape again.[11] The thanks-giving prayers come *at the very beginning* of the account, and the origin of the elements is again not mentioned. Indeed, the prayers both before and after the meal follow Jewish models in acknowledging that the elements are God's gift to us. The reference in chapter 14 similarly says 'gather . . . break bread . . . give thanks'. The production of the bread is not mentioned.

The Acts of John

Michell cites this apocryphal work to display a structure like Justin's: 'Offertory, Consecration, Fraction, Communion'.[12] The work's plausi-bility in relation to catholic tradition is irrelevant as it merely says 'having asked bread, he gave thanks thus . . .'.[13] This alleged 'Offertory' is of no liturgical interest; and the unique occasion of it (the purported farewell of John the evangelist before being taken into heaven) does not even imply that regular eucharists included a presidential request for bread. Nor is significance given to handing it over.

Justin Martyr

In Justin's *First Apology* chapters 65 and 67 give the first description of a real 'bringing in' or 'bringing up' of the elements to the president imme-

---

10 Ignatius nearly compares the eucharist to the incarnation (risky indeed), and it is as the flesh of Christ that he cites it. But he is no more interested in the physical origin of the elements than he would have been in *Mary's* family tree.

11 Cf. Trevor Lloyd, *Agapes and Informal Eucharists*, Grove Booklet on Ministry and Worship 19 (Grove Books, Bramcote, 1973), pp. 9–10.

12 Michell, *Landmarks*, pp. 3–4.

13 *The Ante-Nicene Fathers* (Eerdmans, Grand Rapids, 1994), vol. VIII, p. 562.

diately before he begins the thanksgiving. The description is fleeting, factual and functional. No symbolic significance whatsoever is suggested. In chapter 65 the president does 'take' (*labon*) the elements, which may mean he 'receives' them from the assistants, or may mean he has a separate 'taking'. The elements are 'presented' (*prospheretai*) by the assistants to the president, and, as in Justin's *Dialogue with Trypho* 41, this same verb means bread and wine are 'offered' to God. Dix concludes that 'Justin is quite clear that there is a real "offering" in the rite, specifically of bread and wine; and he uses this technical word for the liturgical offertory.'[14] But, if for Justin it is *not* a 'technical word' but an untechnical general word for offering, then in the *Dialogue* it is the *central* action (comparable to the cleansed leper's offering of the meal-offering) which is the offering to God of the elements, presumably articulated or implied within the great thanksgiving. Dix's school of thought could not conceive of the central action as an offering 'specifically of bread and wine' – reckoning instead that the central action is an offering of the sacrifice of Christ, so there must be a preliminary action of an 'offertory' with the elements. But if we refrain from this latterday theology, *prosphero* functions as an untechnical word, used on one occasion (at the bringing in of the elements) of the handing them over to the president, and on another of his offering them to God.

Irenaeus

Irenaeus is almost the hinge of history for modern Anglican writers on the 'offertory'. Note the following:

1   Dix: 'Irenaeus applied to the liturgical offertory the words of our Lord about the widow's mite – "That poor widow the church casts in all her life (*panta ton bion*, Luke 21.4) into the treasury of God." Thus he stated epigrammatically the essential meaning of this part of the rite. Each communicant from the bishop to the newly confirmed gave himself under the forms of bread and wine to God . . .

   'The offertory in the original view of the rite is therefore something more than a ceremonial action . . . as an inevitable preparation for communion. It is . . . a self-sacrificial act by which each Christian comes to his being as a member of Christ.'[15]

---

14 G. Dix, *The Shape of the Liturgy* (Dacre/Black, London, 1945), p. 111.
15 Dix, *The Shape*, pp. 116–18.

2   Michell: 'St Irenaeus had been prompted by his controversy with the Gnostics to insist that the bread and wine provided by the faithful at the Eucharist were a material offering of the firstfruits of creation.'[16]

3   Henry de Candole: '. . . in the struggle against gnostic ideas . . . the church perceived and asserted, certainly from the time of Irenaeus, the significance of the use in the Christian sacrament of material things, and from that followed the more developed conception of its connection with man's life and labour'.[17]

But what did Irenaeus himself actually say? We take it step by step from *Adversus Haereses* IV.18.

Sections 1–3 are only indirectly about the eucharist. He discusses oblations in general: 'The class . . . in general has not been set aside' (section 2). In this context he says Christians give all their substance (*bion*) for the Lord's purposes, as the widow did. This 'oblation' has *nothing* to do with a liturgical offertory – it is more comparable to Barnabas' action in Acts 4.36–37.

Sections 4–6 are more clearly focused on the eucharist. We are 'offering [to God] the firstfruits of his own created things. And the church alone [i.e. not the Jews] offers this pure oblation to the Creator, offering to him, with giving of thanks, things from his own creation' (section 4). Similarly, the gnostics do not acknowledge the creation, so they ought not to call the bread the Lord's body (section 4), nor continue to offer it (section 5). Irenaeus' consistent picture is that in the giving of thanks we both acknowledge God's creation of the bread and wine, and offer them to him – and he for his part turns them into the body and blood of Christ. The central eucharistic action may be called 'giving thanks' *or* 'offering' *or* 'sanctifying', but these terms then apply specifically to the *central* action. Irenaeus may be more aware of the created nature of the elements than was explicit before (he is contending with gnostics), but he is not shifting the emphasis from the central action to a 'liturgical offertory'. Only a determination that Irenaeus *must* have been implying a liturgical offertory could ever have led writers to conclude he was in fact doing so; and such writers must, from their own convictions, have first determined that Irenaeus *could not* have viewed the central action as an offering to God of the created elements only! But this is what he says – just as Justin does. The second-century writers did conceive that the eucharist was a sacrifice, but each

---

16 Michell, *Landmarks*, p. 43.
17 In an article following the Mascall article cited in n3 on p. 116 above.

had to work out for himself in what sense it was, and (with no scriptural authority behind their exploration) they inevitably came to differing answers. Offering the bread and cup to God recurs, as we shall see, in Hippolytus' text of the anamnesis; but we have to let the second-century writers speak for themselves.[18]

Tertullian

Tertullian has scattered references, which in brief confirm that to him, as with other authors of his time, the eucharist is naturally called a 'sacrifice', fulfilling Malachi 1.11.[19] On one occasion he acknowledges that the elements are part of the created order – unsurprisingly, it is against gnostics.[20] But, while he insists, with others, that the bread and wine become the body and blood of Christ, he nowhere says anything about a liturgical offertory, and all his thinking would naturally relate to the eucharistic prayer itself.

Hippolytus

Hippolytus has the first evidence from a liturgical text:

> And when he has been made bishop, all shall offer him the kiss of peace . . . Then the deacons shall present the offering to him; and he, laying his hands upon it with all the presbytery, shall give thanks, saying . . .[21]
>
> . . . then the offering shall be presented by the deacons to the bishop; and he shall give thanks . . .[22]

This stands in sequence to Justin but has further features. The elements are an 'offering' (*prosphora*), either because they are 'presented' (as in

---

18 Allowing them to be themselves does not imply asserting that they were always *right*. It is very arguable that the reliance on Mal. 1.11 as teaching that the eucharist is a sacrifice actually put them on a misleading path. Their use of 'offering' terminology was entirely innocent, but it has since become impossible to set history aside and go back to their original innocence. Furthermore other uses of the 'sacrifice' terminology exist – e.g. Hippolytus calling *water* an offering (see G. J. Cuming (ed.), *Hippolytus: A Text for Students*, Grove Liturgical Study 8 (Grove Books, Bramcote, 1976), p. 21)!
19 Hanson (*Eucharistic Offering*, p. 83, n40) cites 11 references where Tertullian calls the eucharist a 'sacrifice'.
20 It is in *Adversus Marcionem* – Dix makes much of it (*The Shape*, p. 115).
21 Cuming, *Hippolytus*, p. 10 (at the consecration of a bishop).
22 Cuming, *Hippolytus*, p. 21 (at a baptism).

Justin's *prospheretai*) or because they are offered to God in the eucharistic prayer, as the earlier evidence cited suggests. The use of *prosphora* could well derive from the central event, but be used of the elements as they are brought in. For the moment, we simply note that they are brought in, that this is clearly functional, and that none of the authors cited so far makes anything doctrinal of it.

In the first quotation (i.e. at the consecration of a bishop) there is a second action – the new bishop 'lays hands' upon the offering. There are two possible explanations:

1   It is a regular event, in line with the 'taking' in Jesus' institution, mentioned in Justin, but not well attested otherwise. If so, it would have happened in the baptismal eucharist, but without being identified in the account, and could even have been the practice since the apostles' time.[23] Thus the 'taking' had become a 'laying on of hands' as both elements were 'taken' together, and the sheer amount would not allow them to be lifted – and it reads as though the hands stayed on the elements throughout the thanksgiving.
2   Alternatively, this was an unusual event, determined by the occasion. Perhaps the new bishop established his entry into eucharistic presidency by laying semi-possessive hands upon the 'offering'? It looks less likely, but would account for an action not otherwise attested, but germane to this unique occasion.

Finally, we note Hippolytus' words in the anamnesis paragraph of the thanksgiving:

> Remembering therefore the death and resurrection, we offer you the bread and cup.[24]

This confirms what other authors attest, that in that period the heart of the eucharistic action was seen as the offering of the bread and cup to God (but *as* bread and cup, not in any way as the sacrifice of Christ). It also accounts for calling the elements an 'offering' at the earlier point – for they were indeed to be offered to God.

---

23   Dix treats it as a standard feature of 'The Pre-Nicene Eucharist' (*The Shape*, p. 105 and see also pp. 125–6).
24   Cuming, *Hippolytus*, p. 11.

The *Didascalia Apostolorum*

Hanson cites a passage in the third-century *Didascalia* (and also in the fourth-century *Apostolic Constitutions*) which testifies to a more developed doctrine of eucharistic sacrifice:

> Offer an acceptable eucharist, the likeness of the royal body of Christ . . . pure bread that is made with fire and sanctified with invocations.[25]

But this also addresses the heart of the rite (Hanson's concern), not the preliminaries.

Origen

Origen merely confirms the picture. Hanson calls this passage 'characteristic':

> But we give thanks to the Creator . . . and eat the loaves that are presented with thanksgiving and prayer over the gifts, so that . . . they become a certain holy body . . .[26]

Gifts are here 'presented' to God as the heart of the eucharistic action. But Dix is not citing Origen in connection with the offertory.

Cyprian

Cyprian is famed as the first author to say we offer Christ himself in the eucharist.[27] But Dix has one place where he mentions bringing in the elements. Cyprian 'rebukes a wealthy woman "who comest to the *dominicum* [Lord's sacrifice] without a sacrifice, who takest thy share [i.e. makes her communion] from the sacrifice offered by the poor"'.[28] So the elements were often brought by the worshippers, and in an undifferentiated way were called a 'sacrifice'.

---

25 Hanson, *Eucharistic Offering*, p. 86 (re *Didascalia* XXVI, in n67).
26 Hanson, *Eucharistic Offering*, p. 88 (re *Contra Celsum* VIII.33).
27 *Letter* 63 is the *locus classicus* for this.
28 Dix, *The Shape*, p. 115, citing *De Op. et Eleemos* 15.

Summary

What picture does the evidence give? Initially the people brought food for the agape, and, when the larger meal context had ceased, often still provided the bread and wine for communion. With a single thanksgiving and single distribution, it was appropriate to bring in the elements and hand them over to the president immediately before the thanksgiving. Quite probably the existence of catechumens and people under discipline, who would depart before the meal, confirmed delaying this 'laying up' until only the faithful were present. Then the meal started after the kiss of peace. The 'bringing in' had no greater significance than as a beginning of the meal, though the gifts were called 'offerings' and were 'presented' (or 'offered') to the president. Then, when the eucharistic action began, on one occasion (i.e. in Hippolytus) the president and presbyters laid hands on the elements. The president might 'take' the elements (perhaps by lifting them); but the great presidential action was to articulate the thanksgiving prayer (which certainly often included offering the elements to God). The bringing in of the elements was a functional activity, certainly reflecting the people's provision of them, but without any theological significance attached to it. Nor were other substantial gifts associated with the provision of the eucharistic elements.[29]

---

29 I may lack an exhaustive knowledge of patristic literature, but I suggest (1) that conventionally the communion elements were supplied by the people, with some to spare for the needy, and (2) that the general stewardship of life and goods (in view in Irenaeus *Adv. Haer.* IV.18 cited earlier) should not be automatically read as offering goods *at the eucharist*. I submit that evidence of actual bringing of goods (apart from bread and wine) is not the regular feature of the early eucharist which latterday writers have sometimes asserted.

One text occasionally cited (from the fourth century or earlier) is Canon 3 of the *Apostolic Constitutions* (see *The Ante-Nicene Fathers*, vol. VII, p. 500): 'If any bishop or presbyter . . . offer other things at the altar of God, as honey, milk, or strong beer instead of wine, any necessaries, or birds, or animals, or pulse, otherwise than is ordained, let him be deprived.' But this does not touch on lay people bringing gifts – it is surely a prohibition of clergy 'consecrating' such materials? And if it *did* refer to gifts of the laity, it would only be to forbid a deviant custom. Canon 5 follows with: 'But let all other fruits be sent to the house of the bishop . . . but not to the altar' – which informs us that lay giving could well be exercised in the early church without everything going into an 'offertory procession'. Could Theodor Klauser have had these Canons in view when he wrote, 'We should not be surprised . . . if the sources for our knowledge of the offertory procession in the early centuries mention cheese, poultry, and other gifts in kind' (*A Short History of the Western Liturgy* (OUP: Oxford, 1969), p. 109)? Cf. Cheslyn Jones, G. Wainwright and E. J. Yarnold (eds), *The Study of Liturgy* (SPCK, London, 1978), pp. 189–90.

THE LATER DEVELOPMENT OF EAST AND WEST

In the Eastern tradition, there is little evidence from before the fourth century, the most notable earlier account being in the *Didascalia*. Dix cites the following:

> As regards the deacons, let one of them stand continually near the offerings for the eucharist . . . Then, when you have made the offerings, let them serve together in the church.[30]

So then the elements were brought by the worshippers and handed to the deacons at the door on the way in – far from a preparation of the table.[31] But from the fourth century onwards the whole focus of the preparation of the elements moved from their original provision to the procession with them known as the 'Great Entrance'.[32] Dix's problem in the East is the two stages – the people giving elements to the deacons before the liturgy and the deacons bringing them up at the Great Entrance. He wants to say that the people's giving of them is the 'offertory', and the deacons' role at the Great Entrance is not – but this does not square well with his assertion that the offertory is the first action in the 'shape'. The East (using leavened bread) clearly *practised* the giving of the elements by the people, yet equally clearly had no *theory* about it! From the fourth century to the present day, eastern focus has lain not in the elements' point of origin, but in their acquired

---

30 *Didascalia* II.57.

31 Dix (*The Shape*, p. 122) is still wanting to make this 'the people's offertory'. But it can hardly be classifiable as the first action of a four-action 'shape', as that was obviously done later by the deacons; and there are no liturgical texts to give it significance.

32 Gabriel Hebert, writing years before Dix, similarly finds in the Liturgy of St Mark an impressive offertory (*Liturgy and Society* (1935; Faber and Faber, London, 1961), pp. 76–7). But the passage of text he quotes, referring to 'those who have made their offerings here this day' (F. E. Brightman, *Liturgies Eastern and Western* (Clarendon Press, Oxford, 1896), p. 129), occurs within the anaphora, and Hebert should not call it an 'offertory-prayer'. It may well imply that the worshippers brought the bread and wine, and that is not denied here. But there is no liturgical act, no symbolic significance, implied by it – and the earlier prayer at the Great Entrance (Brightman, *Liturgies*, pp. 124–5) reads more like a preliminary petition for consecration, with no more reference to the provision of the elements or to an 'offertory' than the phrase '[the elements] which the all-holy table receives'.

significance – for the ceremonial entry, far from representing the action or the devotion of the people, represents a dramatization of the carrying of Christ's body to the tomb – with the anaphora to come as the point of resurrection.[33] And so the East continues to this day.

So Dix's main sources are in the West. Acknowledging there is no early evidence, he asserts:

> It seems unlikely that the later 'Western' rite of the offertory first arose in the fourth century. It is too deeply rooted in the ideas of the pre-Nicene fathers about the people's oblations for that (cf. Irenaeus *supra*).[34]

What that sort of conjecture is worth is anybody's guess, though the Irenaeus citation gives only doubtful support. For the Western evidence is scanty. The earliest 'clear picture . . . is derived from incidental references in the works of St Augustine [i.e. by the end of the fourth century]'.[35] Augustine tells us the people brought their gifts to the deacons, who then presented them to the president. This fits Dix's – and a host of others' – theory that in some way this represented the gift of themselves.[36] But it does no more than 'fit' it – there is no indication that Augustine himself held the theory. He tells us of a psalm sung at

---

33 Compare Dix (*The Shape*, pp. 285–6) with Nicholas Cabasilas, *A Commentary on the Divine Liturgy* (ET: SPCK, London, 1960/1977), pp. 65–6. Cabasilas mentions why 'we offer the first fruits of human life' before the liturgy begins; but it seems to be from his need to say something about everything in the rite, rather than from a normal devotional understanding, and his 'first fruits' do not mean in context what we would expect. The main Eastern thrust remains the 'processional' concept deriving from Theodore of Mopsuestia's *Catechesis*.

34 Dix, *The Shape*, p. 123.

35 Michell, *Landmarks*, p. 45.

36 I must purge another patristic 'offertory mythology' from our systems. Augustine (in *Sermo* 129) said. '. . . there you are upon the table, and there you are in the cup'. Dix (with others) seizes on it:

> The offertory in the original view . . . is therefore something much more than a ceremonial action . . . it is . . . the 'rational worship' by free reasonable creatures of their Creator, a self-sacrificial act by which each Christian comes to his being as a member of Christ in the 're-calling' before God of the self-sacrificial offering of Christ on Calvary. 'There you are . . .'. (*The Shape*, p. 118)

the 'offertory', an innovation in his time.[37] But his description is solely functional.

We may add other negative Western evidence. Ambrose is the earliest commentator on the Roman canon in his *De Sacramentis*. In this and in his *De Mysteriis* he writes on consecration, comparing the eucharist to the manna given in the wilderness. In both he states that, in line with the manna, the sacrament is a gift of God from heaven.[38] This does not preclude the provision of the elements by the people – and it was presumably still happening, though Ambrose does not mention it – but it seems to rule out much significance attaching to that provision.

The psalm attested by Augustine was augmented in the West by a series of 'offertory' prayers. These just possibly derive from Innocent I's letter to Decentius, Bishop of Eugubium, in 416, where he mentions 'the prayer which commends the oblations to God', but even Dix admits this may be the canon.[39] Srawley suggests they are 'secreta' prayers,[40] but Innocent appears to be writing about the canon.

The canon, traceable back to the time of Ambrose, regularly calls the elements 'oblations' and they are offered to God *in the canon*.[41] The

---

Yet on inspection Augustine was saying *nothing* about 'offertory' at all. Neophytes have just been initiated into a unity with older members of the body (and the 'you' are the newcomers, as over against the older members). 'You' have, after arduous preparation, 'at last come to the cup of the Lord: and there you are on the table, and there you are in the cup. You are with us. For we take this [bread] together, we drink together; because we live together.' There is *nothing* here about the origin of the bread and cup or their symbolizing the self-offering of the worshippers: the emphasis is all upon their destination – 'Nam et nos corpus ipsius facti sumus et . . . quod accipimus, nos sumus.' Augustine obviously enjoys the punning oscillation between two meanings of 'body' (cf. 1 Cor. 10.16–17), and squeezes fruitful exhortation from it. *Sermo* 227 actually cites 1 Cor. 10.16–17 and airs the pun: 'Si bene accepitis, vos estis quod accepitis . . . et efficimini panis, quod est corpus Christi.' But in both cases the pun moves in the area of fraction (cf. our own use of 1 Cor. 10) and communion – there is not a hint of 'offertory' theology. And Dix must have known this. (The latest to follow his 'there you are on the table' as implying 'offertory' is Wainwright, Jones and Yarnold (eds), *The Study of Liturgy*, p. 190.)

37 *Retractationes* II.7.

38 R. C. D. Jasper and G. J. Cuming (eds), *The Prayers of the Eucharist* (Collins, London, 1975), p. 98; cf. *De Mysteriis* VIII in *The Nicene and Post-Nicene Fathers*, Series Two, vol. X, pp. 323–4.

39 Dix, *Shape*, p. 118, n3, asserts it is an offertory prayer, but on p. 500 concedes it may be part of the canon.

40 J. H. Srawley, *The Early History of the Liturgy* (Cambridge, 2nd edn, 1947), p. 173.

41 This is demonstrable in *Te Igitur, Memento, Hanc Igitur, Quam Oblationem, Unde et Memores, Supra Quae* and *Supplices*.

term 'oblations' may derive from an original presenting of them by the people to the president (as in Justin and perhaps Hippolytus), though the offering of them to God in the canon presumably institutionalized the term 'oblations'.[42]

Ordo Romanus Primus portrays Western development around AD 700.[43] 'If ever there was a real offertory procession of the laity it occurred during the following centuries [viz. after the fourth and fifth] at the papal stational liturgy in the city of Rome. *Ordo Romanus Primus* describes the action in detail.'[44] Now the pope and his assistants descend from the altar to the people and collect the 'offerings' from them. The pope says 'Let us pray', but then the choir sings a chant. When the elements are ready, he 'looks at the choir and nods them to be silent'. A 'procession'? Yes, but no significance.

This pattern was no sooner developed than it began to wither, for two main reasons:

1   There was a falling away of the people from communion (traceable to the seventh century in the West), which meant people would not be bringing bread and wine for themselves, and the priest would provide for *his* reception.
2   The wafer replaced leavened bread in the West from the eighth century onwards. So the provision of 'home-made' bread by the worshippers ended, and the specialized wafer was produced by ecclesiastical professionals, and started its churchly life within the sanctuary.

So *Ordo Romanus Primus* does indeed represent a highwater mark – of a shortlived highwater – in the offertory procession of the laity. The emphasis moves to the priestly prayers over the offerings, and, as they are systematized over the next four centuries, the medieval pattern is completed. The 'offertorium' of psalm verses is sung first, and then the celebrant uses 'offertory prayers' while preparing the elements. The first and famous one, 'Suscipe, sancte Pater . . . hanc immaculatam hostiam . . .', derives from an earlier text for the *laity* to use when making their

---

42 Within the canon they are called 'dona', 'munera', 'sacrificia', 'oblatio', 'hostia' with little difference in significance as between them at any one time (though in origin 'hostiam puram' must go back to the use of Mal. 1.11 in the second century, though it later changed its meaning to become Christ himself).

43 The text is in Jasper and Cuming (eds), *Prayers*, pp. 111–15.

44 T. Phelan, 'Offertory' in J. G. Davies (ed.), *A Dictionary of Liturgy and Worship* (SCM Press, London, 1972), p. 283. Note the 'If ever'.

offering, but the actual form and use of these 'orationes super oblata' is for the priest to pray that our sacrifice (here or about to come) may be acceptable to God – very like prayers in the canon itself.

From the ninth century onwards another factor asserted itself. An ever-increasing stress was laid upon the efficacy of 'This is my body' and 'This is my blood' in the narrative.[45] It reached its doctrinal climax with the definition of trans-substantiation in 1215 at the Fourth Lateran Council. But liturgy was changing in line with the doctrine, and, as the climax in receiving communion disappeared, a new climax of adoration asserted itself in the narrative. This had further consequences:

1   The fixing of a 'moment' of consecration meant that no earlier prayers about God receiving the sacrifice could be deemed effective until the consecration had occurred. In Peter Lombard's famous phrase: 'For when these words are uttered, then takes place the change . . . the rest is said to the praise of God.' In other words, the rest is window-dressing.[46]
2   Although the doctrine was that the *word* effected the change, yet manipulation of the elements became dominant. From around the twelfth century the priest with his back to the people would be lifting (or 'taking') the elements at 'accepit', and then elevating them above his head after 'Hoc est enim corpus meum'. He genuflected and the people bowed or genuflected in adoration. The same followed for the cup. The 'taking' here was preliminary to the consecration, and separable from the elevation for adoration. There seems little precedent for it earlier.

Thus the medieval mass had words dating from Ambrose or earlier, but with a wholly different structure imposed on it. Consecration, adoration and mass-sacrifice were the constitutive features of the mass, and the person of the priest was the sole necessity for the correct ritual performance. The 'offertory' too was his, in the build-up towards the canon. The people, whether to 'offer' or to 'receive', were actually strictly redundant.

---

45 There is patristic precedent, even just arguably from Justin and Irenaeus, but specifically from Ambrose in *De Mysteriis* and others after him – but the emphasis changes greatly later in the first millennium.
46 This is well set out in John Wilkinson, *The Supper and the Eucharist* (Macmillan, London, 1965), p. 84, quoting Lombard, *Sententiae* 4.8.1.

THE REFORMATION AND THE ANGLICAN PRAYER BOOKS

The continental Reformation

The Reformers all over Europe opposed any notion of substantial sacrifice made by us to God in the eucharist. However innocent the origins of the terminology of oblation, the wording of the canon could hardly have been more provocative to them. Luther's famous phrase that 'from the offertory onwards it stank of oblation' meant that from the offertory onwards it had to be changed. He himself both reduced the canon to little more than Sursum Corda and the narrative, and eliminated the offertory (*offertorium* and *secreta* included) altogether. Consecration and distribution were all – there were no instructions about laying the table at all. Nor was Calvin far behind – the point of origin of the elements was of no interest or significance, and the rubrics assumed they were on the table before the abbreviated eucharistic 'action' began.[47]

What the reformers did want to be 'offered' was money. This was to be a liturgical act, in a way it had probably never been before. A formative instance of this occurs in Hermann's *Deliberatio*:

> Therefore, while the Creed is in singing, let the faithful offer their free oblations . . . And that this work of religion may be conveniently done and rightly commended to the faithful, we will that there be some notable place appointed in every temple, not far from the altar, which every man may comely go to, and where the faithful may offer their oblations openly before the whole congregation.[48]

England 1547–1549

In England the changes came in a slightly more measured way, with a visible continental influence behind them.[49] The first step, not obviously connected to the liturgical offertory, came in the Royal *Injunctions* of August 1547:

---

47 See, e.g., the descriptions in G. J. Cuming, *A History of Anglican Liturgy* (Macmillan, London, 1969), pp. 33–5 (2nd edn, 1982, pp. 15–17).

48 Cuming, *A History*, p. 353.

49 Continental liturgical change began about a quarter of a century before reform in England started, thus providing good liturgical precedent for virtually everything that might be considered in England after 1547.

Also they [the clergy] shall provide and have . . . a strong chest, with a hole in the upper part thereof . . . which chest you shall set and fasten near unto the high altar, to the intent the parishioners should put into it their oblations and alms for their poor neighbours.[50]

This replicates Hermann, save that there is no mention yet of its use during service time. That was still to come.

The Order of the Communion in 1548 had little to bear upon the offertory (save that the priest had now to provide wine as well as bread for the congregation[51]). But the 1549 Prayer Book ushered in a vast change. The 'offertory' continued with the old title and in the old place, but with no other continuity. The opening rubric read:

Then shall follow for the Offertory,[52] one or mo, of these Sentences of holy scripture, to be song whiles the people doo offer, or els one of them to bee said by the minister, immediately afore the offering.

Thus far it might still have been the 'people's offering' of eighth-century Rome. But the 20 sentences which follow are in each case about giving *money*. The rubrics read:

Where there be Clerkes, thei shall syng one, or many of the sentences aboue written, according to the length and shortnesse of the tyme, that the people be offering.

In the meane time, whyle the Clerkes do syng the Offertory, so many as are disposed, shall offer unto the poore mennes boxe every one accordynge to his habilitie and charitable mynde. And at the offeryng daies appoynted, every manne and woman shall paie to the Curate, the due and accustomed offerynges.

Then so manye as shal be partakers of the Holy Communion, shall tary still in the quire, or in some convenient place nigh the quire,[53] the

---

50 *Miscellaneous Writings and Letters of Thomas Cranmer* (Parker Society, Cambridge, 1846), p. 503.

51 1548 worked on the assumption that the people had previously wanted communion, but had been denied it by an unwilling clergy. By 1549 the reality had broken through – the people themselves were unwilling (see Chapter 5, n72).

52 'Offertory' is used here in the technical sense of the medieval *offertorium* – the psalm chant – with the 'sentences' replacing the psalm verses. But the term was also used for the whole event, i.e. the putting of money into the box.

53 Presumably, if the 'quire' were full, others would have to gather outside the screen.

> *men on one side, and the women on the other syde. All other (that*
> *mynde not to receiue the said holy Communion) shall departe out of*
> *the quire, except the ministers and Clerkes.*

As in Hermann, the people leave their places in the nave to put their 'offerings' in the 'poor men's box' which is 'near unto the high altar'. They are then in the right place to receive communion, and remain there for that purpose. However, non-communicants depart – and, as in 1548, this is the regular practice![54] So a closing rubric after the service provides:

> *And thoughe there be none to communicate with the Prieste, yet . . .*
> *the Priest shall . . . say al thinges at the altar (appoynted to be sayed at*
> *the celebracyon of the lordes supper), untill after the offertory. And*
> *then shall be added one or two of the Collectes . . . And . . . shall let*
> *them depart with the accustomed blessing.*

So the 1549 offertory belonged to the ante-communion, operated equally even when there was no communion (for almsgiving was ordered anyway), and was wholly separate from preparing the table when there was a communion. This last point was reinforced by the fourth of the rubrics within the rite:

> *Then shall the minister take so much Bread and Wine, as shall suffice*
> *for the persons appoynted*[55] *to receive the holy Communion . . . And*
> *setting both bread and wyne upon the Alter: then the Priest shall saye.*

The preparation of the elements is (as in the medieval use) the priest's responsibility, but done with a minimum of fuss and no *secreta*. It could have been done before the rite began, save that it is only now that he knows how many will be communicating.[56]

The eucharistic prayer follows, structured like the traditional canon, but retaining only two 'manual acts' during the narrative – '*Here the priest must take the bread into his handes*' and '*Here the priest shall take the Cuppe into his handes*' – and the narrative is followed by '*These words . . .*

---

54 See n51 on p. 131 above.
55 The rubrics require heads of households to 'appoint' someone to communicate, to ensure enough were present, but the provision here will include any who had signified their names in advance and were remaining in the chancel.
56 Numbers remaining in the chancel should match those who had signified their names overnight.

are to be saied, turning still to the Altar, without any eleuacion, or shewing the Sacrament to the people.' So there continues a clear 'taking' in the narrative, but no elevation and no adoration. Whether the 'taking' alongside the words of institution should be viewed as consecratory remains debatable.[57]

England 1552

The 1549 rite lasted its brief hour and was gone;[58] 1552 altered the rite's structure and the place of the offertory in it. The prayer for the church was removed from the canon and came, as a separate prayer on its own, to follow the offertory. So the offertory was separated from the beginning of the sacramental section. After the sermon the rubrics said the curate was to exhort the people to remember the poor, using one or more of the sentences, broadly as in 1549. The next rubric said:

> *Then shal the Churche wardens, or some other by them appointed, gather the deuocion of the people, and put the same into the pore mens box: and upon the offering daies appointed, every man and woman shall paye to the curate.*

The people were gathered near the table (itself movable) and did not move to give their money.

After this came the prayer for the church, and in that position it now included a new petition that God would 'accepte our almose'. An indented rubric directed '*Yf there be none amosen geuen vnto the poore, then shal the wordes of accepting our almes be lefte out vnsayde.*' The title 'offertory' did not occur in the main text, but recurred (as in 1549) at the end in '*Collectes to be saide after the Offertorie, when there is no Communion*' – a rubric which clinches the argument that in Cranmer 'offertory' has nothing to do with the sacramental action or elements. Moreover, when 1552 comes to the sacramental action, there is no mention of preparing bread and wine at all. As there are no indented rubrics for a 'taking' in the narrative either, it would be rubrically consistent for the elements to be in the vestry till the distribution – distribution is the sole authorized eucharistic 'action'.

---

57 It is doubtful whether 'consecration' is to be predicated of the 1549 rite (see Chapter 5, p. 90 above).

58 Its offertory method probably helped its demise. Was not the offertory the 'Christmas game' which the west country rebels attacked? (Cf, Dix, *The Shape*, p. 661, and p. 106 above.)

England and Scotland 1559–1662

The Elizabethan era saw a returned emphasis on 'consecration' (by means of the narrative), and may well have led to a visible 'taking' within the narrative – not only a 'high' church practice, but also a Puritan one.[59]

The 1637 Scottish liturgy is intriguing at both points which concern us. Its ante-communion has the same structure as 1552, and after the sentences about giving money the next rubrics include:

> [*during the sentences, the deacon or a churchwarden receives the devotions of the people*] . . . *and when all have offerd, he shall reverently bring the said bason with the oblations therein, and deliver it to the Presbyter, who shall humbly present it before the Lord, and set it upon the holy Table. And the Presbyter shall then offer up and place the bread and wine prepared for that Sacrament upon the Lord's Table, that it may be ready . . .*

The prayer for the church follows, with a bracketed '(to accept our alms, and) to receive these our prayers' and a rubric to omit the bracketed words when there are no alms. So 1637 retains the 1552 offertory, solely of money, and mentions only money in the prayer for the church. On the other hand, it now prescribes a point (within the ante-communion[60]) for placing the elements on the table – and further, surprisingly, says the presbyter is to 'offer up' these elements. But further on, in the 1549-shape '*prayer of consecration*', the presbyter is to stand '*where he may with the more ease and decency use both his hands*'; and, within the narrative, rubrics order manual acts, a 'taking' which is integral to the eucharistic action, and wholly separate from preparing the table.

---

59 This is found in the Genevan Service Book of 1556 and in the 1618 draft Scottish liturgy, in which the text of the narrative has accompanying rubrics about the minister 'taking' the bread and cup into his hands (see G. W. Sprott, *Scottish Liturgies of the Reign of James VI* (Edmonton and Douglas, Edinburgh, 1871), pp. 66 and 71) – this at a time when the Book of Common Prayer had no such taking. The later evidence of the Savoy Conference confirms the picture. The 1637 Scottish Liturgy had something near an inevitability if two schools of thought were combined in their *desideratum*.

60 Why in the ante-communion? Well, preparing the elements had followed the offertory in (differently structured) 1549, and 1549 had some impact on the Scottish liturgy (and in this case upon 1662 also). But it could surely have been that collecting the money provided the numbers (indeed the reporting by the wardens of the numbers) for communion, thus facilitating the preparation of the elements?

The Puritans desired a proper 'taking', and this *may* have influenced 1637. It is explicit in the *Westminster Directory*,[61] in the Puritan 'Exceptions' at the Savoy Conference,[62] and in Baxter's *The Reformed Liturgy*.[63] When it came to the Savoy Conference and 1662 they were being met by stiff churchmen who for their own reasons would meet the Puritan concerns – though not of course in the Puritan way. 1662 saw the following relevant changes from the 1552/1559 service:

1   The money is now offered: '. . . *[deacons etc.] . . . shall receive the Alms for the poor, and other devotions of the people, in a decent bason . . . and reverently bring it to the Priest, who shall humbly present and place it upon the Holy Table.*'

2   The bread and wine are now placed: '*And when there is a Communion, the Priest shall then place upon the Table so much Bread and Wine as he shall think sufficient. After which done, the Priest shall say* [Prayer for the Church militant].'

3   The petition in the prayer '[to accept our alms]' is now '[to accept our alms and oblations]' and the rubric beside it says, '*If there be no alms and oblations, then shall the words* [of accepting our alms and oblations] *be left out unsaid.*'

4   The bread and wine are 'ordered' after the prayer of humble access: '*When the Priest, standing before the Table, hath so ordered the Bread and Wine, that he may with the more decency break the Bread before the people and take the Cup into his hands, he shall say . . .*'

5   The bread and wine are 'taken' during the narrative. The rubrics beside the narrative read. '*Here the Priest is to take the Paten into his hands*', etc.[64]

---

61   The *Directory* provides for a long prayer of consecration and follows it like this: *The elements being now sanctified by the Word and Prayer, the Minister, being at the Table, is to take the Bread in his hand, and say, in these expressions (or other the like . . .):*
       According to the holy institution, command, and example of our Blessed Saviour Jesus Christ, I take this Bread, and, having given thanks, break it, and give it unto you.

62   Edward Cardwell, *Conferences* (Oxford, 1840), p. 321. 'We conceive that the manner of the consecrating of the elements is not here explicit and distinct enough . . .'

63   This included an optional bringing of the elements to the minister, then a setting of them on the table, then a prayer, the narrative of institution, and a direction to the minister to take the bread and break it. See E. C. Ratcliff, 'Puritan Alternatives to the Prayer Book' in *The English Prayer Book 1549–1662* (SPCK/Alcuin, London, 1963), pp. 77–8, or as reprinted in A. H. Couratin and D. H. Tripp (eds), *E. C. Ratcliff: Liturgical Studies* (SPCK, London, 1976), p. 236.

64   The 'laying' of the hand on the elements (with the words 'This is my body' etc. cueing these third and fifth manual acts) appears actually to effect the consecration.

6   Other changes introducing an objective consecration do not relate to the present theme.

So what are we to make of this? Some simple conclusions arise:

1   The 1662 offertory is about money only, and is wholly separate from preparation of the elements.[65]
2   In reinforcement of (1), 'alms and oblations' refers solely to money.[66]
3   Money is 'offered' or 'presented' to God; bread and wine are 'placed' and 'ordered' on the table.
4   In reinforcement of (3), bread and wine are never called our gifts to God, and interest is shown in neither their point of origin, nor their route to the table.[67]
5   The bread and wine are 'taken' during the narrative, and the eucharistic action begins then.

Thus the Puritans' desires were met by the stiff churchmen's mood and language – a real '*via media*'.

During the next two centuries, it looks as though the elements were on the table when the service began. After the offertory, the right quantity was put onto the paten and into the chalice. At the 'ordering' these were moved to the north side of the table. During the narrative they were 'taken' and consecrated. Credence tables had been favoured by Lancelot Andrewes in the early seventeenth century, but are then little in evidence until promoted by the Camden Society and *The Ecclesiologist* in the 1840s. The rubric certainly required the priest to get the elements from *somewhere* before 'placing' them on the table; and the high-church credence tables made it clear that, although a server might help, yet in essence the priest provided the elements without recourse to the congregation. This matched Roman Catholic usage closely.

The fifth rubric actually says '. . . *in which there is any wine to be consecrated*'. Thus the 'taking' must have been preliminary.

65 Note the rubric before the final collects, '*Collects to be said after the Offertory, when there is no Communion.*' When the money is in, the offertory is *over*.

66 The case is made irrefutably and exhaustively in J. Dowden, *Further Studies in the Prayer Book* (Methuen, London, 1908), pp. 176–223. There have of course been notable commentators who understood 'oblations' as the bread and wine – as, e.g., Charles Wheatly in 1710 citing Cyprian calling the elements 'oblations', or Michell citing the Archbishops' reply to Leo XIII in 1897. But Dowden's careful work addresses the full text in a way these ventures fail to do.

67 The elements are characterized solely as 'these thy creatures of bread and wine'.

Further Anglican revisions to 1950

The Scottish rites from 1764 to 1929 present a progressive muddling of the distinctions made above. The elements are 'offered up'; the 'oblations' in 'alms and oblations' are referred to the elements; words from 1 Chronicles 29 (which is clearly about *substantial* giving to God), which had first been used in the 1764 rite after the collecting of money, were in 1912 switched to follow the offering up of the elements.[68] In America 1 Chronicles 29 came in in 1789 at the end of the (monetary) offertory sentences, and the distinctions of 1662 remained, until in 1928 the Scottish pattern was largely followed, though 1 Chronicles 29 was not moved. The general pattern round the Anglican revisions (though not in Ireland nor in the English 1928 'Deposited Book') was that elements were being 'offered' up, and 'offertory' was extending its scope to include this ceremonial preparation of the elements.[69]

So, if we stop the clock around 1945, when *The Shape* was published, the following general conclusions are to be drawn:

1   In 1662 'offertory' means the giving of money, and belongs in the ante-communion.
2   This sense of 'offertory' has historically carried over into collections of money at non-sacramental services, and in the Free Churches.
3   Anglican circles have nevertheless had the thought drifting around that the elements at the point of provision are 'oblations' offered to God by the priest, for no very obvious purpose (save as under (4) below).
4   There has been some credence given to the Roman Catholic notion that this 'offering' is an anticipation of the eucharistic sacrifice yet to be offered.

---

68 The full passage is 1 Chron. 29.11–14, but in different rites thereafter not all four verses are invariably employed, and so different forms appear. The phrase '1 Chron. 29' is used in this Study without further distinction.

69 A curious variant came in the 1924/1929 South African rite:

> *And the Priest shall place upon the Table so much Bread and Wine as he shall think sufficient, saying:*
> Bless, O Lord, we beseech thee, these thy gifts and sanctify them unto this holy use, that by them we may be fed unto everlasting life of soul and body; through Jesus Christ our Lord. Amen.

This seems to have originated in the English Coronation service. The South Africans must have been somewhat confident that God would not answer this prayer before they reached the 'Prayer of Consecration'.

5   Both from the 'thought drifting around' and from the example of
     Rome, 'offertory' was growingly used to mean 'preparation of the
     elements'. An obvious illustration is the allocation of hymns for the
     offertory in *The English Hymnal*![70]

6   Until the time of Dix no one much thought of the offertory of
     bread and wine as being the *people's* provision. Even the conflation
     of the offering of money and of the elements still distinguished
     between them in point of origin – the money came from the
     people, the elements were simply brought into use by the priest
     without mention of their origins.

7   If there was popular teaching around that the elements *represented*
     the people and their self-offering to God, it is poorly attested, and
     never became fixed or constant. It is hard to prove a negative, but
     the hymnbooks and commentaries on the liturgy suggest the
     negative strongly.

AFTER DIX

Dix is a turning-point in 'offertory' history. In the 'shape' he propounded – a 'fourfold' one – the first action, which he equates with
Jesus' 'taking' of bread and wine, is the bringing in of the elements, the
offertory. In so doing he pegged down the 'drifting around' concepts
and gave them a formal status. From now on 'offertory', promoted as
part of the instituted eucharistic action, purported to be as crucial a part
as the further three parts of the fourfold shape. Cinderella was being
retrieved from the liturgical cinders and sent to the ball.

What then did Dix actually say? Two quotations will suffice:

> . . . the offertory of the liturgical tradition . . . is itself a ritual act
> with a significance of its own. It is an integral and original part of
> the whole eucharistic action, not a preliminary to it, like the kiss
> of peace. This is not to say that its significance has always been
> sharply distinguished from that of what followed upon it . . .
> Nevertheless, from before the end of the first century the offertory
> was understood to have a meaning of its own, without which the

---

70 I trace in my successive volumes of Anglican eucharistic liturgy the collapse of
the 1662-type 'offertory sentences' summoning the people to give money. Instead
1 Chron. 29 appears after the 'offertory' is done (however inappropriate it is for
placing bread and wine on the Table) – and a new breed of seasonal sentences, i.e.
without money reference, appears in several rites.

primitive significance of the whole eucharist would not be incomplete but actually destroyed.[71]

The offertory is not, of course, the eucharistic oblation itself, any more than the last supper was itself the sacrifice of Christ . . . The offering of themselves by the members of Christ could not be acceptable to God unless taken up into the offering of himself by Christ in consecration and communion. Nevertheless, though this distinction can readily be made in theory, it is one which is easier to see than to express by the actual prayers of the liturgy. The primitive rites had nothing corresponding to an offertory prayer at the moment of the offertory, but the meaning . . . was nevertheless formally expressed in word in '*the*' prayer, the eucharistic prayer itself.[72]

So – this section of liturgy is 'integral and original' and without its particular meaning the significance of the eucharist would be 'actually destroyed'. But this significance is one which, while it is easy to 'see', is not actually expressed in words in the rite! We have to look through Dix's eyes to see it – and it is in fact a will o' the wisp. If, alternatively, there is an offertory significance which is derived from verbal expressions in '*the*' prayer, then we are still unable to distinguish that separate identifiable significance of the offertory within that prayer.[73] Until Dix tells us, we cannot know it is there.

This must be fatal to Dix's theories. But his role in history is not that of a high-profile teacher of error who needs to be cut down to size (on this point at least); it is more that of a beacon which has led a whole fleet astray, and thus we have both to adjust the beacon and also to recover the fleet. There have been two convergent courses followed by different squadrons of ships, both guided by Dix's seductive light.

The Parish Communion people

The Parish Communion started before the Second World War, and even had offertory processions before the war.[74] However, after 1945

---

71 Dix, *The Shape*, p. 110.
72 Dix, *The Shape*, pp. 118–19.
73 This is in curious contrast with later developments where sacrificial language at the offertory is said really to apply to the significance of the eucharistic prayer itself.
74 See W. S. Baker's chapter on St John's, Newcastle upon Tyne, and Dix's own chapter 'The idea of "the church" in the primitive liturgies' in A. G. Hebert (ed.),

Dix and *The Shape* gave doctrinal undergirding to the practice, and expanded its use as the Parish Communion itself spread during the 1950s. The practitioners *knew* that, even using the 1662 text, they were following a 'fourfold action', and that the first action was the 'offertory', and this was the 'people's liturgy'. Thus the procession developed – lay persons 'bringing up' the elements along with the alms, and presenting them to the officiant in front of the table. Some extracts from the 1950s illustrate this:

> Parish Communion exponents . . . lay most of the emphasis on the Offertory, with its connection with work, home, etc. at the expense of the mystery . . .[75]

> Into that loaf of bread goes the whole working life of the world – all the complicated processes of production, distribution and exchange. And in the bottle of wine we have the symbol of all life's joy and leisure . . . As the offertory goes up, we say in effect 'there you are, God – my brains, my brawn, my friendships and contacts . . .'[76]

> Moreover . . . the Offertory is the layman's liturgy *par excellence* . . . by the giving of these symbols of our life . . . we express our intention to offer ourselves.[77]

As offertory theology was being elaborated, a good friend of the Parish Communion called, 'Hold, enough.' Michael Ramsey said this:

> Here [in the doctrine of sacrifice] there is too often a most alarming one-sidedness. The new movement places much emphasis upon the offertory, as the offering to Almighty God of

---

The Parish Communion (SPCK, London, 1937). Dix actually there describes the eucharist as having 'four *momenta* only – Offertory, Thanksgiving Prayer (Canon, Anaphora), Fraction, Communion – and nothing else'; and he interprets offertory as corresponding to the gospel account that Jesus 'took bread'.

75 *Parish and People*, vol. 1, no. 2 (September 1950), p. 14. This was the journal of the pressure group Parish & People, and other extracts followed in the original Liturgical Study.

76 J. A. T. Robinson, *Liturgy Coming to Life* (Mowbray, London, 2nd edn, 1963), p. 62 – an address from the 1950s.

77 J. G. Davies, *Parish and People*, no. 22 (Spring 1958), p. 6. See from the same time G. Cope, J. G. Davies and D. A. Tytler, *An Experimental Liturgy* (Lutterworth, London, 1958).

the bread and wine . . . Appropriate ceremonial brings out this moment in the rite: layfolk carry the elements in procession from the back of the church . . . And the point is a true and Christian one, for though its place in the New Testament is a little obscure it finds vivid expression in St Irenaeus . . .

By itself, however, this sort of teaching about sacrifice can be a shallow and romantic sort of Pelagianism . . . For we cannot, and we dare not, offer aught of our own apart from the one sacrifice of the Lamb of God.[78]

This is a 'catholic' protest – evangelicals were not closely engaged with the Parish Communion,[79] and for them 'its place in the New Testament is a little obscure' would have finished the question. As it was the phrase 'shallow and romantic sort of Pelagianism' (with the weight of its author) probably did more to restrain the inherent excesses of the movement than any amount of other discussion.

Ramsey was not alone. Mascall added serious weight.[80] Then Henry de Candole, J. G. Davies and George Every pitched in from various standpoints from which it became generally acknowledged – and Mascall's advocacy must have some credit for this – that the 'offertory' and the 'taking' were in some way distinguishable. At the very least, if the 'taking' was part of the 'offertory' it was not the same thing as the procession (the people's part). Dix was being queried, possibly a corner was being turned.

However, despite a move away in some minds, Dix had sown a romantic theology which ran on by acquired momentum. Three instances will illustrate this:

1   The 1958 Lambeth sub-committee on liturgical revision wrote of 'The Offertory, with which the people should be definitely associated, to be more closely connected with the Prayer of Consecration.'[81] Clearly they thought, unlike Cranmer, that the 'offertory' belonged to the eucharistic action.

---

78 A. M. Ramsey, 'The Parish Communion' in his *Durham Essays and Addresses* (SPCK, London, 1956), p. 18.
79 See P. J. Jagger, *A History of the Parish and People Movement* (Faith Press, Leighton Buzzard, 1978), which records how those in the movement kept insisting they were uniting catholics and evangelicals, when in fact the latter shunned them! The reasons would be easy to spell out.
80 In the article 'The Offertory in the Eucharist' in *Parish and People* cited on p. 116 above.
81 *The Lambeth Conference 1958* (SPCK and Seabury, London, 1958), 2.81.

2   In 1971 the semi-official booklet *The Presentation of the Eucharist*,
     purporting to accompany Series 3 Communion, had a chapter
     entitled 'The Offertory'. This reproduced 1950s theology entire:
     '. . . the other action is symbolical . . . The symbolic action is the
     offering of our lives and the fruits of our labour to God.'[82]
3   With Series 2 and Series 3 Communion there developed a rash of
     communion picture books, and they tended, at the 'offertory', to
     have pictorial representations of Dix's thesis. One which caught the
     eye had a great procession of all ages and colours, starting out in the
     fields, or near factories, and bringing everything imaginable before
     God – including bread and wine amid the vegetables and marrows.

Dix had set in train this romanticism. It goes back to his insistence that
the 'offertory' is the first of the instituted acts, and is in some way the
people's offering of themselves.

The modern liturgical texts around the Anglican Communion

The treatment in the Church of England follows in the next chapter.
Elsewhere in the world, the Church of South India was the first church
on earth to provide a eucharistic liturgy prepared with *The Shape of the
Liturgy* open before the compilers (some being ex-Anglicans). They had
a section, immediately before the Great Thanksgiving, called 'The
Offertory' which included placing the bread and wine on the table and
receiving money and using a prayer drawing upon 1 Chronicles 29 to
include both elements and money. The texts from Canada, Japan, West
Indies and India, Pakistan, Burma and Ceylon which were finalized in
1959 and 1960 retained a 1662 position for the 'offertory'. But
revisions which began after the 1958 Lambeth Conference largely had
the 'offertory' where South India had it, and Lambeth had recommended.[83]
     Two exceptions to this should be noted. Australian revisions retain

---

82 *The Presentation of the Eucharist* (SPCK, London, 1971), p. 14. It came from a
joint working party of the Liturgical Commission and the Council for the Care of
Churches — but the Commission at large never saw it, and it here ran counter to the
Commission's mind.
83 These rites are reproduced in the first of my collections of Anglican eucharistic
liturgies, *Modern Anglican Liturgies 1958–1968* (Oxford University Press, Oxford,
1968), and they tend to use the term 'offertory', to conflate the provision of
elements and of money, and to use the 1 Chron. 29 motif to say what we are to say
to God about it. The New Zealand rites of 1966 and 1970 have a kind of epiclesis a
little like the South African one (see n69 above). But see the exceptions in the main
text above.

'offertory' solely to mean money offerings, though the 1978 rite includes an adaptation of the Roman 'offertory' prayers at the presenting of the 'gifts of the people':

> Blessed are you, Lord God our Father;
> through your goodness we have these gifts to share . . .[84]

There is then a separate heading 'The Thanksgiving' and a rubric '*The priest takes the bread and wine for the communion, places them upon the Lord's Table, and says . . .*'

In Scotland (1970) and South Africa (Liturgy 1975) the offertory prayers from the 1970 Roman Catholic mass were adopted unamended. In Scotland they came as an optional alternative under the rubric '*At the offering of the Bread and Wine these prayers may be said*'. In South Africa an initial one of three had the innovation 'Through your goodness we have this money to offer'; and the second and third were introduced by the rubrics '*Taking the bread*' and '*Taking the wine*'.

LITURGICAL REVISION IN THE CHURCH OF ENGLAND

Dix exerted his influence in England also. The first report from the Liturgical Commission was *Prayer Book Revision in the Church of England* (SPCK, London, 1957), prepared for the 1958 Lambeth Conference. This referred in passing to Dix (p. 22) and in a factual way to 'offertory processions' which involve increased 'lay participation in the presentation of the elements' (p. 24). But 'fourfold' is not mentioned. However, after Lambeth 1958 Arthur Couratin commented on its report, 'surely they might have had the courage to say that Offertory,

---

84   The Roman Catholic texts, to which we return below, seem to have taken Dix aboard. They are:

> Blessed are you, Lord, God of all creation.
> Through your goodness we have this bread to offer,
> which earth has given and human hands have made.
> It will become for us the bread of life.
> **Blessed be God for ever.**

> Blessed are you, Lord, God of all creation.
> Through your goodness we have this wine to offer,
> fruit of the vine and work of human hands
> it will become our spiritual drink.
> **Blessed be God for ever.**

Consecration, Fraction, Communion . . . might follow one another in a clearly defined sequence'.[85] So here was a fourfold (Dixian) shape, with 'Offertory' clearly the first action of the four. But Couratin was more restrained when he wrote with Henry de Candole the Commission's later report, *Reshaping the Liturgy* (Church Information Office, London, 1964), as they merely opened questions about where 'the offertory' occurs in the 1662 rite (though, as we have seen, this was actually decided in 1662). To them 'offertory' is the preparation of bread and wine.[86]

In the next 16 years old eucharistic texts – viz. those of both 1662 and the 'Interim Rite', which became in due course Series 1 Communion (1966) and then Series 1 & 2 Revised (1976) – were retouched. In 1966 there was a last-minute inclusion of an option to locate the preparation of the bread and wine just before the eucharistic action started, with the use of 1 Chronicles 29. In 1976 this option became mandatory, and the title 'offertory' was inserted by the House of Bishops at the last minute.

The Commission's own rites (Series 2 authorized in 1967, and Series 3 authorized in 1973) never used the term 'offertory', but Series 2 presented a misleading first part of a fourfold pattern with 'The Prepa-ration of the Bread and Wine'.[87] The money could also be presented then, and initially 1 Chronicles 29 was provided, but this was removed after the Liturgical Conference in February 1966. However, in Series 3 the Commission started to distinguish between placing the elements on the table, and 'taking' them. In the initial text the heading became 'The Taking of the Bread and Wine', and the rubrics under it ran as follows:

23 *A hymn may be sung, and the offerings of the people may be collected and presented.*
24 *The bread and wine are brought to the holy table.*
25 *The President takes the bread and wine.*

---

85 Arthur Couratin, *Lambeth and Liturgy* (Church Union, London, 1959), p. 9.
86 See Arthur Couratin and Henry de Candole, *Reshaping the Liturgy* (Church Information Office, London, 1964), p. 26.
87 Arthur Couratin explained: 'They say we ought to have used the proper words: the offertory, the consecration, the fraction, the communion . . . but we really did not think we need worry them with ecclesiastical words.' *The Liturgical Conference 1966* (Church Information Office, London, 1966), p. 72. He thus advertised the 'Preparation' as the 'offertory', clearly on this basis the first of the instituted acts.

Alms were thus distinguished from elements, and preparing the table from 'taking' the bread and wine. Rubrics about manual acts during the narrative were omitted, thus allocating the 'taking' clearly to Section 25 (as above). They wrote:

> To suggest a 'taking' half-way through the Thanksgiving is to frustrate the fourfold sequence which we follow . . . We have therefore provided a heading and a rubric for a 'taking' before the Thanksgiving begins; and we have distinguished this from the preparing of the table.[88]

So far, so good. However, Synod attached 1 Chronicles 29 as an option to Section 24, suggesting that the elements are an offering to God (though speakers referred to both stewardship (Section 23?), and 'the first action of the fourfold sacramental action' (Section 25?)). This muddled both the Synod and the authorized text.

Revision of Series 3 began in 1977 and the Commission's report (GS 364) was published in May 1978, just before this Study went to press. The Commission emphasized the distinctions between collecting money, preparing the table, and 'taking' the bread and wine as the first action of the dominical sequence. The word 'offertory' returned, following the House of Bishops' insertion of it into Series 1 & 2 Revised. The arrrangement looked like this:

THE OFFERTORY
26 *The bread and wine are brought to the holy table. A hymn may be sung. The offerings of the people may be collected and presented. These or other appropriate words may be used.* [1 Chronicles 29]

The taking of the bread and cup and THE THANKSGIVING
27 *When the offertory has been completed, the president takes the bread and cup into his hands . . .*

The Commission's Introduction said: 'The Taking is a solemn action in its own right after the bread and wine are already on the Table.'[89] Thus, although 'offertory' had returned, it was distinguished totally from the

---

88 Liturgical Commission, *A Commentary on Holy Communion Series 3* (SPCK, London, 1971), p. 21.
89 *Alternative Services Holy Communion Series 3 Revised*, GS 364 (SPCK, London, 1978), p. 7.

'taking'; and 1 Chronicles 29 was attached particularly to the money. In this form the text went to General Synod.[90]

SOME THEOLOGICAL POINTERS

The ramble through history should now lead to some guidelines for the future. I offer:

1   The preparation of the elements is not an 'instituted act'. It does not matter *when* the elements are put on the table – nor *how* the elements are put on the table. They simply need to be there – provided *by* God *for* us.

2   The word 'offertory' is inappropriate in relation to the elements.[91] It might be relevant to giving money, but should be restricted to that. Its use in GS 364 could best be eliminated.

3   Collecting alms has no relationship to preparing elements. The two functions have been juxtaposed in Anglican history, and the vogue for processions has often brought the two functions close together. But their roles are completely different.

4   1 Chronicles 29 ought to be confined to money. Its original context demands that it is only used when gifts of *enormous substantial value* are being provided for God's purposes. Bread and wine for communion are of little substantial value; and there is, of course, no biblical ground for thinking that a *symbolic* offering of them to God is appropriate.

5   Giving thanks for the bread and wine before the thanksgiving is misleading. Thus the new Roman offertory prayers overtly bless God for the provision of the elements. But is this not anticipating *the* thanksgiving – and, if consecration is by thanksgiving, have we not already taken that action if we say such prayers?[92]

---

90 This retains the cut-off point of the original Study, as the revision of Series 3 (to become Rite A) began in Synod. For the later history of the issue see the 'Postscript' on p. 147 opposite.

91 This is not just an 'evangelical' point: 'the question presses, what *can* we offer at the Eucharist? Not mere bread and wine – even the term "offertory" sounds an odd note.' C. O. Buchanan, E. L. Mascall, J. I. Packer and the Bishop of Willesden, *Growing into Union* (SPCK, London, 1970), p. 59.

92 Roman Catholics of course have generally believed that consecration came via the formula 'This is my body', and expressions of thanksgiving at the preparation of the elements would not be consecratory. Anglicans have been moving to seeing consecration as effected by thanksgiving.

6   We do not need redundant processions to enable active lay participation in the liturgy. If leading the eucharistic prayer is reserved for
the ordained president, *yet virtually nothing else is*. The whole event,
and each part of it – the word, the prayers, the music, the greeting
of peace, the distribution of the elements – are all the 'layman's
liturgy'. This has precedent and not only in 1 Corinthians 14, but
also in Justin's 'we all rise together and make prayers' (1 *Apol.* 67).
Fancy getting specialized elements from the vestry, taking them to
the back, and then having two or more silent laypersons carry them
forward, for a period of 45 seconds while a hymn is sung, and
calling *that* the 'layman's liturgy'! How could we ever have been so
blind?

POSTSCRIPT

*The story stopped in Chapter 6 when GS 364 was published in May 1978.
Before final authorization of 'Rite A' in November 1979, much was changed
(and I was myself deeply involved). 'Offertory' disappeared, 1 Chronicles 29
was properly allocated to money, and the distinguishing of 'preparation' from
'taking' the elements as a dominical act was reinforced. Conflict moved to the
Roman Catholic 'offertory prayers'. However, when the Common Worship
texts originated in the 1990s, there was no corporate memory about earlier
issues in Series 3 and Rite A, and the Commission muddled the order. It also
fell for Michael Vasey's persuasion that 'we have this bread to set before you'
could harmlessly replace '. . . this bread to offer', and be safely printed and recommended. I was now not on the Commission, but on the House of Bishops,
and have recorded the developments in* Taking the Long View *(Church
House Publishing, London, 2006), pages 81–4. The treatment above of
patristic evidence about 'offertory' drew from Simon Jones, in his 2005 Introduction to a new edition of* The Shape, *the comment '. . . it is probably true
to say that Dix is as guilty of Buchanan's charge [i.e. in the original study] of
"finding an 'offertory' in every rite" (p. 14) as Buchanan is of finding an
equally ubiquitous absence of one' (note 57, p. xx). Disclaiming any 'guilt', I
put it to Simon Jones that Dix was finding what was not there, while I was
not finding what was not there. His reply neither challenged this nor tried to
justify the imputation of scholarly 'guilt'.*

*Indeed I would now go further in relation to the patristic evidence than I
did in 1978. I have learned from Paul Bradshaw to be wary of 'lumping'. I
try to show above that the patristic evidence, even when 'lumped', hardly
amounts to a row of beans. But, as a convinced 'splitter', I now say that,
even if some scraps of 'offertory' evidence were to exist here or there among
the patristic writers, they would still be but disconnected scraps and could by
no legitimate means be arbitrarily 'lumped'.*

Chapter 7

Priesthood and sacrifice and the ordained ministry

FOREWORD

Being invited to give this 'patriarchal' lecture to the Society for Liturgical Study (23 August 2006), I delivered myself of a theological peroration which brought together convictions held for my whole ordained life, supported by illustrations and argumentation which had accumulated over the years. I have tightened up the lecture, but its lecture character remains.

INTRODUCTION

I greatly value the opportunity to give this lecture.[1] If there is any value in the superannuated, it is more likely to lie in their witness to history than in their insights into the future. So I have endeavoured to bring together two items which have been significant in my own theological life, and have recurred in my consciousness strongly in the last 15 months, while I have been writing my synodical memoirs in *Taking the Long View: Three and Half Decades of General Synod*. There is a chronological tidiness about the invoking of these two items, which I set out in brief before probing more deeply within them.

The first item is the occasion 40 years ago when I was forced into dissent by the Archbishops' Liturgical Commission.[2] The draft Series 2 eucharistic prayer included an anamnesis in which, in alleged obedience

---

[1 I referred to being a founder member of the Society for Liturgical Study in Summer 1978, when it originated from the sustained prompting of Geoffrey Cuming. I had addressed that first conference, and another later. I recalled Charles Whitaker summoned from retirement around 1984 to give a 'patriarchal' paper, the precedent for my paper. Patriarchally I was free to expatiate on whatever subject I wished, untrammelled by a conference theme.]

[2 See Chapter 1 above.]

to our Lord's command, we were to 'offer this bread and this cup' to God. The departure from 1662 was breathtaking; the rationale given to throw dust in our eyes was that we would thus 'get behind the Reformation';[3] and the unanimity with which the Commission, including even the supposed near-evangelicals, had bought the notion was appalling. I do not know why Donald Coggan entrusted eucharistic drafting to Arthur Couratin; but the upshot was bound to be disruptive, and so it was.

The second item just splits the 40 years. Twenty years ago the Faith and Order Advisory Group produced a report requested by the Synod, entitled *The Priesthood of the Ordained Ministry*. The title is precise and identifies a problem exactly; the report is prejudiced and compounds the problem distressingly. Synod virtually rejected the report, so it should have gone to the great filing cabinet in the sky, but in fact it defied its own inbuilt self-destruct mechanisms, and has been quoted as authoritative in later official documents. So its prejudiced contents, and its perverse survival from near-slaughter in Synod, should be exposed before they do further damage.

My desire to pick up these priesthood-and-eucharist doctrines has been reinforced by working on Justin Martyr on baptism and eucharist, work which has itself prolonged the itch that I experienced when writing *Taking the Long View* last year. You will have detected my Anglican provenance, and I speak from that provenance with few apologies to other Christian traditions.

Then I offer a caveat. Not all language necessarily embodies what its own linguistic form suggests. A 'black cab' is a type of London taxi, and may actually be any colour under the sun – it is still a 'black cab'. And when, as an Oxford undergraduate, I ordered a mixed grill for 2/11d at the Stowaway Cafe, the order the waitress shouted down the hatch to the kitchen below was, by an unsophisticated synecdoche, 'one egg' – its Stowaway code title. My digsmate accordingly revelled in ordering 'a mixed grill with no egg', simply to hear the waitress's paradoxical shout of 'one egg, no egg'. This introduces the paradoxes in my lecture title.

I begin with the English Reformation. Cranmer inherited three related terms, each of which, from a possibly innocent origin, had later acquired a substantially erroneous meaning: first, the mass was a sacrifice; second, it was offered on an altar; and third, it was offered by a priest.

Each term is connected with both Jewish and pagan systems – priests existed to offer sacrifices on altars (cf. Hebrews 5.1). That is what the terminology meant. Such sacrifices were usually propitiatory or at least

---

[3 On this principle, see my *Justin Martyr on Baptism and Eucharist*, Alcuin/ GROW Joint Liturgical Study 64 (SCM-Canterbury Press, London, 2007), pp. 52–3.]

impetratory, though there were also sacrifices of thanksgiving for benefits rendered. The medieval religious system centred in the mass – a propitiatory (and votive) sacrifice, offered at the altar by a priest who represented the people (with his back to them).

For Christians none of this has scriptural warrant. The scriptural references to the eucharist, however strong they are about what we receive, nowhere suggest that either the elements or some action with the elements are in any way a sacrifice (and later attempts to read such meanings into *poieo* or *anamnesis* or 'make the memorial' are counsels of despair); the scriptural references nowhere suggest that the meal is conducted on or from a physical altar; and not only nowhere suggest that any Christian ministers have a special priesthood, unique to their ordination, but do not even link such Christian ministers with eucharistic presidency. Well, with these kinds of evidence under his nose, and preferring the authority of scripture over the received traditions of the Church, Cranmer put through a two-and-a-half-fold reform of the triple error.

Is the eucharist a sacrifice?

First, the eucharist ceased to be a sacrifice. It commemorated the sacrifice of Christ, 'there' upon the cross, once in history. It occasioned the offering of the responsive sacrifices we make, 'here' of ourselves, our souls and bodies, as a living sacrifice in line with Romans 12.1–2, and the sacrifice of praise and thanksgiving, in accordance with Hebrews 13.15. This distinction remains fairly clearly in all Church of England revised rites, though in the Scottish Episcopal Church a curious assimilation of two distinct entities is found in their anamnesis:

Made one with him, we offer you these gifts
and with them ourselves,
a single, holy, living sacrifice.

I am conscious of this text, as it was slipped into the liturgy for the proposed English ecumenical covenant in 1981, and was provided again by Alastair Haggart in the official worship book for the Lambeth Conference in 1988. I do not see how the 'gifts' can be called a 'living sacrifice', and although we are responsively to offer ourselves to God in Christ and through Christ, it is going far beyond the evidence to say that we do so in some union with this speculative offering of the eucharistic elements to God in the eucharistic prayer.

Is the table an altar?

Second, at the Reformation the table ceased to be an altar. Edward's reign clearly distinguished between an altar and a table, and the one was removed in 1550 and the other introduced. The table was entrenched in the rubrics, and the terminological distinction remains so to this day (though today we lack defined physical distinguishing of the table from a medieval altar). I recommend persevering with the sometimes slightly pedantic-sounding term 'table'.

Is the presbyter a priest?

Third, at the Reformation the presbyter ceased to be a priest with a cultic sacrifice to offer. Not only was the eucharistic rite radically changed to expunge any notion that the Lord's Supper is itself a kind of sacrifice, but the ordinal was even more radically changed. There, not only was the previous delivery of the paten and chalice with the injunction to receive power to offer sacrifice for the living and the dead removed, with the delivery of a Bible replacing them; but the new exhortation, setting out at great length the pastoral role of the minister, and the need to be well versed in the scriptures and to fulfil a teaching role, *did not in all its length even mention* the eucharist. This, hardly changed, became the 1662 rite by which I was ordained, the only rite of the Church of England until less than thirty years ago, the rite still cited in Canon A5 as our doctrine and in the Declaration of Assent as part of our historic witness to the Christian faith.

So, I submit, there was a half-reform here – a reform of substance, unmatched by a reform of terminology. For whatever reason, the Reformers translated *presbuteros* as 'elder' in the Bible, but left 'priest' (which in the Bible translated *hiereus*) untouched in the Prayer Book rubrics. We know what they meant, and I cheerfully quote Hooker to elucidate that:

> Wherefore to pass by the name, let them use what dialect they will, whether we call it a Priesthood, a Presbytership, or a Ministry it skilleth not: Although in truth the word *Presbyter* doth seem more fit, and in propriety of speech more agreeable than *Priest* with the drift of the whole Gospel of Jesus Christ. (*The Laws of Ecclesiastical Polity*, V.lxxviii.3)

Thus began the era of 'one egg, no egg' terminology, where 'priest' was used, as by synecdoche, but erroneously, as the term 'priest' indicated a function which the presbyters no longer had – offering sacrifice. Thus *sotto voce* the formularies would have had us saying 'a priest, no priest' – until, that is, a new school of ecclesiastical thought insisted that there *was* a distinct priesthood of the ordained ministry. This priesthood had unique powers to bless and absolve as well as confect (a choice verb) the sacrament of the altar, and offer the eucharistic sacrifice. The Reformers' terminological shortcoming had apparently left the door open for reviving medievalisms. It is of passing curiosity that Leo XIII's *Apostolicae curae* suspended the validity of orders for 'priests' on whether the ordinal 'intended' to ordain priests to offer that sacrifice of the mass; and it then decreed that Cranmer's ordinal had failed to confer true orders, supremely because eucharistic sacrifice had been excised from the communion rite, though also because all reference to the power to offer sacrifice had gone from the ordinal. The Archbishops' reply in *Saepius officio* (1897) astonishingly accepted the Pope's criterion and unhelpfully insisted that our eucharistic rite *does* meet it – when they should have rejected that definition, which was foreign to the 1550 and 1552 ordinals, let alone to the 1552 eucharist.

EUCHARISTIC SACRIFICE

For the moment, *Saepius officio* was leading us into a 'sacrifice, no sacrifice' era. While Cranmer had cleanly distinguished between the sacrifice of the cross ('there') and the responsive sacrifices we offer ('here'), wholly in line with the New Testament, an Anglican school of thought had arisen in the nineteenth century which wanted in some way to offer Christ, or at least to offer to God symbols of Christ's sacrifice which in some sense partook of the reality of that sacrifice 'here'. There had of course been precedents, not least in the nonjurors, but also in the established Church, but there had not before the nineteenth century been a sustained mainstream of teaching, nor one which owed so much to Rome. I went back to W. H. Frere's famous *Some Principles of Liturgical Reform* published in 1911. This is generally named as the place where the 'Interim Rite' originated – the rearrangement of the Canon to run as a single prayer from Sursum Corda through the 1662 Prayer of Consecration to the Prayer of Oblation, relocated there from its post-communion position. It had begun there in 1549, and some seventeenth-century persons had wanted it there (and Frere quotes Cosin's famous reference to Overall). However, Frere's fathering of the 'Interim Rite' should not be misunderstood – it is not the main subject of his book; it occupies a little over two pages; and he commends it chiefly as being the most modest of reforms, with a brusque critique of

1662, and a brief rationale of the gains his proposal will bring. The crucial phrase, however, is this:

> for he [the celebrant] inevitably occupies a prominent place during the recital of the Institution and performance of the manual acts; while the relation of the whole Church and the present congregation to this Sacrifice of Praise and Thanksgiving does not find expression till the Prayer of Oblation.[4]

Note how Frere gives 'Sacrifice of Praise and Thanksgiving' capital letters. Part of the not-always-discerned programme of such catholics was to make 'sacrifice of praise' mean a 'praiseworthy (or meritorious) sacrifice' rather than 'praise offered as sacrifice'. Frere had written in 'Procter and Frere' about 1549:

> it is carefully explained that this is the 'memorial' which Christ ordered, and the phrase, 'the sacrifice of praise', the biblical term for the Eucharistic sacrifice, is transferred here from the first *Memento* . . .[5]

This is breathtakingly perversive of scripture. Frere's predecessor, Procter, had said nothing about it.[6] Certainly the old Latin Canon so located *sacrificium laudis* as to present it as a substantial impetratory or intercessory offering, but Cranmer knew what he was doing – and, of course, he moved it to after communion in 1552, where, as simply an optional alternative, it might even not be used at all. Frere's 'interim rite' makes our request that God would accept 'our sacrifice of praise and thanksgiving' follow immediately upon the narrative of institution, and his wording quoted above might suggest that he was more interested in keeping 'sacrifice of praise and thanksgiving' in the canon in 1928, than in keeping 'we offer thee our souls and bodies, to be a living sacrifice' which evangelicals had striven to keep out of it.[7] I have two further comments on this 'sacrifice of praise'.

---

4 W. H. Frere, *Some Principles of Liturgical Reform* (Murray, London, 1911), p. 193.

5 F. Procter and W. H. Frere, *A New History of the Book of Common Prayer* (Macmillan, 1901), p. 459.

6 F. Procter, *A History of the Book of Common Prayer* (Macmillan, London, 17th edn, 1884), pp. 343, 361.

7 Gregory Dix finally undermined the 'Catholic' case for self-offering in the Canon – and so its post-communion position in Series 2 in 1964–6 was surprisingly easily agreed on the Liturgical Commission.

First, its New Testament origins are very clear indeed. In Hebrews 13.15 comes, 'Through him let us offer the sacrifice of praise continually, that is, the fruit of lips which give praise to his name.' While the various Old Testament references (such as in Psalms 50 or 116) may have been in the writer's mind, he is as clearly presenting a changed nature of this sacrifice as he has done throughout with the Day of Atonement sacrifices. Indeed he tops up verse 15 with verse 16 saying: 'Do not forget to do good and to share, for with such sacrifices God is well pleased.' Here then are sacrifices which are responsive and grateful, disconnected from any atoning or redeeming sacrifice. Praises are also, *pace* Frere etc., without any visible relationship to the eucharist. They are offered *with our lips*. Nor are the New Testament authors alone, for the point is almost as clear in the few writers of the hundred years following them. Thus Justin says in *Dialogue with Trypho*: 'Now, that prayers and giving of thanks, when offered by worthy people, are the only perfect and well-pleasing sacrifices to God, I also admit' (117). This exposition is remarkably juxtaposed with Justin's statement that the eucharist itself is a kind of sacrifice – and with no apparent sense of inconsistency. He derived the eucharist as a sacrifice from Malachi 1.11, a stock in trade prophecy for early Christian writers, teaching that the gospel among the Gentiles had been prophesied in the Old Testament, and this Gentile dispensation outstripped the worship of God made by the Jews of Malachi's time. The Malachi text is found in the *Didache*, five times in Justin's *Dialogue with Trypho*, and again, after Justin, in Irenaeus and elsewhere. Yet two or three scraps of evidence, from a century and more of Christian worship across the whole Roman empire and beyond, are a poor sample on which to base a doctrine totally absent from the New Testament. The common factor motivating these early authors is the distancing of Christianity from Judaism, whether, as in Irenaeus, as a development or as a revolutionary replacement.[8] Their concern is the fulfilment of prophecy in that a universal gospel supersedes the tribal salvation of the Old Testament, with the side implication that the 'sacrifice' – the *thusia* – is pure when the lives of worshippers are pure.

Malachi 1.11 is nowhere quoted in the New Testament, despite all the dealings of Paul with Judaizers. But, once shipped in aid by post-apostolic authors, even while they referred it to holy lives, nevertheless, probably because of its cultic terminology, they also referred it to the eucharist, or to holy lives at the eucharist. Thus the eucharist became in

---

[8 See my later discussion in *Justin Martyr on Baptism and Eucharist*, pp. 27–9.]

regular nomenclature a 'sacrifice'. But, in the light of the New Testament, this was 'a sacrifice, no sacrifice'.

Because the terminology of eucharistic sacrifice has run strongly in the life of our church, the Group for Renewal of Worship (GROW) endeavoured years ago to put it in context. We republished Richard Hanson's very thorough review of the early evidence;[9] and, seeking a representative anglo-catholic to respond to Hanson, after difficulty we found a young Westcott tutor, Rowan Williams. He gave a very subtle exposition of what his title placards as a 'metaphor'[10] – but declined to be seen as a representative anglo-catholic, and wrote simply as himself. GROW then sponsored an overnight conference, leading to a symposium reflecting further on Rowan Williams' exposition.[11]

In Hebrews 13.16 pure lives are the sacrifices Christians offer, but they follow the 'sacrifice of praise' in verse 15. And I had a second comment to make on 'sacrifice of praise', for the Frere exposition ran into my own time. Arthur Couratin once said to me, 'the sacrifice of praise is, in the Old Testament, a four-footed animal'. He was implying, I assume, that the antitype of that animal slain is Christ himself, in some way offered to God in his passion, as our 'sacrifice of praise'. Sure enough, Bryan Spinks titled his Festschrift for Arthur in 1981 *The Sacrifice of Praise*, echoing a famous sermon of Arthur's in 1955, in which, despite the title 'The Sacrifice of Praise', he left it curiously unclear what content he intended 'sacrifice' to have. He concluded, 'we should be able to stand before God united, and to minister to him as priests, by offering the sacrifice of praise and thanksgiving, and by confessing to the Name of God . . .'. He does not expound 'sacrifice of praise and thanksgiving', but Geoffrey Willis's chapter in the Festschrift is entitled 'Sacrificium Laudis' (Geoffrey thought largely in Latin), and here he discusses Hebrews 13.15, and cites Arthur's sermon as back-up for his own tendentious finding:

> [The metaphorical sense of *thusia*] would seem to fit well with the rest of the sentence in Hebrews 13.15, where the words, 'the fruit of lips giving praise to his name' stand in apposition to the words

---

9 R. P. C. Hanson, *Eucharistic Offering in the Early Church*, Grove Liturgical Study 19 (Grove Books, Bramcote, 1979), a slightly expanded version of the lecture he had given in 1976 in Dublin, published as 'Eucharistic Offering in the Pre-Nicene Fathers' in the *Proceedings of the Royal Irish Academy.*

10 Rowan Williams, *Eucharistic Sacrifice: The Roots of a Metaphor*, Grove Liturgical Study 31 (Grove Books, Bramcote, 1982).

11 Colin Buchanan (ed.), *Essays on Eucharistic Sacrifice in the Early Church*, Grove Liturgical Study 40 (Grove Books, Bramcote, 1984).

'sacrifice of praise' . . . However *thusia* may well not be metaphorical, but literal and in this case . . . it will mean a sacrifice expressive of praise or a thankoffering. This is how Canon Couratin, among others, takes *thusia* in Hebrews 13.15, and the Christian sacrifice is clearly the Eucharist.[12]

We are not *quite* told what this 'literal' sacrifice is. The nearer it comes to being an offering of Christ himself, or of his body and blood, or of his sacrifice, not only has it no New Testament support, but the harder to understand is (what the authors quoted above ignore) that Hebrews exhorts us to offer '*through him*' the sacrifice of praise. If the sacrifice is 'literally' Christ or his work, then it is odd, if not circular, to offer it 'through him'. If it is 'literal' but is simply bread and wine, then we can understand it, but it is an over-dignification to call that 'eucharistic sacrifice'. However, with a metaphorical sacrifice, that is, a godward responsive expression of praise from our lips, it is entirely natural to offer it 'through Christ'. Interestingly, when we were drafting Series 2 Communion over 40 years ago Arthur himself drafted, in the post-Sanctus, this lead-in to the petition for consecration: 'Through him accept our sacrifice of praise . . .'. It is there today in the Order One Prayer A, in the reduced form 'Accept our praises', which helps explain its meaning originally. In Series 3 the request that God would accept our sacrifice of thanks and praise passed to the petition for fruitful reception after the anamnesis. In the original report in September 1971 it said simply, 'Accept this our sacrifice of thanks and praise', which, I suppose, could just have been expounded Couratin-wise – though personally I had no problem in signing that text. However, in the passage through Synod and the Steering Committee it emerged as 'Accept through him, our great high priest, this our sacrifice' – and, if this phrase has any sense that we offer Christ himself, I cannot see how that is done 'through him'. The phrasing goes back to Hebrews 13.15–16, and does of course echo 'It is right to give thanks and praise' in the opening dialogue, and it can *only* mean a metaphorical sacrifice consisting of articulated thanks and praise. While Frere originally wanted to move it (with the whole prayer of oblation) from the post-communion into the Canon, we still do not know what 'literal' content could be given to this 'sacrifice'. Now that it is in the eucharistic prayers, I submit that it must, like Hebrews 13.15, indeed mean 'a metaphorical sacrifice consisting of articulated thanks and praise'. The text ran on in the

---

12 Geoffrey Willis, 'Sacrificium Laudis' in Bryan Spinks (ed.), *The Sacrifice of Praise* (Centro Liturgico Vincenziano, Rome, 1981), pp. 74–5.

Second Eucharistic Prayer, but in Prayer C today it is in the form 'through him we offer you this our sacrifice of praise and thanksgiving' – and in Prayer B, it continues (as from the Brindley–Beckwith improper deal in 1978) without the 'through him'. Is it for the sake of *this* phrase that that particular prayer has been treated by Anglican catholics as 'our' prayer? Yet, from my point of view, the metaphorical meaning, drawing on Hebrews 13, can well continue unshaken, especially if no literal meaning of a substantive offering can be attached to the phrase. And this metaphorical 'sacrifice of praise and thanksgiving', we should note, though appropriate at the eucharist, is *not* a statement about the eucharist, nor limited to it (which is exactly the case in Hebrews 13.15, where the eucharist is not in view). In the 1662 Book of Common Prayer, slightly amusingly, 'our sacrifice of praise and thanksgiving' comes not only in the post-communion, but also in the collect of thanksgiving to be used at sea for deliverance from a storm – perhaps hundreds of miles and, in 1662, months of time from any eucharistic celebration. So, although the terminology is fine, we should handle it quite separately from eucharistic doctrine and not fall for any paradox of the eucharist as 'a sacrifice, not a sacrifice' here.

I append a small diversion. Geoffrey Willis in that same chapter has a footnote about those who decline to see Hebrews 13.15 as about the eucharist:

> Cf. A remark of Dr. H. E. Savage, Dean of Lichfield, recorded by R.Wilson in *Theology* 55 (1952), p. 298: 'Bishop Westcott always seemed to me to be quite unable to understand what was meant by the sacrificial aspect of the Eucharist. In fact, he appeared to me to have no conception of the principles of sacrificial worship, and that, to my mind, is what makes his commentary on . . . Hebrews so disappointing, though I heard him more than once refer to it as being his best bit of work.'[13]

Poor old Westcott – his *summum opus* was impoverished by his not knowing what he was talking about.

I need hardly add that, if the eucharist is no ritual sacrifice, the communion table is no altar. Nor is there mileage in trying to make the reference to an 'altar' in Hebrews 13.10 mean an altar of ritual – it is consistent throughout Hebrews that the place of Jesus' death (a place emphasized in the following verses here) is the altar at which we worship, from which we are 'fed'.

---

13 Willis, 'Sacrificium Laudis', p. 74, n3.

PRIESTHOOD

We come then to priesthood. You know that Jesus Christ is our high priest according to Hebrews, that he fulfils and winds up any role for earthly priests within the life of the church, and that, although the whole church is occasionally viewed as priestly, no ministers of the church are in the New Testament ever called priests. I found it fascinating when studying Justin to find how deeply Hebrews had sunk into his system, how often the high priesthood of Christ is emphasized, how fully the significance of the order of Melchisedek is aired. Furthermore, in those very passages we have noted where Justin calls on the prophecy of Malachi (viz. in *Dialogue with Trypho* 116), he says:

> . . . we are the true high priestly race of God, as God himself bears witness, saying that in every place among the Gentiles they are presenting to him well-pleasing and pure sacrifices. Now God receives sacrifices from no one, except through his priests.

On a natural reading, this makes the corporate church priestly, able to offer its sacrifices because it is priestly. It also confirms the given fact from Hebrews that offering sacrifice is what being a priest entails (it may have other functions, but this is the non-negotiable defining function). But in Justin, as in Hebrews, there is no mention of a category of *ordained* Christian priests – Justin is remarkable for never mentioning any Christian ministers at all, save the deacons who take sacramental elements to those absent, and the 'presider' at the eucharist, who seems to be known by his function rather than his order. While there are hints of levitical rankings to be discerned in the first-century Letter of Clement of Rome to the Corinthians, it is not until the third century that we find the bishop being called the 'high priest'. And it is not only that there is no scrap of biblical evidence for calling ministers 'priests', it is that the Letter to the Hebrews, by its teaching, absolutely precludes such a category. All Old Testament sacrificing priesthood is consummated in the person of Jesus, and all Old Testament sacrifices are consummated in his sacrifice of himself once for all for ever. We have then a cumulative, yet relatively unconnected, set of problems: the error of the third century, the failure to grasp the terminological nettle at the Reformation, and the nineteenth-century resurgence of medieval ideas giving us today's 'priest, no priest' paradox.[14]

---

14 Anders Bergquist revived this paradox for me: he spoke about ordained 'priesthood' at a Southwark study day; I asked him about the teaching of Hebrews; he

The determinative character of Hebrews is well recognized by Roman Catholics who will think 'outside the box'. I can quote you from Küng, Tillard[15] and Bob Taft. Wonderfully, the original Anglican–Roman Catholic Statement on Ordination in 1973 acknowledged that in the New Testament ministers are never called 'priests', and went further and said 'their ministry is not an extension of the common Christian priesthood, but belongs to another realm of the gifts of the Spirit'.

However, the subject has been well muddled by a General Synod document of 20 years ago. Through the initiative of a layman, the Faith and Order Advisory Group (FOAG) had to write a report on *The Priesthood of the Ordained Ministry*. This report, published in 1986, I revisited when writing my book about General Synod, and so I checked out its contents more carefully. In brief it begins with four chapters which acknowledge that there is no ministerial priesthood in the New Testament. The largest wobble is on page 28:

> No priesthood is attributed to the distinctive ministry. This latter fact is not surprising since the early church developed within Judaism and the sacrificial system of the Temple continued until the destruction of the Temple in 70 AD.

This suggests that the apostolic church would have liked to call its ministers 'priests', but refrained lest there be confusion. But the surer answer is that their beliefs would have ruled out using the *hiereus* stem about their ministers, and the suggestion that they had even an option about it, and a decision to take about it, arises from the conclusion FOAG was seeking, and not from the New Testament evidence.

We go on to Chapter 13. On page 102 the rabbit comes out of the hat:

> Although the terms 'priest' and 'priesthood' are not used in the New Testament with reference to the work of the Church's special

---

replied that his doctrine was a legitimate development of the 'potentialities' (that was his word) of Hebrews; I wrote to him, asserting that his 'potentialities' are, according to Hebrews, 'impossibilities' – the letter leaves no room for developing a 'priesthood' of ordained ministers. In four years Anders has not replied. I have seen him – indeed he was the 'theological consultant' to the Revision Committee on the Ordinal – and I have reminded him I have had no answer, and he has agreed that he ought to write, but he has not. So I have yet to learn about this 'development'.

15 I published his *What Priesthood has the Ministry?*, Grove Booklet on Ministry and Worship 13 (Grove Books, Bramcote, 1973).

ministry, nevertheless in the way they have been used . . . they indicate essential aspects of the ministry of bishops and presbyters.

This is *not* now 'priest, no priest'. No, it is 'priest, real priest – *essential* priest'! General Synod stuck in its toes with a blocking amendment citing the contradiction between the first four chapters and the last one, and referring the report to the House of Bishops. That amendment failed by 224 votes to 207, but the report then lost all credibility. Synod finally allowed it was a 'stimulating contribution' to Anglican thinking, not a summary of it. So far, so good – indeed better than might have been expected, once such a report was in the public arena. I wrote up the process in my Synod book. However, I bring this poor specimen before you for two further reasons, one of its contents, one of its use; and if I can nail the error in those two categories, then perhaps we can bury it for ever.

What further content then? Well, in Chapter 8 on pages 71–3 the writers call in aid two learned nineteenth-century evangelical Anglicans – Dean Goode and Nathaniel Dimock. Goode wrote *The Effects of Infant Baptism* (1849), assisting Gorham win his case on appeal to the Judicial Committee of the Privy Council. Dimock wrote a great series of books (I think I have 12) on the liturgy and sacraments of the Church of England a generation or so later (he died in 1909). Both were very scholarly, unwavering protestants. So, having mentioned the bare-faced deceit of FOAG in calling these authors in aid, I followed up the references. The result is in an appendix here (see pp. 163–5).[16] Goode virtually condemns the position which the report attributes to him. The Dimock reference is less perverse, but has no reference to ministers being 'priests', nor to the eucharist being a 'sacrifice'. Did some bright spark draft these paragraphs and the others accept them without checking? No theological group, met to study the Goode and Dimock texts, could ever have come up with anything that would match this report. It confirms how partisan the report is – the drafters must have decided their conclusions before they started, and then twisting these authors as evidence was fair game. Or am I the first actually to check their references?

My complaint is not only about the content of the report, but is as much directed to the later use of it. At least two major later reports treat it as a sound source for authoritative statements on the Church of England's ordained ministry.

---

16 At the lecture the appendix was a duplicated hand-out.

The first of these is *Eucharistic Presidency*, the 1997 report from the House of Bishops which was compiled to set out why only bishops and presbyters can preside at communion. The passage concerned is quoted partly to preclude some more extravagant notions of priesthood, but it leaves a strong unbiblical residuum, thus:

> . . . in so far as its [the special ministry's] ministry is priestly, its priesthood is not simply derived from the priestliness of the whole community. Rather the common priesthood of the community and the special priesthood of the ordained ministry are both derived from the priesthood of Christ.[17]

You will see the giveaway – in what sense dare we say that the presbyteral ministry has a 'special priesthood' (an *hierosune*), 'derived from the priesthood of Christ'? Does not this spring from our half-reformed language 'priest, no priest'?

The other instance of reliance upon the FOAG report – and, indeed, on precisely the contentious parts of the report – comes in the Anglican–Methodist Covenant of 2001: '153 The Church of England also believes that there is a distinctive priestly ministry which is also derived from Christ himself and which is exercised by those ordained priest.'[18] It then quotes precisely the same extract from *The Priesthood of the Ordained Ministry* which *Eucharistic Presidency* had quoted, and it looks as though it got it from there. And again we are left with two serious problems – one of substance, that is, whether the Church of England generally does believe anything of the sort, and one of Commission procedure, that is, how they came to quote from such a damaged source to make their contentious point. Let me emphasize that it is entirely appropriate to say that ministry is derived from Christ himself, and even that a 'distinctive' ministry is exercised by those ordained presbyter, but it is contentiously unbiblical to derive a supposed 'priestly' ministry of the presbyterate from Christ's priesthood – if these sentences were couched in Greek, the sleight of hand would be quickly exposed.

Curiously, although this 'distinctive' statement about the Anglican 'priesthood' was presumably included to distinguish Anglican priests from unpriestly Methodist ministers, the report cheerfully continues:

---

17 House of Bishops, *Eucharistic Presidency* (Church House Publishing, London, 1997), pp. 29–30, quoting *The Priesthood of the Ordained Ministry*, p. 99.
18 *An Anglican–Methodist Covenant* (Epworth, London, 2001), p. 47 – followed by the above quote from *The Priesthood*, p. 99.

'We believe there is a common understanding of the presbyterate.' My comment: 'So, despite all the tangles, with one bound Jack was free.'

Sorting out this wretched report of itself imperils neither the threefold ministry, nor the nature of episcopacy, nor the presbyteral presidency of the eucharist. Those are not at issue here. But clearly we should complete the reform of the translation of *presbuteros*. The quagmire of 'priest, no priest' is totally avoided if we stick to 'presbyter' in English. It is there, but rare, in history. The bishops at the Savoy Conference use it (see the quotation at p. 52 above). Newman uses it in Tract 1; Dimock himself uses it throughout; the Scottish Episcopal Church has used it since the Reformation; and it was part of the basis of union in South India. But it has often been belittled as pedantic and obscure in the life of the Church of England, almost certainly by those who could see that its coming into currency would drive out the word 'priest'.

Yet we make progress. In the ASB ordinal we got 'presbyters' into the title of the rite as an equivalent to 'priests'. We also, of course, got 'priest' out of the rubrics of Rite A, by using 'president', the functional word.[19] Soon after, the Lima document in 1982 discusses throughout its ministry section 'bishops, presbyters and deacons'. It charitably allows that 'priest' may be used, though its basis is weak. Common Worship provides a larger mixing of the two words in the ordinal, so that 'presbyter' gains in currency. I have used 'presbyter' unvaryingly throughout the larger books I have written in recent years, and have naturally offered this kind of explanation in my entries for 'priest' and 'presbyter' in my *Historical Dictionary of Anglicanism*. There is a dawning awareness that the second order of ministry is 'priest, no priest' – and that may assist real clarification. It is progress if the Church of England can recognize that 'priests' may be equally called 'presbyters'; but I hope we can move on to the Lima stage, where they are 'presbyters' who *may* be called 'priests'.[20]

---

19 The ASB has one small exception to this, for, when we were pressed on the Revision Committee that 'priest' was the Prayer Book word (and therefore obligatory), we smiled to ourselves and put it into the rubrics for the form of Rite A *'following the pattern of the Book of Common Prayer'* – the smile arising from doubts whether our objectors were going to be endeared to that form.

20 This approach was endorsed by the sixth International Anglican Liturgical Consultation in its Berkeley Statement. See Paul Gibson (ed.), *Anglican Ordination Rites: The Berkeley Statement 'To Equip the Saints'*, Grove Worship Series 168 (Grove Books, Cambridge, 2002), pp. 7–8. The Statement, allowing the term 'priest', then uses 'presbyter' throughout.

It is foreign to the New Testament to teach that in the eucharist a substantial sacrifice, in some sense the sacrifice of Christ, is offered to the Father; so no priestly role of offering sacrifice exists to be fulfilled by the eucharistic president. We encounter not only no need but some harm through mixing 'priestly' words into the presbyter's role. Leadership in worship, and presidency at the eucharist, are *not* specifically *priestly* activities, and it is unhelpful to confuse those roles with priestly ones. The Roman words 'May the Lord receive the sacrifice at your hands' is a ghastly intrusion which distorts both eucharist and ministry. For my part on the day I was ordained a presbyter 44 years ago, I presided at communion that evening and preached on 'priest, no priest' at that very Cranmerian rite which removed all suspicion of eucharistic sacrifice from the Anglican settlement.

'One egg, no egg' amused because it was self-contradictory. But 'a priest, no priest' and its kindred do not amuse. So bring out your biblical reasons why the eucharist is a sacrifice, or cease from the misleading language. Bring out your biblical reasons why the presbyter is a priest, or cease from the misleading language. Bring out your biblical reasons why a communion table is an altar or cease from the misleading language. Let not the self-contradictory language linger solely through mistaken charity, a half-loyalty to Rome, or an Anglican love of fudge. We hold a higher responsibility before God than that.

APPENDIX

(a) *The Priesthood of the Ordained Ministry* and Dean Goode

The Priesthood of the Ordained Ministry (p. 71): **'Evangelical Contribution'**	Dean Goode, *The Divine Rule of Faith and Practice*, vol. 2, pp. 354–5
(107) Among the Evangelical critics of Tractarianism, a special place is occupied by one of the most learned, William Goode, author of *The Divine Rule of Faith and Practice* (second enlarged edition 1853, three volumes – the second of which discusses priesthood and sacrifice). Goode's critique contained many positive statements, and his position is summarized in what follows. Under all ordinary circumstances,	We have already observed, that there are senses in which the word sacrifice may very properly be applied to the eucharist. The whole action of the eucharist is a sacrifice of thanksgiving, and such 'sacrifice of praise' (Heb. xiii.15), as being a sacrifice of the heart, is one more acceptable to God than any material or external offering. Moreover, the elements themselves may be called a sacrifice to God, not as things offered up as a propitiatory sacrifice to God, but as oblations to God, or things given and set apart for the service of God. Thus Cyprian rebukes the wealthy for coming to church 'without a sacrifice', and 'taking

---

The Priesthood of the Ordained Ministry (p. 71): **'Evangelical Contribution'**

Dean Goode, *The Divine Rule of Faith and Practice*, vol. 2, pp. 354–5

---

he believed, the ordained ministers of the Church are the only proper dispensers of the sacraments, but that is not to say there can never be exceptional circumstances. The threefold ministry has good scriptural support, and all ordinations not performed by a bishop are irregular, which is not to say that episcopal ordination in due succession is a rigid necessity for validity. Succession is valuable, but (as Bellarmine conceded) no infallible guarantee of truth in the Church. Evangelicals generally affirmed the worth of episcopacy but felt it could not be said to belong to the essence of the Gospel. Granted that the Christian priesthood is not without Old Testament analogy, the action of the eucharistic celebrant is not to be understood levitically. The eucharist is indeed a sacrifice – first and foremost a thanksgiving of the heart rather than a material or external offering. Yet the elements are also offered to God and set apart for their holy end, and the consecrated elements represent and symbolically set forth the sacrifice of Christ. We should not think there is one moment when the priest offers consecrated elements to the Father as a propitiatory sacrifice, but say rather that 'by the whole eucharistical act we represent Christ's passion to the Father.' The consecrated elements 'are solemnly offered as a memorial of the Cross', not by the priest alone for the people, but by all

part of the sacrifice which the poor offered'; it being customary then for the bread and wine to be brought by the communicants.

So also the consecrated elements might be called a sacrifice *figuratively*, as they *represent* and symbolically set forth the sacrifice of Christ; although it is evident, from the deductions of our opponents from such language, that it is inconvenient and dangerous phraseology. However harmless in its original use and signification.

Ibid., pp. 364–5

[There are four erroneous propositions set out by the Tractator]

1st. That the bread and wine, after consecration, are to be offered up to God by the minister, as a sacrifice commemorative of the sacrifice of the cross.

2dly. That the minister performs this act in a strictly sacerdotal character.

3dly. That by *this* sacrifice so offered by a priest, remission of sins is obtained for the whole Church.

4thly. That by this sacrifice so offered an additional refreshment is obtained for the souls of the dead in the intermediate state.

All these propositions, then, we maintain to be contrary to the testimony of Scripture and the earliest Fathers.

1st. That the bread and wine, *after* consecration, are to be offered up to God by the minister, as a sacrifice commemorative of the sacrifice of the cross.

Whether there is any *intrinsic evil* in such an oblation, is *not here the question*. That the bread and wine, after that they have obtained by consecration a peculiar character, as things set apart as emblems of Christ's body and blood, should be solemnly offered up to God, as a memorial, as it were, of the sacrifice of the cross, may not be itself an improper act, if it be understood that the offering is made, not by the priest as a propitiation for the people, but by all the congregation by the hands of the priest as a commemorative representation of the sacrifice of Christ. And by this act the body and blood of Christ might be said to be offered up, that is *figuratively* and *symbolically*, which is the only way in which they could be offered up by elements which, as the Fathers

| *The Priesthood of the Ordained Ministry* (p. 71): **'Evangelical Contribution'** | Dean Goode, *The Divine Rule of Faith and Practice*, vol. 2, pp. 364–5 |

the congregation at the hands of the priest. The true Body and Blood of Christ are spiritually offered to the Father in prayers and praises as the only propitiation for sins; and this spiritual sacrifice is 'the soul of the service'. Goode affirmed that the eucharistic intercession may have a propitiatory effect with God, but this effect is not automatically attached to the performance of the rite as such. The people are as much sacrificers as the priest, offering up the sacrifice of the cross 'not by iteration but in the prayers of the faithful.'

testify, are still bread and wine. And this was perhaps done by some in the fourth or fifth century, and was admitted into our first reformed Liturgy, but was done simultaneously and correspondently, as far as the succession of time would admit, with that act of the heart by which the true body and blood of Christ – the true sacrifice of the cross – were spiritually offered up to the Father in prayers and praises, as the only propitiation for our sins; which spiritual sacrifice is that which at all times is, as it were, the soul of the service, and that upon which its value altogether depends. But, though the offering up of the consecrated elements may not be in itself improper, yet there are objections to it, and our Church has thus judged. We have not the testimony of Scripture, or of the Primitive Church, in its favour. And there is no inconsiderable danger, as I think facts teach us, that this external offering made through the hands of the minister, may be substituted for that spiritual offering up of the sacrifice of the cross upon the altar of the heart of each individual, upon which the value of the service to each individual communicant wholly depends. Nay more; *as we have no authority for so doing, it is an act which appears to savour strongly of presumption.*

(b) *The Priesthood of the Ordained Ministry* and Nathaniel Dimock

| *The Priesthood of the Ordained Ministry* (p. 72) | Nathaniel Dimock, *Our One High Priest on High* |

(108) Nathaniel Dimock, to whom we have already referred,[21] in his *Our One Priest on High* (1899), was anxious to distinguish (whilst holding indissolubly together) the completed propitiatory work of Christ on the cross and his continuing work of intercession in heaven. 'All that we

COB states:
(a) This Dimock book is a supplement to tidy up two loose ends left by his major work, *The Sacerdotium of Christ*. Read that also.
(b) The quotation is from p. 85. Its context is the assertion (at vast length

---

21 This reference must be to the paragraph on pp. 65–6 of *The Priesthood*, which says:

The Priesthood of the Ordained Ministry (p. 72)	Nathaniel Dimock, *Our One High Priest on High*

claim for the present is founded on that which we claim for the past.'

Accordingly, Christ's ministers have a task of high dignity to perform in that they minister the fruits of a sacrificing priesthood, they are called in Christ himself to a subordinate function in an 'applicatory and consequent work'. It was in the light of this understanding of Christ's work that Dimock and others of his persuasion wished the eucharistic celebration to be understood.

and depth) that Christ's sacrifice was made once for all on earth, and that Jesus' high priesthood is currently exercised for us in heaven, not in any sacrificing work, but in interceding.

(c) The 'applicatory and consequent work' (p. 86) of Christian ministers is the general task they have. It is specifically denied by Dimock that they are 'priests', and he does not relate their work to the eucharist (which is hardly mentioned in the book).

(d) The FOAG summary is initially not far from Dimock, but the last sentence asserts that Dimock is writing about the eucharist when he is not; so, because pp. 85–6 as quoted above have *no eucharistic reference*, quoting Dimock is useless for FOAG's purposes, and it is deceptive (or desperate) to include it as an 'evangelical contribution' to a conclusion the opposite of that to which Dimock clearly adhered.

POSTSCRIPT

This lecture is published here to trail a theological coat. The comeback could lead to a real theological encounter – and we need it.

Daniel Waterland also admitted a wider sense of 'offer' as meaning commemorating or presenting to the divine consideration (*Works* V.286). The theme appears several times in the writings of the nineteenth century Anglican Evangelical, Nathaniel Dimock (1835–1909). Dimock was convinced that to admit any priestliness in the ordained ministry must dishonour the uniqueness of Christ's high priesthood. But he freely granted that in the Eucharist there is a pleading of the Cross before the Father. Dimock's discussion of the Jesuit, J. B. Franzelin (1816–86), shows both how sympathetic he found his work and how narrow the divide could be.

The report gives no references in Dimock, and the 'several times' looks unsubstantiated. That which Dimock 'freely granted' will prove, I suspect, to have been very carefully hedged. But I have not found his discussion of Franzelin in the ten volumes of Dimock I possess.

Liturgical Journalism

Twenty-nine years of *News of Liturgy*: the late twentieth-century liturgical blog (1975–2003)[1]

James Steven

INTRODUCTION

One of the interesting developments that has accompanied the explosion in communication and information available on the Internet is the huge popularity of personal weblogs, better known as 'blog' sites. A survey in April 2005 estimated there to be 43 million blogs worldwide, and 56 new blogs were being posted each minute! A blog is simply a series of updated posts on a web page in the form of a diary or journal, often including commentary on, and hypertext links to, other websites. Posts are in chronological order and can contain anything, from simple text to music, images and even streamed video. As one website puts it, 'A blog is a personal diary. A daily pulpit. A collaborative space. A political soapbox. A breaking-news outlet. A collection of links. Your own private thoughts. Memos to the world.'[2] Blogging is an opportunity to communicate, to express oneself, to test ideas and connect to those people who might be listening and might want to begin a conversation. The personalized nature of blogs means that they can be 'opinionated, ranting, often incoherent and frequently biased with little regard for accuracy or balance.'[3] But one of the attractions of blogging lies in its unmediated and dynamic quality. With no official agenda or editorial stance blogging can provide reportage in a raw and exciting form, and people will visit weblogs for sceptical analysis, critical commentary, and alternative perspectives rarely seen in mainstream media.

---

1 An earlier version of this chapter was delivered as a paper at the Society for Liturgical Study Conference, August 2006.

2 <www.blogger.com>.

3 <www.newsgroup.co.uk>.

No collection of essays that relate to Colin Buchanan's contribution to Anglican liturgy would be complete without a discussion of his editorship of *News of Liturgy* (*NOL*), the monthly liturgical journal that ran for 348 editions from January 1975 to December 2003. In reviewing the contribution of *NOL* to the liturgical life of the Church,[4] I want to suggest that it is best understood as a late twentieth-century liturgical blog. Despite being non-web based (an eight to twelve A5 page leaflet[5]) in character *NOL* is all that one might expect and hope for in a blog. As Colin himself admitted in the editorial celebrating the three hundredth edition, *NOL* has

> provided a platform where I have great freedom to express my own mind and judgment . . . *NOL's* only angle on the charge of twisting or creating news is to admit it – this has been and remains a transparently biased and prejudiced publication . . . *NOL* has tried to be a 'journal of record' – just slightly spiced![6]

Whence did the blogger emerge? There was an occasion: when the first *NOL* was published in 1975 the Church of England was in the middle of its first period of sustained liturgical change for over four hundred years and there was a need for its worshipping community, lay and ordained, to be informed of the changes and issues at stake. Second, there was the means. An evangelical group of liturgists, a rare breed hitherto in the Church of England in the twentieth century, had formed by the name of the Latimer House Liturgy Group (to be reconstituted in 1976 as Group for Renewal of Worship (GROW)). This Group had already started the Grove Books series in 1971 and was committed to providing evangelical comment and perspectives on contemporary liturgical issues. From within this Group emerged the blogger, Colin Buchanan, who was then himself deeply engaged with the processes of liturgical revision by dint of being on the Liturgical Commission and the newly formed General Synod of the Church of England. An astute synodical politician, thriving in the field of public debate, and an informed liturgical historian with theological convictions to boot, Colin found in *NOL* an ideal blogging outlet for his engagement with liturgical revision. And so, as the first editorial of *NOL* stated, the aim was to include the Church in a fast-moving situation and to provide

---

4 I became an *NOL* subscriber in 1988. A period of sabbatical leave in 2005 provided me with the occasion to review the journal from its beginnings in 1975.
5 Special editions could run to 20 pages, as in the case of the last edition.
6 *NOL* 300.1.

evangelical comment, with an 'irenic and ecumenical stance' on the process and content of liturgical change.

NOL AND REPORTING: THE 'FIRST-HAND' BLOG

The reporting of events as they happened was one of the most universally appreciated characteristics of *NOL*. Responses to a questionnaire circulated at the annual meeting of the Liturgical Commission and representatives of diocesan liturgical committees in October 1999 placed 'up to date liturgical news' as the most valuable feature of *NOL*. Liturgical business at every successive Synod was previewed, reported and then commented upon; no liturgical matter was too small or insignificant to be overlooked and so the readers could be assured that they missed nothing. *NOL*'s boast was that 'every text from the Liturgical Commission, every motion or amendment in General Synod, every vote, even complaints in Parliament, have been recorded verbatim, and errors corrected in later editions'.[7] For the seasoned *NOL* subscriber official initiatives, such as the Church House Publishing advertisement in a 1998 edition of *NOL* offering a service for keen liturgists to keep up to date with Synod Papers, would always be a pale imitation of the full-bodied version you received in *NOL*! In this sense of 'catching all things liturgical' (which of course would include not just liturgical textual revision but matters ranging from changes to the canons to debates surrounding the publication of new texts) *NOL* can be legitimately regarded as an unbiased and dispassionate publication.

However, no sooner has this judgement been made than it needs to be qualified by the fact that the value of this reporting lies in the reporter being involved at first hand in the processes of revision, whether it was as a member of the Liturgical Commission, or a revision committee, or as a bishop in Synod. Colin could claim to have been there in some way or the other, and this gives the reporting in *NOL* a level of authenticity that other commentators would always find it difficult to imitate. Even the deepest secrets of the synodical processes were laid bare for all to see by 'our man on the inside' in the occasional *NOL* double-page spread-charts outlining the timetable for liturgical revision (which the editor happily assumed would end up on readers' kitchen fridge doors!). On some occasions the speed and manner in which materials were published bordered on liturgical 'piracy', as *NOL* happily conceded; when challenged by the secretary of the Liturgical Commission for releasing liturgy that had not yet been seen in the

7 *NOL* 348.3.

public arena, Colin would always give a carefully argued rationale for the publication, an apology when called for, and then, as happened on one occasion, a reminder of the benefits of *NOL*: 'If you want to buy the news before it happens, then *NOL* is for you'![8] This mirrors the spirit of Grove Books publishing enterprise (whose liturgically related publications are faithfully previewed and advertised in *NOL*), which promotes itself as 'Not the last word but often the first'. *NOL*'s 'piracy' also allowed access to documentation that would never have been seen, an example being the Appendix drafted for the Lambeth Conference (1998) Report, 'Current Anglican Concerns in Liturgy', which was cut (or 'butchered', as *NOL* delicately put it) from the final Report, thereby rescuing mention of the significant work done by the International Anglican Liturgical Consultations in the 1990s.

So, although closely involved with synodical business, *NOL* could never be regarded as an official publication. Yet those responsible for national liturgical matters could not ignore its unique value as a means of disseminating useful information, as evidenced in the request made by the Liturgical Commission for *NOL* to carry liturgical news from the dioceses. The request was granted and from 1988 *NOL* began publishing reports from diocesan liturgical committees, a practice that lasted more or less uninterrupted for the remaining years of the journal; Colin cheerfully acknowledging that such an addition might have toned down *NOL*'s independence 'by a whisker'! Even after *Praxis News* began its quarterly updates on the new Common Worship liturgies in 1998, *NOL* still carried regular official bulletins from the Liturgical Publishing Group, headed by David Green in Church House.

Alongside its extensive coverage on synodical matters, *NOL* addressed all sorts of wider concerns and events. Liturgical changes throughout the Anglican Communion were reported. Revisions in Wales, Ireland, Scotland, Australia, New Zealand, Nigeria, Kenya, South Africa, Zaire, USA, Canada, South and North India, and the Mar Thoma Church were all addressed, together with news and published statements from the International Anglican Liturgical Consultations (IALC). True to its ecumenical intentions, *NOL* reviewed the liturgies of other denominations, ranging from Roman Catholic revisions to those of the Methodists, and it also carried the occasional report from the ecumenical Joint Liturgical Group (JLG). The meetings of major liturgical societies, such as the British-based Society for Liturgical Study (SLS) and the international *Societas Liturgica* were advertised and conference reports received.

---

8 *NOL* 276.3.

First-hand reporting of events, accompanied by liturgical comment, was one of the hallmarks of *NOL*. High-profile liturgical events featured, such as successive archbishops' enthronements, the royal wedding, the Pope's visit to Canterbury Cathedral in 1982, and the events surrounding the millennium celebrations. There is report and comment by the editor on worship at Catholic–Anglican conferences, Anglican evangelical conferences, and Billy Graham rallies. Here was liturgical journalism (or, as I am suggesting, liturgical blogging) with an insatiable appetite for reporting events as they happened. Colin's personal liturgical diary became a feature of *NOL*, such as the launch of the ASB in London,[9] and subsequent 'Liturgical Scrapbooks', a series of reports on the liturgical life as Bishop of Aston in the mid-1980s. By this means *NOL* created and fostered a culture of reporting and comment on special or more general run-of the-mill liturgical events, unconsciously creating a style of liturgical reporting that is now used to great effect in the 'mystery worshipper' web entries on the Ship of Fools website. Other *NOL* readers caught the blogging bug and it became commonplace for ordinations, inductions and various ecumenical gatherings to be reported upon. A Deacon's Liturgical Diary (Charles Read) and an Ethiopian Liturgical Diary (Phillip Tovey) feature, together with contributions from Mark Earey on his visits to charismatic congregations, which range from Spring Harvest eucharists to a child dedication in a Vineyard church. At his own consecration as Bishop of Aston 'the blogger was blogged' when Geoffrey Cuming, long-standing friend and colleague on the Liturgical Commission, wrote a report for *NOL!* Following some innocent comments on the nature of the occasion and congregation, he writes, with tongue in cheek: 'Colin arrived in time for the beginning of the service and stayed until the end (though when he retired to put on Episcopal garb there was a long pause and we all began to wonder!).'[10]

But it is the less official and more eccentric events that often catch the reader's interest. One of my favourites is the article entitled 'Eucharist on the Move' in which a group of adult education officers, returning from a conference in Paris, celebrate a eucharist on the train in the Channel Tunnel. As the correspondent records:

> Getting out of the coach we stood in the bare compartment with one of our number acting as the altar/table (holding the elements) with another leading. Starting near Calais we finished just before

---

9 *NOL* 71.
10 *NOL* 127.8.

surfacing on the English side. We resisted the temptation to sing old favourites like *Make me a channel of your peace* and *For those in peril under the sea*. Whose See were we in or under? It was a meaningful occasion because of the group dynamic but one could not help commenting 'it was a moving occasion'.[11]

EDITORIALS: THE BLOGGER'S AGENDAS

Colin's natural talent for debate was harnessed in many a *NOL* editorial and, in the true spirit of blogging, Colin used *NOL* to air his concerns and personal agendas. In the debates surrounding the arrival of the *Alternative Service Book* in the late 1970s and early 1980s, Colin defended the new provisions from both progressive and conservative attack. The editor and contributors to the periodical *Theology*, representatives of the progressive agenda, were of the view that the liturgies that formed the ASB were compromised by theological conservatism and patristic fundamentalism. Conservatives, in the form of members of the Prayer Book Society, fronted by David Martin and aided from time to time by Prince Charles, formed the other flank of opposition; they regarded the ASB as the sign that the Church had committed an act of 'Great Forgetting'.

However, any thoughts of the editor of *NOL* being a mere lapdog of the Liturgical Commission, based on his defence of the liturgies of the ASB, were soon to be dispelled in the vigorous and sustained argument that he launched in response to the form of absolution in the proposed liturgy for the Reconciliation of a Penitent ('I absolve you from all your sins'). In the *NOL* editorials from January to June 1981 Colin's opposition to this wording was spelt out in typically clear and robust fashion, and there was, no doubt, some satisfaction on his part when the proposed liturgy was debated but then voted down in the February 1983 Synod. In popular interpretation this failure is often remembered as being an occasion which marked the growing political influence that *NOL* was capable of exerting, and may have contributed to a number of evangelicals and like-minded Christians 'voting with Colin' on subsequent issues in Synod. *NOL* was not beyond exhorting its readers to lobby their Synod reps or, if a Synod member, to vote against an issue, though it is difficult to be certain about the degree to which *NOL* has influenced synodical decisions. Colin himself identifies the absolution debates of 1983 and 1987, together with the debates on the priesthood of the ordained ministry in 1986, as occasions of *NOL* influence, and it

11 *NOL* 296.11.

is interesting to note that the debates in 1986 and 1987 fell in a period when he was not a member of Synod.

Along with the absolution issue, regular readers of *NOL* would have become familiar with Colin's other major liturgical concerns which appear during the four decades spanned by the publication. These include the conviction that initiation is fully complete in baptism (with a strong encouragement to submerge baptismal candidates if at all possible, together with information on where you can hire your birthing pools), the support of children to receive communion and the questioning of the initiatory status of confirmation and a deep-seated suspicion of the eucharistic offertory. Colin was also mystified by what he regarded as the eccentric and romantic attachment to the Book of Common Prayer, focused in his well-documented dislike of retaining the traditional version of the Lord's Prayer. In its recommendation for the use of candles at the turn of the millennium, the New Start millennium liturgical provision had unwittingly given Colin an opportunity to express his prophetic zeal, as was evident in the following recommendation he made to his readers:

> Wrap the traditional version of the Lord's Prayer round the top of the candle and the modern form (with 'Save us from the time of trial') round the bottom. You would then read the old form aloud around 11.50 p.m., light the candle and watch it burn down to halfway consuming the ancient text as it went and arrive there as the new millennium began: you would then blow it out, say the modern text, and keep the bottom half of the candle by you thereafter to mark a liturgical New Start.[12]

Colin's wider ecclesiological concerns were also represented in *NOL* editorials. For example, the nature of ordination, women and ordination (in favour), deacons (let's not have a too romantic and catholic view of this order) and presbyters (yes, the word priest is too heavily laden with theological freight really to command acceptance). As *NOL* readers will know, there were other less obviously liturgical items that also received a regular airing, such as his support of disestablishment (when challenged as to its appropriateness for *NOL* the editor was perfectly capable of mounting an argument to back a proper liturgical foundation for such a concern).

---

12 *NOL* 286.3.

NOL READERS: THE BLOGGING COMMUNITY

The fact that *NOL* has its own distinct editorial style attracted some, frustrated others and perhaps sometimes did both. I have a liturgical friend who enjoyed the news but allowed himself periodic *NOL* 'sabbaticals' when he grew weary of Colin's old chestnuts! The most ambivalent results of the sample questionnaire completed by diocesan liturgical committee representatives mentioned above were those recorded for the questionnaire entry, 'Colin Buchanan's idiosyncratic editorial style' (a loaded category description if ever there was one). On a scale of 1 (low) to 4 (high) there were as many 1s as 4s, and even a 10, who was presumably in the 'can't get enough of this' category! Perhaps most surprising of all, given the evangelical concerns represented in *NOL* editorials, is that among the fans of *NOL* were a number of catholic Anglicans. For example, among those offering support to the editor upon his consecration as Bishop of Aston is a correspondent who remarks that he will be saying mass for him on the day 'whether he likes it or not'! This support may have been because *NOL*'s theological and liturgical agendas encouraged and sparked genuine debate, but there was also a recognition among catholic Anglicans that, while they would not agree with the editor, *NOL* was making a significant contribution to contemporary liturgical education and conversation, and a far superior one than any offered by catholic Anglicans. Here is an article by *NOL* subscriber Frank Pickard in the Spring 1982 edition of the *Server*, and subsequently recorded in the pages of *NOL*:

> . . . it is undoubtedly true that for anyone who wants to follow easily what is going on liturgically these days, Colin Buchanan's monthly *Notes on Liturgy* [well he got one word out of three right in the title – keep at it, FEP – editor], and his Grove Book publications represent the only possibility. (I tried unsuccessfully to make the Bishop of Chichester and the Church Union produce something from the catholic stable by means of occasional papers from a catholic 'shadow' Liturgical Commission . . . but I left the executive of the Church Union and it was quietly dropped. Alas!) . . . But as Fr Heidt taught us last issue with another of Colin Buchanan's books, one has to watch for party political bias (and why not indeed – all credit to the evangelicals).[13]

---

13 *NOL* 86.8.

The ability of a blog to stimulate conversation by inviting visitors to post their own comments is replicated to a large degree by *NOL* in its encouragement of readers to exchange ideas and news. Kenneth Stevenson contributed as a guest columnist in the mid-1980s and Bryan Spinks ran a series of journal reviews in the late 1980s and into the 1990s. Members of GROW supplied a steady stream of liturgical publication reviews. Colin, who was naturally suspicious of liturgical practices that were regarded as indispensably Anglican and yet whose rationale was to many a trade secret, started a series in the early 1980s appropriately entitled 'coelacathines' (a term used to describe animals that have a hollow spine). In this and subsequent *NOL* discussions readers were invited to discuss the origin and meaning of liturgical practices that receive little or no coverage in mainstream liturgical journals: the blessing of non-communicants at the communion rail, wearing of mitres, mixing of water with wine in the chalice, turning east for the creed and bowing towards the table or to one another. Often these conversations were started by *NOL* readers; the disposal of ASBs, for instance, generated a long-running correspondence as the period of ASB authorization drew to a close in the year 2000. Complaints with the new Common Worship texts were aired by readers, usually constructively, in the pages of *NOL*. For example, one incumbent with strong objections to the new collects (which he viewed as 'mock-Tudor gibberish') also offers some of his own rewritten texts. Similarly, errors in the publishing of texts, poor formatting of texts and even odd theology are commented upon ('true errors' in Common Worship texts, those committed in the production of texts after authorization, were awarded a £2 prize by the editor). On occasion readers would use *NOL* as a means of requesting help from others, such as requests for burial rites (for pets or for the burial of retained organs in a pre-existing grave) and sample orders of service (by Mark Earey when, as the national Praxis Officer, he was preparing material for training on producing local orders of service). When I requested help with liturgical material to accompany the celebration of the anniversary of baptism I received a reply from a *NOL* reader in Canada, which indicates the global reach of the publication. Readers would also offer their own contributions to liturgical celebration, and among the more unusual were David Stancliffe's guidance on the techniques of presidency at large gatherings of eucharist, how to receive relics (Truro Cathedral), services of thanksgiving and blessing of animals, and the pastoral provision of a prayer to be used for the removal of an old wedding ring for a widow or widower preparing for a new marriage.

THE BLOG'S 'ODDS AND ENDS'

Four further features of *NOL* deserve comment, if only briefly, if I am to capture the true spirit of this late twentieth-century blogger. The first is Colin's skill and scholarship as a liturgical historian. When there was no fresh liturgical news for comment in the editorial, Colin's regular standby was 'Anniversaries'. Whether it be the 250th anniversary of John Wesley's Aldersgate experience, or the 40th anniversary of the Church of South India, Colin would have all the relevant historical data at his finger tips and would present them in a way that enabled him to make a point or two about what we could learn. Second, and related to this, is his interest in those who have been involved in making liturgical history, reflected in the large number of obituaries that appeared regularly in the pages of *NOL*. The influence of both well-known and lesser-known liturgists is acknowledged, and we learn something of Colin's eye for historical detail combined with a generosity of spirit; I note, for example, that even those with whom he disagreed were honoured. Third, *NOL* was the place where Colin took the liberty of airing his pet hates in liturgy; readers will be familiar with such things as his dislike of collects being announced as the collect 'for' rather than 'of' (lest leaders find themselves praying the collect 'for' the conversion of St Paul or the Beheading of John the Baptist!), a service ending two or three times and the congregation changing posture during the eucharistic prayer. A full list of 16 pet hates can be found in the final edition of *NOL*, reflecting his most recent experience as suffragan bishop among anglo-catholic parishes in South London.[14] In this, we recognize in Colin a reflection of ourselves, those who are from time to time intensely irritated by public worship. Fourth, one of the ubiquitous features of *NOL* was its ability to find something that could make you laugh. It has been suggested by more than one regular subscriber that collecting all the humour in *NOL* would justify a separate publication ('Laughter in Liturgy: 29 Years of Chuckling in the Pew'?). A brief sample hardly does this justice, but here are a few of my favourites:

- Reported from one of the first SLS conferences: 'Does putting on a chasuble at the Offertory mark a liturgical change of gear?'

- In a draft infant baptism rite from the Church of Ireland at the newly inaugurated presentation of the candle the rubric reads: 'Then shall the priest give the godparents a light'. The editor adds that presumably the Irish know what they meant.

---

14 *NOL* 348.19–20.

- Why does the Pope kiss the ground when arriving in a new country? So would you if you flew Air Italia!

- Among many glorious and not so glorious examples of typos from service sheets in the Liturgical Spellchecker series was 'Blessed be the Lord, the Cod of Israel', to which the editor adds mischievously, 'the origin of *ichthus*, no doubt'.

- Living proof that liturgical terminology is never self-evident comes from a correspondent who freely admits that prior to subscribing to *NOL* he always assumed that an epiclesis was the medical procedure given to his wife during childbirth.

AND FINALLY . . . THE BLOGGING LEGACY

No doubt each *NOL* reader would have his or her own reasons for looking back in gratitude to Colin for the monthly journal. If I were asked to name my own I have three to offer.

First, *NOL* is an unrivalled journalistic history of liturgical revision in the C of E in the late twentieth and early twenty-first centuries and as such provides a rich resource for students of liturgy. Along with the detailed report on the process of revision, together with incisive, robust and often witty comment, laced with historical references to previous revisions in Anglican liturgical life, *NOL* has the added bonus of allowing the reader access to the unofficial yet no less real liturgical changes in the Church of England. The evolving character of charismatic worship, for example, is a topic that maintains a profile throughout the life of *NOL*, from the report on the meeting in 1975 between the Latimer House Liturgy Group and charismatic clergy to editorial comment and assessment of the Toronto Blessing in the 1990s.

Second, *NOL* has been an important catalyst for evangelical involvement with liturgical revision. Along with GROW, which has served to launch a number of evangelical liturgists into mainstream Anglican liturgical life, *NOL* represents Colin's faithful and creative fulfilment of the decision made by evangelicals in 1967 at the National Evangelical Anglican Congress at Keele to shed their identity as critics on the margins of the Church of England and embrace and engage with the process of reform within the Church and its structures. *NOL* has given confidence that involvement in liturgical revision is a properly evangelical exercise, encouraging the Church to celebrate its identity as a community shaped by the gospel, a tradition that goes all the way back to the work of Thomas Cranmer himself, as Colin regularly reminded his readers.

Third, and returning to my main thesis, *NOL* represents some quality blogging. Unlike official liturgical documentation, which tends to iron out all the rough edges, *NOL* has thrived on the controversial, contradictory and generally untidy aspects of liturgical revision. *NOL* embodies the spirit of blogging perfectly, and it was this quality that engaged the reader who was looking for the unmediated and uncensored comment that has a raw yet dynamic quality to it. *NOL* liked to be at the place where tectonic plates were colliding and tremors of liturgical debate and controversy were to be felt; indeed, as he himself confesses in one edition of *NOL*, high on Colin's editorial wish-list would be the chance to time-travel and run *NOL* in the 1870–80 era at the height of the ceremonial law-breakers controversy.

The last word goes to one correspondent whose letter is posted on the final blog in *NOL* of December 2003:

Dear Colin

Congratulations on so many years of *NOL*. I'm going to miss your regular construction of liturgical barricades and thorough-going demolition of earthworks thrown up by more primitive tribes, the gossip (parochial ministry is so devoid of good honest-to-goodness such), also the spur to purchase the occasional book, the odd groan as one of your chestnuts comes out for a grooming, some good ideas and insights ready for application.

Thank you.

Blessings
Matthew Grayshon, Hanwell[15]

---

15 *NOL* 348.15.

Liturgical bibliography of Colin Buchanan

Note: This listing omits various publications over the years from 1961 to 2009 in the fields of ecclesiology (including Anglicanism worldwide), employment of the clergy, ecumenism, church and state, electoral reform, and even mission and biblical scholarship.

1961 'The Bible and the Prayer Book' (Pamphlet for the Bible Churchmen's Missionary Society for 350th anniversary of the Authorized Version)
'The Church of England and Apostolic Succession' in *The Churchman*, August 1961

1966 'Prayer Book Revision in England 1906–1965' in R. T. Beckwith (ed.), *Towards a Modern Prayer Book* (Marcham Manor)
The New Communion Service – Reasons for Dissent (Church Book Room Press) (reprinted in *The Churchman*, Summer 1966)
A Guide to the New Communion Service (Church Book Room Press)

1967 (with R. T. Beckwith) '"This Bread and this Cup": An Evangelical Rejoinder', *Theology*, June 1967
Drafting Statement on Worship in preparation for the First National Evangelical Anglican Congress at Keele, April 1967

1968 (ed.) *Modern Anglican Liturgies 1958–1968* (Oxford University Press)
(ed. with R. T. Beckwith and K. F. W. Prior) *Baptism and Confirmation* (Latimer Monograph, Marcham)
A Guide to Second Series Communion Service (Church Book Room Press)
'An Evangelical Looks at Sacramental Initiation' in *Faith and Unity*, May 1968

1969 (with the Bishop of Willesden (Graham Leonard)) 'Intercommunion: Some Interim Agreement', *Theology*, November 1969
'Liturgical Reform in Anglicanism' in *Concilium*, vol. 2, no. 5

1970 (with E. L. Mascall, J. I. Packer and the Bishop of Willesden (Graham Leonard)) *Growing into Union: Proposals for Forming a United Church in England* (SPCK)

1971   Review of Peter J. Jagger (ed.), *Christian Initiation 1552–1969* (Alcuin/SPCK) in *Journal of Theological Studies*, October 1971
Beginning of Grove Booklets on Ministry and Worship (hereafter 'MW' with a number) – no. 1 on 31 December 1971

1972   (ed. and contr.) *Evangelical Essays on Church and Sacraments* (SPCK)
(arts) 'Burial: Anglican' and 'Liturgies: Anglican' in J. G. Davies (ed.), *A Dictionary of Liturgy and Worship* (SCM Press)
Review article on J. D. G. Dunn, *The Baptism in the Holy Spirit* (SCM Press, 1970) in *The Churchman*, Vol. 86, no. 1
MW3, *Baptismal Discipline*
MW4, (contr.) *Reservation and Communion of the Sick*
MW9, *Patterns of Sunday Worship*

1973   (art.) 'Liturgy' in J. C. King (ed.) in *Evangelicals Today* (Hodder & Stoughton)
MW14, *Recent Liturgical Revision in the Church of England*
MW20, *A Case for Infant Baptism* (see also under 2009)

1974   (art.) 'Series 3 in the Context of the Anglican Communion' in R. C. D. Jasper (ed.), *The Eucharist Today: Essays on Series 3* (SPCK)
MW24 (with David Pawson), *Infant Baptism under Cross-Examination*
MW14A, *Supplement for 1973–74 to Recent Liturgical Revision in the Church of England*
MW32, *Inaugural Services*

1975   (ed.) *Further Anglican Liturgies 1968–1975* (Grove Books)
MW37, *Liturgy for Infant Baptism: The Series 3 Service*
Began editing (monthly) *News of Liturgy* (which ran for 29 years – 348 issues – to 2003)
Began editing (quarterly) Grove Liturgical Studies (hereafter 'LS', which ran to 1986)

1976   (art.) 'Twenty Years of Anglican Liturgy' in *English Church Music*
(art.) 'The Holy Spirit and Liturgy' in *Theological Renewal*, no. 2
MW14B, *Supplement for 1974–76 to Recent Liturgical Revision in the Church of England*
LS7, *What Did Cranmer Think He Was Doing?*

1977   (art.) 'The Sacraments are Developed' in *The History of Christianity* (Lion)
MW51, *Encountering Charismatic Worship*
LS9, 'Lay Presidency: Some Anglican Historical Perspectives' in Trevor Lloyd (ed.), *Lay Presidency at the Eucharist*

1978   MW61, *One Baptism Once*
MW14C, *Supplement for 1976–78 to Recent Liturgical Revision in the Church of England*
LS14, *The End of the Offertory: An Anglican Study*

1979   MW65, *Liturgy for Initiation: The Series 3 Services*
MW68, *Liturgy for Communion: The Revised Series 3 Service*

LS17, 'The Pentecostal Implications' in Kenneth Stevenson (ed.), *Authority and Freedom in the Liturgy*
LS20 (ed.), *The New Eucharistic Prayers of the Church of England*
'Back to the Stained-Glass Window?' in *The Times Higher Educational Supplement* 21, December 1979

1980 (ed. with Trevor Lloyd and Harold Miller) *Anglican Worship To-Day: Collins Illustrated Guide to the Alternative Service Book 1980* (Collins)
LS21 (ed.), *The Directory of Public Worship*
(drafted) Two chapters in Liturgical Commission, *A Commentary on the ASB* (SPCK)

1981 (drafted) General Synod Working Party report, *The Charismatic Movement in the Church of England* (Church Information Office)
MW76, *Leading Worship*
LS27, Appendix 'Infant and Child Communion in the Church of England' in David Holeton, *Infant Communion – Then and Now*
'The Church and Worship' and 'Baptism, Confirmation and Communion' in Alan Nichols and John Williams (eds), *Agenda for a Biblical Church 2* (Anglican Information Office, Sydney)

1982 'Liturgical Revision in the Church of England in Retrospect' in Kenneth Stevenson (ed.), *Liturgy Reshaped* (SPCK)
'Christian Worship' in *Lion Handbook of the World's Religions* (Lion) Grove Worship Series (hereafter 'W')
W80, *The Kiss of Peace*

1983 'The Lord's Supper according to the Book of Common Prayer' in I. Pahl (ed.), *Coena Domini 1* (Universitats-verlag, Freiburg, Schweiz)
W84 (with David Wheaton), *Liturgy for the Sick: The New Church of England Services*
W86, *BEM and ARCIC on Baptism and Eucharist*
LS33 (ed.), *Anglo-Catholic Worship: An Evangelical Appreciation after 150 Years*
LS34 (ed.), *Eucharistic Liturgies of Edward VI*
LS35 (ed.), *Background Documents to Liturgical Revision 1547–1549*

1984 W90, *Evangelical Anglicans and Liturgy*
LS39, *Latest Liturgical Revision in the Church of England 1978–1984*
LS40 (ed.), *Essays on Eucharistic Sacrifice in the Early Church*

1985 (ed.) *Latest Anglican Liturgies 1976–1984* (Alcuin/SPCK)
W91, *Adult Baptisms*
LS41, *Anglican Eucharistic Liturgy 1975–1985*
LS43 (ed.), *Liturgies of the Spanish and Portuguese Reformed Episcopal Churches*
LS44 (ed.), *Nurturing Children in Communion: Essays from the Boston Consultation*
(drafted for Standing Committee of GS) 'The Worship of the Church' (the end-of-term report of the Liturgical Commission of 1981–6)

1986 (arts revised from 1972) 'Burial: Anglican' and 'Liturgies: Anglican' and (new) 'Cremation' in J. G. Davies (ed.), *A New Dictionary of Liturgy and Worship* (SCM Press)

W96 (contr.) D. Smethurst, *Extended Communion: An Experiment in Cumbria*

LS48, *Anglican Confirmation*

1987 W98, *Policies for Infant Baptism*

W101, *Anglicans and Worship in LEPs*

Alcuin/GROW Joint Liturgical Studies (hereafter 'JLS'), (series editor from 1987 onwards)

JLS3 (ed.), *Modern Anglican Ordination Rites*

'The Renewal of Baptismal Vows' in *Studia Liturgica* (vol. 17 – *Gratias Agamus*)

1988 'The Liturgist as Theologian' in Peter Eaton (ed.), *The Trial of Faith* (Churchman Publishing)

(arts) 'Confirmation', 'Penance', 'Sacrament' in S. B. Ferguson and D. F. Wright (eds), *New Dictionary of Theology* (InterVarsity Press)

JLS6 (ed.), *The Bishop in Liturgy: An Anglican Study*

(drafted) Statement on Liturgy of 1988 Lambeth Conference

1989 'Music in the Context of Anglican Liturgy' in Robin Sheldon (ed.), *In Spirit and in Truth* (Hodder & Stoughton)

W106, *Lambeth and Liturgy 1988*

W107, *Revising the ASB*

JLS10, 'Adult Initiation and the Anglican Churches' in Donald Withey (ed.), *Adult Initiation*

1990 W112, *Children in Communion*

(essays) 'Infant Baptism – the Atomized Sacrament' and 'A Ghost in the Grove: An Exercise in Exorcizing' in Clifford Owen (ed.), *Reforming Infant Baptism* (Hodder & Stoughton)

1991 'Epilogue' in Clifford Owen, *Baptise Every Baby?* (Marc)

1992 W121, *The Heart of Sunday Worship*

(16-page pamphlet) *Infant Baptism in the Church of England* (Grove Books)

'The Boston Consultation: A New Introduction to the Essays' in Ruth Meyers (ed.), *Children at the Table: The Communion of all the Baptized in Anglicanism Today* (Church Hymnal Corporation, New York)

1993 W124, *The Renewal of Baptismal Vows*

'Worship and Doctrine' in G. Kuhrt (ed.), *Doctrine Matters* (Hodder & Stoughton)

'Confirmation' in David Holeton (ed.), *Growing in Newness of Life: Christian Initiation in Anglicanism Today* (Anglican Book Centre, Toronto)

'The Threefold Order in Question: An Anglican Perspective' in Paul Beasley-Murray (ed.), *Anyone for Ordination?* (Marc)

Infant Baptism and the Gospel: The Church of England's Dilemma (Darton, Longman & Todd)

1994 JLS27, 'Future Directions in Eucharistic Revisions' in David Holeton (ed.), *Revising the Eucharist: Groundwork for the Anglican Communion*
JLS28, 'Issues of Liturgical Inculturation' in David Gitari (ed.), *Anglican Liturgical Inculturation in Africa*
'Anglican Confirmation: Recent Trends' in Angela Berlis and Klaus-Dieter Gerth (eds), *Christus Spes: Liturgies und Glaube im Oekumenischen Kontext – Festschrift fur Bischof Sigisbert Kraft* (Peter Lang, Frankfurt am Main)
'Christian Worship' – revised article for 2nd edn of *The World's Religions* (Lion)

1995 W131, *The Lord's Prayer in the Church of England*
'Worship in an Anglican Context' ('Gottesdienst in anglikanischen Kontaxt') in Hans-Christoph Schmidt-Lauber and Karl-Heinrich Bieritz (eds), *Handbuch der Liturgik* (Evangelische Verlagsanstalt, Leipzig, Germany and Vandenhoeck and Ruprecht, Göttingen)

1996 W136 (with Trevor Lloyd), *Six Eucharistic Prayers as Proposed in 1996*

1997 JLS38, 'The Next Coronation' in Paul Bradshaw (ed.), *Coronations Past, Present and Future*
JLS39, 'Anglican Orders and Unity' in David Holeton (ed.), *Anglican Orders and Ordinations*
'Some Loose Legal Cannons' in *Ecclesiastical Law Journal*, no. 20, January 1997
'Anglican Ordination Rites: A Review' in *Visible Unity and the Ministry of Oversight: The Second Theological Conference Held under the Meissen Agreement between the Church of England and the Evangelical Church in Germany* (Church House Publishing)

1998 W145 (with Michael Vasey), *The New Initiation Rites*
W148, *Eucharistic Consecration*
'Henry de Candole' in Christopher Irvine (ed.), *They Shaped our Worship* (Alcuin/SPCK)
Is the Church of England Biblical? An Anglican Ecclesiology (Darton, Longman & Todd)
(comp.) *Lambeth Prayer* (worship book of the 1998 Lambeth Conference)
Listed as contributor re the BCP to E. A. Livingstone (ed.), *The Oxford Dictionary of the Christian Church* (3rd edn, Oxford University Press)

1999 (ed.) *Michael Vasey – Friend and Liturgist* (Grove Books)

2000 W158 (with Charles Read), *The Eucharistic Prayers of Order One*
W161, *Services of Wholeness and Healing*
'Gregory Dix – The Liturgical Bequest' in *Churchman*, vol. 114, no. 3
'Eucharistic Prayer H – An Unauthorized Account' in *Ushaw Library Bulletin* (and offprinted pamphlet by the author)

'"Do this in remembrance of me" – But what do we do?' (Vasey Memorial Lecture for 2000), *Anvil*, November 2000
Proofreader of *Common Worship* main book

2001   W163, *Infant Baptism in Common Worship*
Consultant editor and contributor in Mark Earey and Gilly Myers (eds), *Common Worship Today* (HarperCollins)

2002   W171 (with Mark Earey, Tim Stratford and Gilly Myers), *Collects – An Alternative View*
(arts revised from 1972 and 1986, and others added new) 'Books, Liturgical: Anglican'; 'Charismatic Worship'; 'Eucharist: Anglican'; 'Funerals: Anglican' and House Church Worship' in Paul Bradshaw (ed.), *The New SCM Dictionary of Liturgy and Worship* (SCM Press)
JLS54 (ed.), *The Savoy Conference Revisited*

2003   W175 (contr.) Ian Tarrant (ed.), *Bible-Based Liturgies*
'Worship in an Anglican Context' ('Gottesdienst in anglikanischen Kontaxt') revised from 1995 edn in Hans-Christoph Schmidt-Lauber and Karl-Heinrich Bieritz (eds), *Handbuch der Liturgik* (Evangelische Verlagsanstalt, Leipzig, Germany and Vandenhoeck and Ruprecht, Göttingen)
Finished editing *News of Liturgy* in December after 348 monthly issues

2004   Began quarterly contribution – 'Colin's Column' – in new *Praxis News of Worship*
'Liturgical Uniformity' in (Australian) *Journal of Anglican Studies*, vol. 2, no. 2, December 2004

2005   'The Position of the President: Exploring an Historical Anglican Bypath' in *Studia Liturgica*, vol. 35, no. 1
'Saints in Anglicanism: inherited, and what others, if any?' in *A Cloud of Witness: The Cult of Saints in Past and Present* (Peeters, Leuven, Netherlands)
'Anglikanische Liturgie' in I. Pahl (ed.), *Coena Domini II* (Universitas-verlag, Freiburg, Schweiz)

2006   W186, *Ordination Rites in Common Worship*
Editorial Consultant and Contributor 'The Winds of Change', 'The Legacy of the Church of South India' and 'Preserving the Classical Prayer Books' in Charles Hefling and Cynthia Shattuck (eds), *The Oxford Guide to the Book of Common Prayer: A Worldwide Survey* (Oxford University Press, New York)
Historical Dictionary of Anglicanism (Scarecrow, MD; includes full set of entries on Anglican liturgical matters)
Taking the Long View: Three and a Half Decades of General Synod (Church House Publishing; includes five chapters on liturgical revision in the Church of England)
'David Wright on Baptism', *Evangelical Quarterly*, vol. LXXVIII, no. 2, April 2006

'Flying Bishops' in Ronald Dowling and David Holeton (eds), *Equipping the Saints: Ordinations in Anglicanism Today* (Columba, Dublin)

2007 W190, 'Passiontide and Holy Week' in Phillip Tovey (ed.), *Introducing Times and Seasons: 2 The Easter Cycle*

(contr.) Mark Earey, Trevor Lloyd and Ian Tarrant (eds), *Connecting with Baptism* (Church House Publishing)

Consultant editor and reviser for (revised from 2001) Mark Earey and Gilly Myers (eds), *Common Worship Today: Student Edition* (St John's College, Nottingham)

Author of teaching module on Common Worship for St John's Extension Studies

JLS63 (with David Holeton), *A History of International Anglican Liturgical Consultations 1983–2007* (SCM-Canterbury Press)

JLS64 (ed.), *Justin Martyr on Baptism and Eucharist: Texts in Translation with Introduction and Commentary* (SCM-Canterbury Press)

'Questions liturgists would like to ask Justin Martyr' in Sara Parvis and Paul Foster (eds), *Justin Martyr in His Worlds* (Fortress Press, Minneapolis)

2008 Teaching module on Church of Ireland BCP 2004 for St John's Extension Studies

2009 *An Evangelical among the Anglican Liturgists* (Alcuin/SPCK)

W20, *A Case for Infant Baptism* (a rewritten fresh edition of MW20, *see* 1973)

JLS68 (ed.), *The Hampton Court Conference and the 1604 Book of Common Prayer* (SCM-Canterbury Press)

Indexes